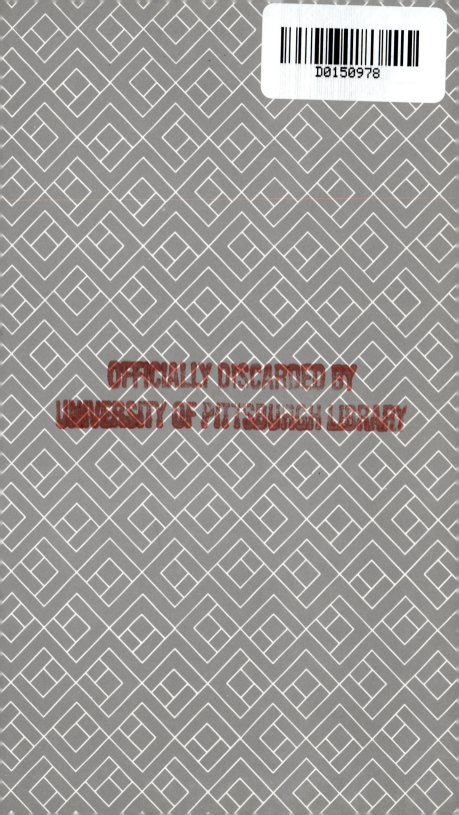

D0150978

OFFICIALLY DISCARDED BY
UNIVERSITY OF PITTSBURGH LIBRARY

Working women

†35.

NIM

Though the female labour market worldwide continues to expand, the terms on which women work remain problematic. *Working Women* is a detailed examination of women's position in a number of countries in both 'North' and 'South'. In particular, it identifies the common cultural and economic factors that create disadvantage.

Through international studies of women's work in diverse contexts, the contributors – all active feminists – give insights into the reasons for unequal conditions, showing that in widely differing locations similar concepts are used to justify women's disadvantage. They explore the extent to which women can challenge their subordinate position by participating in alternative forms of work and collective action, such as co-operatives or feminist enterprises.

Innovative in its study of alternative working practices for women and in its comparative focus, *Working Women* is a unique contribution to the existing literature on women in the workforce and will be particularly useful to students in economics, sociology, social anthropology, gender studies and development studies.

Nanneke Redclift is Lecturer in Social Anthropology at University College, London, and **Thea Sinclair** is Lecturer in Economics at the University of Kent.

Working women
International perspectives on labour and gender ideology

Edited by
Nanneke Redclift
and
M. Thea Sinclair

London and New York

First published in 1991
by Routledge
11 New Fetter Lane, London EC4P 4EE

Simultaneously published in the USA and Canada
by Routledge
a division of Routledge, Chapman and Hall Inc.
29 West 35th Street, New York, NY 10001

© 1991 Routledge, the collection as a whole; the individual
   contributors, each chapter.

Typeset by LaserScript Limited, Mitcham, Surrey
Printed and bound in Great Britain by
Mackays of Chatham PLC, Chatham, Kent

All rights reserved. No part of this book may be reprinted or
reproduced or utilized in any form or by any electronic,
mechanical, or other means, now known or hereafter invented,
including photocopying and recording, or in any information storage
or retrieval system, without permission in writing from the
publishers.

British Library Cataloguing in Publication Data

Working women : international perspectives on labour and
   gender ideology.
   1. Women. Employment – Sociological perspectives
   I. Redclift, Nanneke   II. Sinclair, M. Thea
   331.4

Library of Congress Cataloging in Publication Data

Working women : international perspectives on labour and gender
ideology / edited by Nanneke Redclift and M. Thea Sinclair.
   p.   cm.
Includes bibliographical references.
   1. Women—Employment. 2. Feminism.   I. Redclift, Nanneke.
II. Sinclair, M. Thea.
HD6053.W677   1990
331.4—dc20   90–35047
                                                              CIP

ISBN 0-415-01842-0
      0-415-01843-9 (pbk)

Contents

List of contributors   vii

Preface   x

1 **Women, work and skill: economic theories and feminist perspectives**   1
M. Thea Sinclair

2 **Gender and library work: the limitations of dual labour market theory**   25
Maura Luck

3 **Images and goods: women in retailing**   42
Adelina Broadbridge

4 **Shop floor control: the ideological construction of Turkish women factory workers**   56
Yildiz Ecevit

5 **Prostitution and tourism in South-East Asia**   79
Wendy Lee

6 **Return to the veil: personal strategy and public participation in Egypt**   104
Homa Hoodfar

7 **Women in struggle: a case study in a Kent mining community**   125
Avril Leonard

8 **Women shop stewards in a county branch of NALGO**   149
Jenny Walton

9 **Money and power: evaluating income generating projects for women**   172
Joy Lyon

Contents

10 **Greek women and tourism: women's co-operatives as an
   alternative form of organization**   197
   Mary Castelberg-Koulma

11 **A feminist business in a capitalist world: Silver Moon
   Women's Bookshop**   213
   Jane Cholmeley

   Name index   233
   Subject index   237

Contributors

Adelina Broadbridge is a Lecturer at the Institute for Retail Studies, Department of Marketing, University of Stirling, and is working on the MBA in Retailing and Wholesaling by Distance Learning Course. Prior to this she worked on two projects as a research fellow within the Institute for Retail Studies. A graduate of Stirling University, she gained some experience of working in the retail sector while undertaking an MA in Women's Studies at the University of Kent. Her interests include issues in retail employment and distance learning opportunities, particularly for women.

Mary Castelberg-Koulma completed her BA honours degree in Social Sciences at the Open University while living and working as an English teacher in Greece (1974–87). She decided to come to Britain to do an MA in Women's Studies at the University of Kent. Since then she has lived in Britain. She writes and teaches adult evening educational courses, and intends to do a Ph.D. based on tourism in Greece. She has a six-year-old son.

Jane Cholmeley lives in London and works at the Silver Moon Women's Bookshop. Between 1981 and 1983 she completed an MA in Women's Studies at the University of Kent, supporting herself by working as a Company Secretary for a firm of ecclesiastical architects. In 1982, with Sue Butterworth, the idea of the Silver Moon Women's Bookshop was born. In May 1984 it became a reality. In 1989 Silver Moon Bookshop won the Pandora Award given for 'contributing most to promoting the status of women in publishing and related trades'. In 1990 Jane Cholmeley and Sue Butterworth launched Silver Moon Books, a lesbian publishing house.

Yildiz Ecevit completed her Ph.D. degree in Sociology and Social Anthropology at the University of Kent. Her Ph.D. thesis was on Women's Work in Industry. She is currently lecturing in the Sociology

Department at the Middle East Technical University in Ankara, Turkey. She is involved in women's studies and has published articles on women's issues in Turkey.

Homa Hoodfar has a Ph.D. in Social Anthropology from the University of Kent, and is currently teaching at McGill University, Montreal. Her field interests are the household economy, changing patterns in the distribution of power between husbands and wives and international migration in the Middle East.

Wendy Lee is currently living in New Zealand where she works as a mother and also as part-time co-ordinator of the Auckland Development Education Centre. She previously completed an MA in Women's Studies at the University of Kent and taught in Nigeria, Papua New Guinea and Palestine where she developed an interest in the anthropology of gender and in women and development issues. Her recent work includes articles on the impact of colonialism on gender relations in the Pacific and on the role of women in national liberation struggles.

Avril Leonard is a mental health social worker in Kent. She comes from Dublin and has been living in Kent for the last seven years. During this time she completed an MA in Women's Studies at the University of Kent. She lives with her partner and twelve-year-old daughter and has just had her second daughter.

Maura Luck is an articled clerk with a firm of solicitors in Surrey. She studied law at Newcastle Polytechnic from 1986 to 1988. Prior to this she studied for her MA at the University of Kent whilst working part-time as a secretary. She graduated from Kingston Polytechnic in 1982 with a BA in Social Science.

Joy Lyon completed a BA degree in Development Studies at the University of East Anglia. She lived and worked for three years in Zimbabwe, where she carried out research for an MA in Women's Studies from the University of Kent. She is currently employed by Oxfam, sharing the job of area administrator for Kent and East Surrey. She has two young children.

Nanneke Redclift teaches Social Anthropology at University College London and previously taught on the MA in Women's Studies at the University of Kent. Her main research interest is in gender and anthropology, about which she has published extensively. She has three children.

M. Thea Sinclair teaches Economics and Women's Studies at the University of Kent. She is actively involved in the Tourism Research Centre, which is researching into tourism's growing importance worldwide, and carried out a study of tourism in Kenya in 1990. She has close links with Spain, where she lived and worked during the transition to democracy.

Jenny Walton lives in rural Nova Scotia where she works part time as a social worker in foster care for a child welfare agency. She and her husband have three children and their own business; Wise Acres Produce, Organic Gardening and Epistemology.

Preface

This book is the product of work on women's studies, carried out by students and staff at the University of Kent. We would like to thank all who have provided us with a stimulating and supportive working environment at the University; Sallie Westwood, who provided us with thought-provoking comments and Heather Gibson, for all her editorial support. Much gratitude is due to Yana Johnson, Kate Russell, Marilyn Spice and Carol Wilmshurst who typed the manuscript with wondrous patience and efficiency.

Nanneke Redclift
M. Thea Sinclair

Chapter one

Women, work and skill

Economic theories and feminist perspectives

M. Thea Sinclair

Introduction

Women and men participate in the paid labour market on a very
different basis. Women's employment in both the 'North' and 'South' is
segregated horizontally, in a limited range of occupations and of jobs
within occupations, and vertically, at the bottom of the occupational
ladder. Such segregation almost invariably corresponds to lower
earnings and inferior working conditions for women and is
accompanied by a division of labour within the home which accords
women the major share of childcare and other domestic labour. What are
the forces which serve to perpetuate such inequality, and under what
circumstances is it open to change? In answering these questions
existing studies have tended to emphasize three types of variables:
material conditions, institutional determinants, and 'unobservable'
factors such as preferences, attitudes, and ideologies. Orthodox
economic explanations, for example, have examined the operation and
effects of market forces, concentrating on changes in quantifiable
variables such as wages, income, and family circumstances including
the age and number of children. Segmented labour market theorists, on
the other hand, emphasize the importance of structural differences
within the overall labour market and examine the institutional
determinants of such differences; for example the provision by
employers of a career ladder for (male) workers within the privileged
primary sector of the labour market, pay bargaining procedures, and the
role of trade unions in reinforcing the advantaged role of workers within
the primary sector. Many sociological workplace ethnographies have
concentrated on the role of socialization and culture in forming the
consciousness of working women.

This book shows that uni-causal explanations of women's working
position are over-simplistic. Since the inequality between women's and
men's positions results from and is perpetuated by a complex
combination of factors, it is analysis of the interrelationships between

1

the different factors which is appropriate. Such factors include not only material variables such as wages, but also a range of ideological determinants, among which gender is particularly important. The labour market is not a gender-neutral context to which women simply bring a set of preconditioned attitudes, but is permeated by implicit gender ideology activated through the practices of management, unions, male workers, and women themselves (Cockburn 1985, Game and Pringle 1984). At the same time, women's participation in the world of paid work and their representation within it cannot be understood in isolation from their position in kinship and family structures and their relationship to childbearing and reproduction. Their positions in paid and unpaid work are mutually determining. The significance of women's unwaged labour continues to have a crucial effect on their identity as waged workers, in spite of their integral role within the paid labour force.

In order to understand the ways in which the labour market is gendered, it is necessary to take into account the system of social reproduction, including the division of labour in the family, reciprocal relations in the wider kin group or community, assumptions concerning sexuality, fertility, procreation, and nurturance, and the control over property and income allocation. Also of importance is the construction of subjective identity through the media, the state, and the education system, offering women images of the values of the home, motherhood, and paid work which, like the system of social reproduction, vary between class and race. Such variations mean that although it is possible to make some general statements about the relationship between work and gender, the use of a homogeneous definition of 'women's work' precludes adequate explanation of either the structure of the labour market or the determinants of women's own self-perceptions and consciousness. Explanations of the gendering of the labour market should therefore take explicit account of differences by race and class.

Comparative analysis of the conditions under which women work and the ways in which their work is defined is necessary both for explaining inequality and for shedding light on the ways in which women's inferior position in the workforce is reinforced or can be challenged. Many previous studies have been related to women's position either in the 'North' or the 'South', implying a disjunction between the experiences of women in these distinct contexts. However, the chapters in this book show that by examining women's positions in a variety of circumstances, it is possible to demonstrate the similarities between the concepts which are used to explain women's unequal positions in the workforce in different settings. At the same time, variations in the specific positions of women which relate to differences in economic and cultural contexts can be identified. Although previous work has analysed inequality and women's subordinate position in the workplace and the family, the contributors to the book demonstrate that it is also important to examine some of the attempts which women have made to establish alternative forms of paid work which are not based on inequality.

It has long been assumed that social production is the key to the determination of collective consciousness. Many of the chapters in this book question this view and, while focusing primarily on forms of women's waged labour, show how the world of paid work interacts with domestic ideologies and concepts of gender. In the department store situation as discussed in Chapter 3, for example, the labour force is structured and controlled on the basis of a concept of white femininity which is reinforced by management literature and directives. Gender stereotypes are also associated with a language of control which can be used by employers to achieve a particular form of industrial discipline and flexibility, as is shown in the case of Turkish factory workers in Chapter 4. In another context, the view of women as sexually submissive objects to be used for male release provides the basis for sex tourism as a key feature of South-East Asian 'development' in Chapter 5.

The main themes which the book examines are gender ideology and control, consciousness, and alternative working practices. Although all the chapters in the book are concerned with all three themes, the issue of control and gender ideology is the main focus of the first four chapters. The following two chapters discuss the relationship between women's consciousness and their material conditions. The final four chapters deal with the theme of resistance and examine a variety of ways in which women have challenged their working conditions by industrial action and the establishment of alternative forms of work.

Orthodox economic theories

One of the main topics which is examined in this book is the relationship between gender, definitions of skilled and unskilled work, and associated pay levels. Women generally undertake jobs which are perceived as involving low levels of skill and which are relatively low paid. Among the explanations which have been put forward to account for women's position in the workforce, those of economists have proved particularly influential owing, in part, to the central role they play in determining the ideology and policies according to which the economy is run. Their influence is extensive not only within industrialized countries, but also in non-industrialized countries, via the powerful positions which they hold in international financial and 'developmental' agencies. A review of the most important economic explanations of the relationship between women's jobs, perceived skill levels, and the wages they receive therefore provides a useful context against which to appreciate the ways in which this book contributes to the debate and challenges some of the existing theories. The dearth of intelligible explanations of orthodox and alternative economic analysis constitutes a further reason why such a review is useful. The contributions and challenges put forward by the authors in this collection can then be considered against this background.

Economists argue that an examination of the supply of and demand for labour is essential to any explanation of women's position in the labour market. The usual methodology is to set out a theory to explain the supply or demand for labour as dependent upon a number of observable variables. The variables included in early studies of the supply of female labour (measured by women's participation in the labour market or the number of hours worked), were usually limited to those which are attributed a value by the market, such as wages and other household income (Killingsworth and Heckman 1986: 186–188). The link between women's role in both paid production and reproduction has received greater acknowledgement in more recent studies and has been accompanied by the introduction of other variables such as the number and age of children (Leuthold 1979; Heckman and Macurdy 1980; Joshi 1984).

Studies of the demand for female labour have also estimated the demand for labour as a function of measurable variables such as wages, and recent studies of a variety of industrialized countries have attempted to quantify the degree of substitutability between female and male labour of differing ages (Hamermesh 1985). Particular attention has been paid to young workers, given the context of the current and future effects of demographic changes upon the labour market. All economists agree that the demand for and supply of labour are important determinants of wage levels. However, beliefs about the nature of wage determination differ. For example, those who adhere to the view that the economy operates as a 'perfect market' argue that the wages paid to workers are determined where demand equals supply, with any excess demand bidding up wages and any excess supply lowering them. According to this argument, wage levels correspond to the individuals' productivity levels, with additional amounts being paid to compensate for activities which are particularly unpleasant or dangerous.

Orthodox economists argue that discrimination occurs if employers pay equally productive individuals different wages, or refuse to employ some individuals at any wage, however low, with minority ethnic workers being a possible example of the latter category. Since employers are assumed to aim to maximize their profits, discrimination, according to orthodox reasoning, is unlikely to result, since other employers could increase their profits by employing the lower paid workers. Thus, the operation of market forces is said to eliminate discrimination in a 'perfect' market economy. Since it is argued that differences in wage levels which are not due to differences in productivity levels are eliminated by competition, this theory implies that the reason why women's average wages are lower than those of men is because women are less productive than men.

One theory which has been put forward to explain women's relatively low wage levels is the human capital theory, which relates wage levels to the levels of 'human capital' (education, training, and skill) embodied in individuals. Women are said to have a lower average level of skill than men as the result of a lower level of education and training. The emphasis is thus on the skills which individuals possess, some of which are innate and some of which are acquired at a cost outside the home. There is some acknowledgement that different skills are required for carrying out different occupations. However, it is usually argued that even if wages are associated with jobs rather than with individuals, higher paid jobs are almost invariably carried out by individuals with more human capital.

The reason why women are thought to have less human capital and hence to be less productive than men is the time they spend out of the labour force during the years spent rearing children (Mincer and Polachek 1974). They are also said to choose jobs which require less education and training than men partly because they believe that they will spend fewer years in the labour market obtaining a return on the time spent in such training. Employers assume that women will have a lower degree of attachment to the firm than men, and prefer to train male workers who will wish to work continuously. Women's lower degree of training is said to cause them to be less productive than men, resulting in their lower average wages.

A fundamental problem with this type of reasoning is its circularity, since low levels of human capital appear to be both the cause and the consequence of women's changing participation in paid work during the life cycle (Amsden 1980). It can be argued that skill and productivity levels not only cause but also result from relative wage levels. Since the wage is a key element of the opportunity cost of child rearing, women may decide to obtain lower levels of training prior to and during child rearing as a consequence of the lower level of female wages, since the level of household earnings which are lost during the years of child rearing will be lower if women rather than men leave the labour force during this period. Thus, there is a material incentive for the household, and men in particular, to allocate child rearing to women. The tremendous loss of earnings which women undergo throughout their post child rearing years as a result of interrupting their paid work has only recently been quantified (Joshi 1984).

Orthodox economics acknowledges that people make decisions about their paid and unpaid work activities in the context of constraints, some of which (for example limited availability of paid employment) may be of such great importance as to imply very little actual choice. The choices which women and men make have also been related to variables such as the presence of children and level of education. However, a major limitation associated with the use of a methodology involving the estimation of models including measurable variables is that the nature and effects of non-quantifiable causes of the choices which people make are rarely identified (Mallier and Rosser 1987:2). Given this methodological approach, it is thought to be either impracticable or unnecessary to estimate the relative importance of material and non-material variables (such as voluntary preferences, socialization, perceptions of appropriate roles) in explaining women's and men's generally differing combinations of paid work and home activities during their life cycles.

'Choices' are in fact made within a context of inequality. Women and men enter into and participate in the labour market on an unequal basis owing to pre-existing gender assumptions and an unequal distribution of power. The analysis of interactions and outcomes on the basis of the prevailing ideology and distribution of power means that the ways in which such interactions and outcomes are affected by and, in turn, affect dominant ideological beliefs are rarely considered. In consequence there is a lack of analysis of specific forms of resistance by women to such assumptions and inequalities.

Orthodox economic analysis is useful in shedding light on particular aspects of women's role in the labour market, for example in quantifying the effects of changes in observable variables on the supply of or demand for female labour, and in enabling comparisons to be made with the changes in the supply of or demand for male labour. Most economists agree that higher wages tend to be paid to workers who are more productive and who have higher levels of skill. However, many believe that the use of a 'perfect' market model of the economy is an unrealistic way of explaining the determination of wage levels. Instead they argue that wages in some sectors of the economy are determined by additional variables such as trade union membership (Thomas 1982) and the seniority of workers within the firm (Collier and Knight 1985). Most of the studies which have been carried out have been limited to labour markets in western countries, owing partly to the fact that accurate data relating to women's labour in activities such as agricultural production in low and intermediate income countries are more difficult to obtain than data for women's work in industrialized countries (Beneria 1981).

Alternative economic theories

Segmented labour market economists have charged orthodox economics with failing to account for the ways in which labour markets are structured in terms of horizontal and vertical segregation (Cain 1976). For example, as Hakim (1981) has shown, there has been relatively little decrease in the extent of occupational segregation by sex in Britain since the beginning of the twentieth century. Moreover, approximately 80 per cent of part-time jobs are now carried out by women, most of whom are white (Bruegel 1989). When considered by orthodox economists, such segregation is often said to be caused by differences in the job preferences of women and men, by 'imperfections' in the labour market such as geographical immobility and imperfect information, and by externalities such as firm-specific human capital. Since women and men are employed to carry out different jobs, it is also argued that segregation is consistent with an absence of discrimination by employers (as previously defined).

However, in practice the phenomenon of occupational segregation is likely to cause the demand for labour for particular occupations to be directed towards either male or female workers. It is also likely that the inequality between different groups of workers' positions in labour markets has different effects on the groups' plans and expectations in relation to education and training, fertility, and the combination of labour market and home activities. Thus, instead of constituting the outcome of differences in voluntary preferences, segregation may itself influence such 'voluntary' behaviour. This point is taken up by alternative theories of segmented labour markets.

Segmented labour market and job competition theories are concerned with explaining the structure of labour markets in industrialized countries, and bear some resemblance to the dual economy models which have been applied to industrializing nations. Both theories co-incide in challenging the human capital theory of wage determination, although job competition theory is closer to orthodox theories of the labour market (Cain 1976). Job competition theory argues that the number and type of jobs in internal labour markets in large, unionized firms are technologically determined. Employers hire workers to fill them on the basis of their perceptions of the workers' future 'trainability' using indicators such as past education as a screening device. If the supply of skilled workers is greater than employers' demand for such workers, workers cannot obtain jobs by working for lower wages as orthodox economists argue, owing to the job competition theorists' view that the number of jobs is given. Thus workers do not always obtain a job or wage in accordance with their skills, and some skilled workers can only find jobs in the external labour market – in firms which are usually smaller and less likely to be unionized – where wages are determined on the basis of the market forces of demand and supply.

Unlike workers in the external labour market, workers in the internal labour market are offered a career ladder with inducements to remain within their firm so that the firm can retain the returns from their training and experience (Hamermesh and Rees 1988). Thus, wages in the internal labour market are seen as institutionally determined on the basis of custom and the procedures agreed by employers and unions, so that institutional rules are substituted for market processes and the wage differential between the internal and external labour markets is not eliminated. Decisions about the acquisition of skills via training within the internal labour market are also made on the basis of institutional procedures. Workers in the external labour market are unlikely to be able to enter the internal labour market, in a way which is comparable to the lack of mobility between the 'modern' and traditional sectors suggested by dual economy models.

Segmented labour market models also examine the way in which the labour market is structured, but focus particularly upon the issue of inequality (Cain 1976; Taubman and Wachter 1986). Unlike orthodox economic models, they do not concentrate on the analysis of labour market interactions *given* the existing distribution of resources and power, but instead aim to examine the nature of such inequality and its effects upon labour market behaviour. Workers in the primary sector of the labour market tend to receive higher wages, have better working conditions, more stable work, and superior promotion possibilities, with union bargaining reinforcing their position. Workers in the secondary sector are subjected to the opposite conditions and, although they may enter the secondary sector with skill levels comparable to those of workers in the primary sector, they are said to be 'moulded' into the inferior skill and working characteristics of the jobs in the secondary sector. Thus, workers' consciousness and work behaviour result not from their own preferences but from their unstable, inferior jobs. The 'insider – outsider' theory of employment (Lindbeck and Snower 1988) is similar to the previous segmented labour market models in positing a divided labour force. In this case 'insider' workers who have received in-firm training are able to extract relatively high wages from employers who wish to avoid the costs associated with recruiting and training replacement workers. Workers in the secondary sector and the unemployed are 'outsiders' who lack formal training and the associated wage bargaining power.

The radical economists' theory of segmented labour markets emphasizes the role which the socialization of individuals prior to entering the labour market, via the education process and community culture, plays in conditioning them for their future roles in paid work (Cain 1976: 1224). This analysis is related to Marxist theory in that both identify the role of class conflict in the historical determination of structured labour markets. In a context of deskilling and the 'homogenization' of workers, the separation of the labour market into a hierarchical primary sector, within which workers are provided with incentives, and an unstable secondary sector, within which high turnover acts as a disincentive to unionization, is said to be functional to capitalism (Reich *et al.* 1973); such divisions prevent workers from uniting to strengthen their bargaining position. However, the theory does not explain why some capitalists refrain from undercutting others by employing more low paid workers, and the role of workers within this scenario is little more than that of passive spectators.

None of the preceding theories concerned with explaining structural differences in the labour market and their related effects adequately addresses the question of why virtually all the workers who are recruited and trained in the internal labour market (or primary sector) are men, and why almost all working women are employed in the external labour market (or secondary sector). Subsequent studies have tended to use the theories to describe women's position in the labour market without explaining the gender composition of the sectors. The studies by Cockburn (1983) and Rubery (1978) are exceptions, highlighting the role of male-dominated trade unions, as well as employers, in structuring the labour market. Using a historical approach, Cockburn shows how pressure from male trade unionists resulted in union/ employer agreements to exclude women from the printing industry and how male trade unionists subsequently exercised considerable influence over access to particular jobs and over the skill definitions and wages associated with them. Thus, the effect of economic power is explicitly introduced as a component of the institutional determination of skill definitions and wage rates.

Rubery explains how control of the female labour supply and the confinement of women to one sector of the labour market serves the material interests of male trade unionists. If women's access to the primary sector can be restricted by such means as bargaining over recruitment procedures, downward pressure on the wage level which would otherwise occur because of the additional supply of labour can be limited. The large supply of women workers who are available to carry out secondary sector occupations means that, in the absence of a minimum wage, there is a tendency for wage levels in the secondary sector to remain low.

Both orthodox and segmented labour market theories have tended to draw a clear distinction between the theory of production in the market and the theory of consumption in the home, the focus of analysis usually being the sphere of production. Past models of female labour supply, for example, have usually assumed the number and age of children (if any) to be determined independently of labour market participation, and have then analysed their effects upon women's participation in the labour force (Montgomery and Trussell 1986:205). The importance of considering the interrelationship between the paid labour market and the home has, however, been recognized in the economic theory of home production (Gronau 1986) and in life cycle theories of labour market participation (Joshi 1984). Bargaining theories of family behaviour have also started to examine the nature of decision making by family members (Killingsworth and Heckman 1986: 132-133). However, there is considerable scope for further economic studies of the inter-relationship between childcare and domestic labour, participation in the labour market, and the number of hours worked (Montgomery and Trussell 1986: 248).

Whereas Marxists initially viewed the labour market as the site of production and the home as the site of consumption and reproduction, Marxist-feminist analysis has pointed out that the home is also an important site of production (Himmelweit and Mohun 1977). The main Marxist-feminist contributions to the analysis of the interrelationship between women's domestic labour within the home and the capitalist economic process were made during the well-known domestic labour debate. However, as has been pointed out (Molyneux 1979:12), the participants in the debate did not succeed in explaining why it is women rather than men who bear the major responsibility for domestic labour and childcare.

Marxist-feminist debates have also been concerned with women's role as a possible reserve army of labour for employers (Beechey 1978; Bruegel 1979; Somerville 1982). Such discussions have proved problematic given the absence of an objective definition of a 'reserve army', and the context of women's increasing participation in the paid labour market in industrialized countries. The fundamental role which women continue to play in many productive activities in both the market and non-market sectors of industrializing countries, and the contribution which their labour makes to the profits of multinational enterprises, has also been pointed out (Beneria 1981; Boulding 1983; Mitter 1986; Moser and Young 1981). The threat which women's labour market participation has posed to the maintenance of relatively high wages for male workers has been limited by the social and sexual norms and power relations which restrict women's entry into many male-dominated occupations. This can occur in a variety of ways. As Maura Luck shows, jobs can be categorized as part-time. Employers, and sometimes women themselves, justify the employment of women in part-time rather than full-time jobs by referring to women's family responsibilities (Beechey and Perkins 1987). The validity of this argument is, however, challenged by its general lack of applicability to black women, whose full-time work and relatively poor material circumstances are reinforced by the receipt of lower pay for given levels of qualifications (Bruegel 1989). As Maura Luck and Avril Leonard demonstrate in Chapters 2 and 7, white women can also adapt their family duties to suit their outside commitments. Another deterrent to women's entry into particular occupations is the sexual ideology which views women's physical proximity to males who are not kin as a threat to their honour, as is shown by Josephides' (1988) study of Cypriot women in Britain and by Yildiz Ecevit and Mary Castelberg-Koulma in their discussions of Turkish and Greek women in Chapters 4 and 10. These studies also indicate that such ideologies are subject to change, particularly in response to changes in material circumstances.

One of the main implications of the debates to date is thus that women's unequal position in the labour market cannot be explained solely by recourse to an analysis of their role in relation to production and consumption; women's role in reproduction, both biological and social, must also be examined (Harris and Young 1981; Mackintosh 1981). One of the ways in which the debate has usefully, though all too infrequently, been extended is by consideration of the different forms of interaction between gender, class, race and sexuality. In post-war Britain, for example, the gender ideology which reasserted women's appropriate role as that of mothers within the home, though supposedly of general applicability, was in fact specific to white women. During this period, Afro-Caribbean women were encouraged to provide low wage labour in such occupations as the NHS, while their children were fostered or returned to relatives in the Caribbean (Bryan *et al.* 1985). Although the differing treatment of black and white women has sometimes been justified on the grounds that black and minority ethnic women are subject to different cultural norms from those of white women, as Phoenix (1988) shows, cultures evolve over time and young Afro-Caribbean and white working class women are influenced by a similar overall cultural context. Women from different classes and ethnic backgrounds can, however, draw on specific cultural resources such as kinship networks. Thus, culture does not function simply as a means of control, and such stereotypes as the view of Asian women as 'passive victims of their circumstances' are rarely realistic. Cultural resources can also be used as a means of resistance, as is clearly demonstrated by Westwood's (1988) discussion of Gujarati women factory workers' protests against attempts to decrease their control over the production process and Bhachu's (1988) study of Sikh women's role in establishing and running their own enterprises.

Perceptions of skill and pay

Definitions of skill have an important effect on women's and men's relative pay and status in the workplace. However, existing theories have differing views about the nature of the relationship between skill and pay determination. It follows from the human capital theory that if women wish to obtain higher wages they should obtain higher levels of education and training, but this theory fails to distinguish between the actual level of human capital embodied in the individual and the level of human capital which the individual is perceived to possess. Women's relatively low earnings can be explained on the basis of the *belief* that they are less skilled than men, irrespective of their actual skill levels. If women and men are paid according to the skills which they are perceived to possess, the human capital (and 'perfect market') theory of the relationship between skill and pay is only valid if perceived and actual skill levels coincide.

This condition does not always hold true. For example, as Adelina Broadbridge points out in Chapter 3, the actual level of skill possessed by department store saleswomen may well exceed their recognized level of skill, whereas the perceived level of men's skill is more in accordance with their actual skill level. Armstrong (1982) obtains a similar finding in a study of the clothing industry. Women whose actual skill levels are similar to those of men are often paid considerably less, as both Broadbridge, and Zabalza and Arrufat (1985) show. Men's higher basic pay is sometimes said to result from the higher market value of the goods they produce or sell, rather than from differences in job content (Craig *et al.* 1982:82), and may be associated with the use of newer technology or more capital-intensive production methods by men, as is shown by Yildiz Ecevit. Moreover, disparities in basic pay are frequently increased by men's preferential entitlement to overtime earnings and/or commission as Adelina Broadbridge demonstrates.

Yildiz Ecevit's chapter on women's and men's work in the very different context of an urban manufacturing sector in Turkey also shows that the skills which women factory workers require to carry out their jobs are at least as great as the skills which are required of men, and that the women's educational levels often exceed those of the men. Although the actual level of skills possessed by women and men are similar, men's skills are believed to be superior to those of women, and men are paid higher wages. One possible reason for such differences is the non-recognition of the skills which women acquire in the home (Elson and Pearson 1981; Heyzer 1986: 103). Abilities such as dexterity and accuracy are perceived as women's natural characteristics, and the informal 'training' by which they acquire such abilities, at zero cost to their employers, is not acknowledged or rewarded in the paid labour market. This often occurs in a context in which the supply of women workers with such skills is high relative to the demand for their labour. Although wages received by individuals with relatively high levels of formal education and training tend to exceed those paid to individuals with lower levels, as predicted by the human capital theory, skills acquired via informal processes in the home do not tend to be recognized or result in higher wages. Even when women's skills are explicitly recognized, as in the case of the Spanish embroiderers discussed by Lever (1988), the wages which they receive are often incommensurate with the level of their skills, owing to the women's poor bargaining position within their local context. Women themselves frequently view their skilled but low paid occupations as the best option available given constraints such as an actual or perceived absence of alternative opportunities, sometimes related to state policies which prejudice women's position in the formal economy.

Segmented labour market theorists argue that primary sector jobs require significant levels of skill; hence skill is attached to jobs. However, the role of gender in the workplace is not examined and, as Craig *et al.* (1982: 87-88) have argued, the differences in the wages paid to male and female workers in the 'primary' and 'secondary' sectors in a range of British industries did not appear to result from objective differences in job content or skills (see also Phillips and Taylor 1980). Thus, although segmented labour market theory may be applicable to some sectors of the economy, it is not always appropriate. Moreover, employment decisions are not always determined by technological requirements; employers can select their desired labour/machinery combination on the basis of criteria such as the relative prices of labour (i.e. wages) and machinery. This tends to result in production using labour-intensive production methods in low and intermediate income countries and capital-intensive methods in industrialized nations. If trade unions are weak (or non-existent), market forces rather than institutional procedures are likely to play the major role in determining the wages of all employees. For example, studies of women's work in non-unionized firms in export processing zones show that women's work is usually classified as unskilled (or sometimes semi-skilled) and women are paid wages which are significantly lower than those paid to male workers in the zones, or to individuals doing comparable work in industrialized countries (Mitter 1986).

Feminist theorists such as Cockburn (1983, 1985) have examined the role of institutional procedures and trade union bargaining power in determining differences in skill definitions and wages between women and men, pointing to men's greater participation in union-employer negotiations and preferential access to jobs defined as skilled, for example via the promotion system and access to intra-firm training. Not only do employers benefit from women's role as an 'unskilled', cheap, flexible workforce; male workers also maintain their relatively privileged position as 'more skilled' and hence higher status workers, receiving higher wages in the paid labour market and a lower share of domestic labour within the home.

Yildiz Ecevit's account of factory workers in Turkey shows that although the women workers were often unionized, traditional skill definitions and wage differentials between men and women had not been challenged. The male employees' higher relative power, both within the union and in terms of the sexual roles believed to be appropriate to them, enabled them to maintain the institutional determination of skill definitions and wages in their own favour. In addition, the men's 'monopolization' of the use of the more modern machinery introduced into the factory may have resulted in a higher value of production per male employee, contributing to the perception of men's work as more skilled than women's work (see also Armstrong 1982).

Maura Luck's discussion of women workers in a university library examines the issue of women's work in a public sector occupation. The library workers' wages were institutionally determined on the basis of a grading structure agreed by management and unions. The women workers who were allocated to the lower grades had significant actual skill levels, and significant skills were also usually required for carrying out their jobs. However, as in the case of the Turkish workers, these skills were not given formal recognition and did not appear to be rewarded in their pay. Part-time evening and weekend workers, in particular, were always allocated to the lowest pay grades, providing the management with a cheap, flexible labour force which met the library's varying labour requirements during the academic year. The unions did not succeed in challenging the biases embodied within the grading structure, concentrating instead on improving the position of individual workers within the existing structure.

Although the previous examples relate to different countries and different contexts, what is important is that in almost all of the cases the jobs carried out by women tend to be perceived as less skilled than those carried out by men, and the average wages paid to women are lower than those paid to men. Most orthodox and alternative analyses of paid work have implicitly assumed that there is no difference between actual and perceived skills, and have failed to examine the ways in which perceptions of women's appropriate roles affect behavioural decisions and women's material position in the labour market. The contributions of British feminist lawyers in relation to 'equal pay for work of equal value' legislation are, however, important in challenging traditional definitions of the relative values of women's and men's work (O'Donovan and Szyszczak 1988; Szyszczak 1985). Greater attention should therefore be paid to the determination of skill definitions and associated wage levels not only by economic variables such as the supply and demand for labour, level of demand for the commodity produced, extent of formal training and labour-intensity of production, but by factors such as culture, women's and men's relative bargaining power, and state policies towards female and male workers.

Alternatives for women: problems and achievements

All of the contributors to this collection provide considerable material to demonstrate the conditions of women's work. Their aim is to identify the problems which women face in attempting to challenge the balance of power in the workplace, as a prerequisite to the formulation of appropriate resistance strategies. This aim is facilitated by the authors' use of a feminist academic methodology which explicitly acknowledges the researchers' objective of challenging women's subordination. All the authors in the book have been involved in the situations which they write about, either directly as workers and trade unionists, or indirectly as participant observers or in related campaigns. While the later chapters document a variety of alternative working practices, the earlier chapters examine the obstacles to the improvement of women's working positions.

As a number of the contributors show, the structuring of labour markets in both the 'North' and 'South' into women's jobs and men's jobs is one of the most important barriers to women's consciousness of their unequal position in the labour market, since women cannot compare their pay and conditions with those of men doing similar jobs. Labour markets are structured in different ways. For example, the female sales assistants interviewed by Adelina Broadbridge tended to work in departments selling low cost items with a high turnover, while male assistants were employed in departments with the opposite characteristics. Gender characteristics such as a feminine appearance and a submissive and patient mode of behaviour constituted requirements of the female assistants' jobs. The characteristics required could also be argued to involve racist stereotypes since there was an almost total absence of black and minority ethnic women workers at a 'prestigious' London store.

Race and gender divisions overlie class divisions in employment,

15

demonstrating the fallacy of treating class as a unitary category. Such divisions are common in a range of working situations, as is illustrated by the studies of the gender divisions within library work by Maura Luck and of women shop stewards within the social services by Jenny Walton in Chapter 8. The absence of black and minority ethnic women from both library work and the trade union structure is a further indicator of racist stereotyping in relation to 'appropriate' working roles for women, and of the considerable role which race and gender perceptions play in fragmenting social class. A particularly extreme example of the role of racism in relation to women's work is that of South-East Asian women's role as prostitutes in the international tourism industry. Wendy Lee's study of tourism and prostitution clearly demonstrates the usefulness of examining race, gender, and class divisions within a global context.

As many of the chapters in this book show, sexuality is another important barrier to resistance against women's inferior working conditions, because it lies at the heart of women's perceptions of their own bodies and identities in relation to men. Though an intrinsic facet of women's working situations across the globe, it takes specific forms in different contexts. For example, Adelina Broadbridge shows how white sales assistants were expected to display an attractive appearance and to be tolerant of sexual harassment. In a different context, as Yildiz Ecevit explains, the ideology that Turkish women's appropriate place is in a separate sphere from that of men in order for women's sexual reputation to be safeguarded, constituted a barrier to resistance against job segregation and the corresponding wage differentials between women and men. Manual jobs carried out by women in Turkish factories were allocated on the basis of women's assumed dexterity, cleanliness, and patience, while men's jobs were said to require characteristics such as greater physical strength, although the actual characteristics of the jobs did not always coincide with those attributed to them. A variety of arguments were used to maintain the barriers between women's and men's jobs. For example, women in Turkish factories were said to be more concerned with family problems and to be absent from paid work more frequently than men, contrary to the finding that family responsibilities were not, in fact, a constraint on women's labour market activities. The possibility of resistance to inferior working conditions via participation in trade unions was limited since the male-dominated unions formed part of the orthodox pattern of control, reinforcing traditional ideas and perceptions. Sexuality is thus a further feature of class fragmentation.

Homa Hoodfar's discussion in Chapter 6 of veiling among women in Cairo demonstrates the complexity of the re-negotiation of perceptions of women's working role. Women had to balance family financial pressures and the need for a degree of individual economic autonomy against the threat to personal integrity posed by contact with males outside the controlled and legitimated sphere of kinship relations. For women, space was sexualized, and their movements in particular spatial fields defined their acceptance of the norms which gave them social value and respect. In return they could trade this value and conformity for certain rights to male support. Their own overt demonstration that they recognized the moral connotations of public space, through bodily concealment, gave them some guarantee that they could continue to call on male obligations. However, while women's use of this strategy may have enabled them to assert their own interests, it implicitly supports the status quo in which they are already sexualized.

Wendy Lees's discussion of sexuality as an economic commodity in its own right underlines the face that sexuality is not merely a private individual concern, but is closely linked to local economic conditions, international economic exchange, and racist perceptions. As she shows, in some circumstances compliance with racist stereotypes via prostitution is the only alternative which women have at their disposal. On a more optimistic note, Mary Castelberg-Koulma argues that traditional sexual norms can be open to challenge. The contrasting adverse stereotypes of Greek women and female tourists which have accompanied the growth of mass tourism in Greece have been challenged by more positive images as Greek women have started to organize their own economic ventures. These have brought Greek and foreign women into contact with each other on their own terms and have enabled Greek women to contest the sexual connotations of public space.

In the public sector occupation of library work, Maura Luck shows that the distinction between full-time and part-time work was one of the main ways in which library workers were categorized into distinct groups. The main priority of female part-time workers was perceived as being their home activities, in spite of the fact that women's initial organization of their paid work around their domestic commitments was soon substituted by the organization of their domestic role around their paid work. Male library workers were frequently assumed to make more rational decisions, since their decisions were not assumed to be constrained by domestic commitments. Moreover, the men's first priority was never perceived to be related to their potential or actual role as fathers, unlike the perceptions of the women's role.

The structuring of the labour market means that men and women have different material positions and status within the workforce, maintaining divisions between men's and women's interests and limiting the potential for change. Labour market structuring also plays an important role in reinforcing the gender division of labour in the home. Studies of women's work in a variety of countries show that the

17

presence of children is not an obstacle *per se* to the improvement of women's position in the paid labour market; many women in different countries have full-time jobs even if they have young children, as Yildiz Ecevit shows. However, although differences in material conditions (such as the availability of nurseries and the differential between men's and women's wages) affect women's and men's specific roles in relation to childcare and paid labour, the ideology that women have the major responsibility for childcare and the home is common across the globe, adversely affecting their positions in paid employment.

Attitudes towards participation in trade unions constitute a further common obstacle to the improvement of women's position in the labour market. Female library workers on lower grades, for example, did not perceive the union as playing an actual or potential role in affecting their working lives, as Maura Luck demonstrates. Some part-time workers did not even realize that they were entitled to join the union. This situation was reinforced by dual union representation in the library, whereby the AUT represented the higher grade, full-time workers and NALGO represented the lower grades, including all part-time workers. Similar views about the lack of importance of unions in influencing working conditions were held by department store workers in London and factory workers in Turkey. The Turkish women factory workers had presented requests for changes in working conditions to their union representatives, but their requests had been ignored by the union officials.

Even in situations in which female membership of trade unions is relatively high there are still problems. Jenny Walton, for example, shows that women's attendance at union meetings was often poor because women were unwilling or unable to add an additional load to their existing dual burden of paid work and home activities. Those women who did attend union meetings were rarely active participants in discussions owing to the alienating nature of trade union procedures and to frequent informal decision-making by men (for example in pubs) prior to the meetings. The women without children or with older children in Walton's study were more likely to play an active role in the union and to become shop stewards. However, their views of their appropriate role as a shop steward varied according to such factors as who they saw as their reference group (being more active if they felt that they had the support of other women), and whether their job involved a management role. Women shop stewards whose jobs involved some form of supervisory function were likely to see their role of shop steward as that of an unofficial personnel officer, helping to resolve individual members' problems, but often not becoming involved in broader issues. However, the women's material interests did not constitute a simple determinant of their consciousness and actions.

Particular events, such as the dismissal of a male shop steward, could lead to industrial and other forms of action by women which were in contradiction to women's material interests.

Avril Leonard provides a detailed analysis of the relationship between changes in material conditions and changes in consciousness. Prior to the 1984–5 miners' strike, Kent miners' wives defined their identities in relation to their families and the home. The women's activity and experience outside the home during the strike was accompanied by a change in their consciousness so that their views of their appropriate roles both inside and outside the home changed considerably. The women's awareness was no longer limited to white, male, working class interests, but extended, for example, to issues relating to race, 'Third World' campaigns, and the peace movement. Thus, although the women's participation in strike action brought about an increase in class strength, it also had the effect of exposing previously unrecognized gender, race, and class contradictions. Wendy Lee points out that a very different form of material change – the end of the Vietnam War, accompanied by a change in political power and the distribution of resources – resulted in a radical change in the role and beliefs of former prostitutes. She notes that racist attitudes towards prostitution can also be changed by international public awareness campaigns in industrialized countries.

Given the varying relationship between changes in material conditions and changes in consciousness, how effective are the attempts which are made to gain an alternative position in the paid workforce? The authors show that feminist strategies across the globe need not be based on traditional concepts of class resistance via industrial action. Joy Lyon in Chapter 9 demonstrates the importance of an accurate assessment of women's problems as a prerequisite to the formulation of appropriate solutions. Many of the 'development' schemes for women, often initiated or supported by western institutions such as the World Bank, have been based on western perceptions, often involving gender and race-related stereotypes, and have failed to acknowledge the important role which women play in the productive sphere. This has frequently resulted in the introduction of schemes which promote women's role in home-based activities such as basic health care, reinforcing traditional perceptions of gender roles. As the same time, women's positions have often worsened as they have lost the income which they previously gained from agricultural production.

Material changes in the form of the introduction of income generating schemes only succeed in bringing about significant improvements in women's position if women retain control over the production process, the distribution of the commodities produced and the income which is obtained from their sale. They are also more likely to be successful if women have access to material resources such as credit, and to official training services such as government extension services, resulting in the formal recognition of women's skills. If these conditions are not met, traditional attitudes are likely to prevail as men (and sometimes the better-off women) gain control of production and distribution.

Mary Castelberg-Koulma examines an alternative form of income generation scheme for women: the establishment of co-operatives controlled by women, and providing accommodation, meals, and other services for tourists in peripheral areas of Greece. The co-operatives aim to benefit women without any alternative source of income, and are particularly useful to women with children and older women who do not wish to migrate to areas where more jobs are available. An important difference between the income generating schemes and the Greek women's co-operatives is the Greek aim of implanting co-operative working practices. However, the introduction of material change in a specific form, in this case that of co-operatives, is not guaranteed to result in an immediate (or possibly even long term) change in consciousness in a desired direction; many of the Greek women working in the co-operatives aimed to obtain a short term increase in income, but the idea of working co-operatively with women other than kin was alien to them.

The establishment of co-operatives for tourists provides Greek women with work where they can use their traditional skills, which are brought outside the home, given formal recognition, and rewarded. As is the case in many of the income generating schemes for women, the rise in income and status which the Greek women obtain can be offset by the reinforcement of their traditional role in relation to domestic work, although the power which they exert within the home is not eroded. The need to carry out co-operative business legitimates women's entry into public domains which were previously the province of men and this may constitute a first step towards challenging the balance of power outside the home. The contacts established between Greek women and women from other countries can also challenge racist assumptions about both groups and can lead to changes in the understanding, attitudes and practices of each.

Jane Cholmeley's study in Chapter 11 of the establishment of a women's bookshop is set in the context of an industrialized country, but is similar to the previous examples in demonstrating the role which some form of government intervention can play in the market. The aim of the bookshop is to bring about both material and ideological changes. Material changes have been achieved, not only in the form of providing incomes for the women employed in the shop, but for the women writers whose books are sold. A change in consciousness can be achieved by the spread of feminist ideas by such means as the sale of books containing a non-traditional ideology, the shop's role as an information point and resource centre, the readings and discussions which take place in the shop, and the worldwide distribution of an information pamphlet. Both the material and the ideological changes are important in facilitating access to writing and talks by lesbian, black, and minority ethnic women. The establishment of feminist working practices and an egalitarian wage distribution within the shop have therefore been accompanied by the dissemination of ideas which challenge the prevalent ideology in the public and private spheres.

The authors in this book have demonstrated the importance of examining the issues of the control of women's work, consciousness, and alternative working practices both on a global basis and in relation to specific material and cultural contexts, facilitating identification of the similarities as well as the differences in women's positions. This perspective aims to avoid overemphasis on the concept of difference and identity politics, which can stifle co-ordinated action for change. What, then, are the implications for the appropriate role for western feminists in relation to the lives and campaigns of women in other countries? Acknowledgement of the similarities and differences between the positions of women in different countries may enable western feminists to avoid the danger of imposing their own ethnocentric and sometimes racist assumptions and solutions, and increase their awareness of the ways in which women themselves understand and confront subordination in their own contexts. It should also increase awareness of gender in North–South relations, facilitating a dual resistance strategy based on a feminist politics of autonomy and alliance.

Acknowledgements

I would like to thank Steve Bazen, Mary Evans, Ian Gordon, Nanneke Redclift, and Sallie Westwood for their many useful comments on this chapter.

References

Amsden, A.H. (1980) 'Introduction', in A.H. Amsden (ed.) *The Economics of Women and Work*, Harmondsworth: Penguin.

Armstrong, P. (1982) 'If it's only women it doesn't matter so much', in J. West (ed.) *Work, Women and the Labour Market*, London: Routledge and Kegan Paul.

Beechey, V. (1978) 'Women and production: a critical analysis of some sociological theories of women's work', in A. Khun and A.M. Wolpe (eds) *Feminism and Materialism. Women and Modes of Production*, London: Routledge and Kegan Paul.

Beechey, V. and Perkins, T. (1987) *A Matter of Hours*, Cambridge: Polity Press.

Beneria, L. (1981) 'Conceptualising the labour force: the underestimation of women's economic activities', *Journal of Development Studies* 17(3): 10–28.

Bhachu, P. (1988) 'Apni Marzi Kardhi. Home and work: Sikh women in Britain', in S. Westwood and P. Bhachu (eds) *Enterprising Women*, London: Routledge.

Boulding, E. (1983) 'Measures of women's work in the Third World: problems and suggestions', in M. Buvinic, M. Lycette, and W. McGreevey (eds) *Women and Poverty in the Third World*, Baltimore: Johns Hopkins.

Bruegel, I. (1979) 'Women as a reserve army of labour; a note on recent British experience', *Feminist Review* 3: 12–23.

——(1989) 'Sex and race in the labor market', *Feminist Review* No. 32: 49–68.

Bryan, B., Dadzie, S., and Scafe, S. (1985) *The Heart of the Race: Black Women's Lives in Britain*, London: Virago.

Cain, G. (1976) 'The challenge of segmented labour market theories to orthodox theory: a survey', *Journal of Economic Literature* 14 (4): 1215–1257.

Cockburn, C. (1983) *Brothers. Male Dominance and Technological Change*, London: Pluto Press.

——(1985) *Machinery of Dominance. Women, Men and Technological Know-how*, London: Pluto Press.

Collier, P. and Knight, J.B. (1985) 'Seniority payments, quit rates and internal labour markets in Britain and Japan', *Oxford Bulletin of Economics and Statistics* 47 (1): 19–32.

Craig, C., Rubery, J., Tarling, R., and Wilkinson, F. (1982) *Labour Market Structure, Industrial Organisation and Low Pay*, Cambridge: Cambridge University Press.

Elson, D. and Pearson, R. (1981) '"Nimble fingers make cheap workers": An analysis of women's employment in Third World export manufacturing', *Feminist Review* 7: 87–107.

Game, A. and Pringle, R. (1984) *Gender at Work*, London: Pluto Press.

Gronau, R. (1986) 'Home production – a survey', in O. Ashenfelter and R. Layard (eds) *Handbook of Labour Economics* Volume 1, Amsterdam: North-Holland.

Hakim, C. (1981) 'Job segregation: trends in the 1970s', *Department of Employment Gazette* 89 (12): 521–529.

Hamermesh, D.S. (1985) 'Substitution between different categories of labour, relative wages and youth unemployment', *OECD Economic Studies*: 57–85.

Hamermesh, D.S. and Rees, A. (1988) *The Economics of Work and Pay*, New York: Harper & Row.

Harris, O. and Young, K. (1981) 'Engendered structures: some problems in the analysis of reproduction', in J.S. Kahn and J.R. Llobera (eds) *The Anthropology of Pre-Capitalist Societies*, London: Macmillan.

Heckman, J.J. and Macurdy, T.E. (1980) 'A life cycle model of female labour supply', *Review of Economic Studies* 47 (1): 47–74.

Heyzer, N. (1986) *Working Women in South-East Asia. Development, Subordination and Emancipation*, Milton Keynes: Open University Press.

Himmelweit, S. and Mohun, S. (1977) 'Domestic labour and capital', *Cambridge Journal of Economics* 1(1): 15–31.

Josephides, S. (1988) 'Honour, family and work: Greek Cypriot women before and after migration', in S. Westwood and P. Bhachu (eds) *Enterprising Women*, London: Routledge.

Joshi, H. (1984) 'Women's participation in paid work. Further analysis of the women and employment survey', *Department of Employment Research Paper* No. 45 London: Department of Employment.

Killingsworth, M.R. and Heckman, J.J. (1986) 'Female labour supply: a survey', in O. Ashenfelter and R. Layard (eds) *Handbook of Labour Economics* Volume 1, Amsterdam: North-Holland.

Leuthold, J. (1979) 'Taxes and the two-earner family: impact on the work decision', *Public Finance Quarterly* 7(2): 147–161.

Lever, A. (1988) 'Capital, gender and skill: women homeworkers in rural Spain', *Feminist Review* 30: 3–24.

Lindbeck, A. and Snower, D.J. (1988) *The Insider-Outsider Theory of Employment and Unemployment*, Cambridge, Massachusetts: MIT Press.

Mackintosh, M. (1981) 'Gender and economics: the sexual division of labour and the subordination of women', in K. Young, C. Wolkowitz and R. McCullagh (eds) *Of Marriage and the Market. Women's Subordination in International Perspective*, London: CSE Books.

Mallier, A.T. and Rosser, M.J. (1987) *Women and the Economy*, London: Macmillan.

Mincer, J. and Polachek, S. (1974) 'Family investments in human capital: Earnings of women', *Journal of Political Economy* 82(2): 76–108.

Mitter, S. (1986) *Common Fate, Common Bond. Women in the Global Economy*, London: Pluto Press.

Molyneux, M. (1979) 'Beyond the domestic labour debate', *New Left Review* 116: 3–27.

Montgomery, M. and Trussell, J. (1986) 'Models of marital status and childbearing', in *Handbook of Labour Economics* Volume 1, Amsterdam: North-Holland.

Moser, C. and Young, K. (1981) 'Women of the working poor', *Institute of Development Studies Bulletin* 12(3): 54–62.

O'Donovan, K. and Szyszczak, E. (1988) *Equality and Sex Discrimination Law*, Oxford: Basil Blackwell.

Phillips, A. and Taylor, B. (1980) 'Sex and skill: notes towards a feminist economics', *Feminist Review* 6: 79–88.

Phoenix, A. (1980) 'Narrow definitions of culture: the case of early motherhood', in S. Westwood and P. Bhachu (eds) *Enterprising Women*, London: Routledge.

Reich, M., Gordon, D.M., and Edwards, R.C. (1973) 'A theory of labor market segmentation', *American Economic Review* 63(2): 359–365.

Rubery, J. (1978) 'Structured labour markets, worker organization and low pay', *Cambridge Journal of Economics* 2(1): 17–36.

Somerville, P. (1982) 'Women: a reserve army of labour?', *m/f* 7: 35–60.

Szyszczak, E. (1985) 'Pay inequalities and equal value claims', *Modern Law Review* 48: 139–157.

Taubman, P. and Wachter, M.L. (1986) 'Segmented labor markets', in O. Ashenfelter and R. Layard (eds) *Handbook of Labor Economics* Volume 2, Amsterdam: North-Holland.

Thomas, B. (1982) 'Unions and the labour market', in J. Creedy and B. Thomas (eds) *The Economics of Labour*, London: Butterworth.

Westwood, S. (1988) 'Workers and wives: continuities and discontinuities in the lives of Gujarati women', in S. Westwood and P. Bhachu (eds) *Enterprising Women*, London: Routledge.

Westwood, S. and Bhachu, P. (1988) 'Introduction', in S. Westwood and P. Bhachu (eds) *Enterprising Women*, London: Routledge.

Zabalza, A. and Arrufat, J.L. (1985) 'The extent of sex discrimination in Great Britain', in A. Zabalza and Z. Tzannatos *Women and Equal Pay. The Effects of Legislation on Female Employment and Wages in Britain*, Cambridge: Cambridge University Press.

Chapter two

Gender and library work

The limitations of dual labour market theory

Maura Luck

Women have a long history of engagement in economically productive work. Not only have they produced goods and services for the family's own consumption; they also have a long tradition of working for pay outside the home. The growth in the female labour force in the twentieth century needs, therefore, to be seen as a continuation of the long term process of the incorporation of increasing numbers of women into paid employment and not as a distinct change in the pattern of women's productive work. However, the terms on which women participate in the labour force remain a considerable problem for women, one that gains in importance as the female labour force continues to expand. The differences in the earnings and conditions of employment for women and men are intimately related to their differing patterns of participation in the labour force over their lifetimes. Whereas those men who are employed tend to participate in the labour force on a full-time basis throughout their lifetime, women's place in the labour force is characterized by a bi-modal pattern of participation over the lifetime, with a break in employment for childbirth and the early years of child rearing, and a return to predominantly part-time employment thereafter. Women's employment is also segregated, both horizontally, in a limited number of occupations, and vertically, so that the majority of women are employed at the bottom of the career ladder.

It is the concentration of women in predominantly female jobs and the likelihood that, even within relatively integrated occupations, women and men tend to work in different jobs, or jobs classified as different, which is argued by some economists to result in a virtual 'dual labour market' for female and male labour. In its simplest form dual labour market theory states that the labour market can be divided into two quite distinct sectors: a primary sector which is characterized by relatively high wage rates and non-pecuniary rewards, in which the jobs require high levels of skill, there are opportunities for training and promotion, employment stability, good working conditions, and high levels of union activity. The secondary sector is characterized by the absence of these features, so that there are unstable work patterns, acquiescent workers, and a lack of solidarism. A major feature of the secondary sector is a very high level of part-time work, so that a disproportionate number of women are found in the secondary sector.

The aim of this chapter is to examine the propositions which are associated with dual labour market theory and the arguments which a number of feminists have put forward and which are of relevance to the theory, in the context of a case study of women workers in a university library. A library was chosen as an interesting site for the study because library and information work has a high proportion of female workers, with approximately 60 per cent of professional librarians working in English public libraries being women. In setting the study in a university library it is possible to examine the extent to which differently graded jobs within the library are segregated by sex, and the extent to which such segregation is reinforced by both the sexual division of labour within the home and the career development and promotion possibilities which are available to women within the library. Since most of the studies which have used dual labour market theory as a framework for analysis have been concerned with private sector establishments, the choice of a public sector institution is also of particular interest.

All the jobs in university libraries are classified according to a grading system. The 'professional' grades are grades IIA (assistant librarians); III (sub-librarians); and IV (the head librarian). These grades correspond to the grades according to which lecturers, senior lecturers, and professors in the university are paid. The subordinate grading system is a 1–5 grading system where shelving assistants are grade 1, library assistants grade 2, senior library assistants grades 3, 4, and 5, and cataloguers are also grade 5. There is also an administrative grade, IB, which is intermediate to both grading systems and does not appear to be used frequently.

As was seen earlier, dual labour market theory postulates that the labour market is divided into two different sectors which have very different characteristics. It is possible to divide the library broadly into two such sectors. The primary sector consists of workers on professional grades where qualifications in librarianship are deemed essential, and the secondary sector incorporates workers paid on the lower clerical grades 1–5. As Table 1.1 shows, in 1986 ten of the fifteen workers employed on professional grades were men, nine working full-time.

Of the four women employed on professional grades, two worked full-time and two worked part-time. All but two of the seventy-nine workers employed on the clerical grades in the 'secondary' sector were women. Table 1.1 shows that by far the largest numbers of part-time women workers were employed on the lowest grades, 1 and 2, with almost 100 per cent of grade 1 jobs and 67 per cent of grade 2 jobs being carried out by part-time women workers [1]. The secondary sector can be further sub-divided into the relatively more privileged part-time day workers and the less privileged part-time evening and weekend workers. Despite the fact that the part-time evening and weekend workers performed the same jobs as part-time day staff, they were all allocated to the lowest grade 1, while part-time day staff doing the same work were all on grade 2. All the evening and weekend workers, except one, were women. If they want to move up a grade they have to change to daytime work.

Table 1.1 Full-time and part-time day and evening staff, 1986

| | Day staff | | | |
| Grade | Full-time | | Part-time | |
	Female	Male	Female	Male
Librarian				
Grade IV	0	1	0	0
Sub-librarians				
Grade III	0	2	0	1[1]
Assistant librarians				
Grade IIA	2	6	2	0
Grade IB	1	0	0	0
Senior library assistants				
Grade 5	3	1	2	0
Grade 4	1	0	2[2]	0
Grade 3	2	0	1	0
Library assistants				
Grade 2	13	0	26[3]	0
Grade 1	0	0	12[4]	0
	Evening and weekend staff			
Grade 1	0	0	21	1[5]

Notes
1 This post was held on a part-time basis as a prelude to retirement.
2 This figure includes a cataloguer who was employed at grade 4 because her job had been designated a temporary and part-time post.
3 This figure includes three women who were also employed at grade 1 and two women who also worked in the evening.
4 This figure includes three women who also had posts on grade 2 and one woman who was employed in the evening.
5 This employee was a boy who was still attending school.

The structure of employment in the library can therefore be classified broadly into a primary sector consisting mainly of full-time male workers employed on professional grades and a secondary sector consisting almost entirely of part-time women workers employed on clerical grades. Although male employees constituted only 5 per cent of the library's workforce, the highest grade posts were filled by men, while 94 per cent of all women employed in the library worked in the 'secondary' sector.

The vast majority of part-time workers in the library, 97 per cent, were women, while approximately 74 per cent of all women who worked in the library were working part-time. It would appear that all the jobs on grade 1 have been defined as part-time jobs, and 67 per cent of workers on grade 2 were also part-time workers. The advantage of part-time women workers for the library is that they provide a flexible and low cost labour supply, so that the library can increase the supply of labour at periods of maximum demand and reduce it when there is less demand for services, particularly during the long summer vacation. The concept of part-time work is problematic, however, because some women who work in the library do two part-time jobs and part-time work in the library can be as little as 2 hours per week, or as much as 32.5 hours per week.

One of the propositions put forward by dual labour market theory which is of particular importance for women is that certain workers become trapped in the secondary sector because of the existence of mobility barriers between the two sectors. According to Doeringer and Piore (1971), an internal labour market operates within a firm or company and wages and job allocations are governed by a set of administrative rules and procedures. Within the internal labour market, job-specific skills and knowledge have become increasingly important, relative to transferable occupational skills. Thus, employers, in order to retain skilled workers, develop career ladders. The result is that not only do workers who are in the primary sector have a secure future in terms of career progression and wage increments, but they also have the opportunity for further training provided by the employer, which will enhance their initial advantage by maximizing their long run investment in 'human capital'. Employment stability in the primary sector is a crucial factor for employers.

The other side of this dual structure is the secondary sector. Jobs in this sector are perceived as requiring little if any skill, so that employers see no incentive in offering secondary sector workers any opportunities for advancement or training. Secondary sector workers are thus unable to improve their skills and, further, come to be seen as unstable workers, while workers in the primary sector are seen as stable workers. Each sector of the dual labour market seems to reinforce the characteristics of the workers of that sector, so that the structure of the labour market itself is seen to have affected the differing characteristics of the workforce in each sector. Thus, dual labour market analysis offers explanations in terms of barriers to mobility where disadvantaged workers seem, as a group, to obtain employment which differs systematically from that of more 'advantaged' workers. Since disadvantaged workers are employed in jobs for which wages are low, working conditions are poor, employment is unstable, and opportunities for advancement are firmly restricted, it could be argued that it is possible to replace the term 'disadvantaged' worker by 'woman' worker, as virtually all women are employed in jobs which have these characteristics.

Dual labour market theory gives some insight into the experience of women in the labour market due to the fact that decisions taken about individuals are likely to be based on group probabilities (Phelps 1972), and sex is an obvious basis for differentiation on the basis of real or perceived quality differences between female and male labour. Thus, if women are perceived as being less skilled, more unstable workers, they will be excluded from the primary sector. Statistical discrimination in this model is distinguished from the 'pure' discrimination of Becker's (1957) model in which discrimination amounts to prejudice in the sense that employers or employees have a taste for giving relatively favourable treatment to one sex rather than the other. Statistical discrimination occurs because of employers' desire to select workers who are perceived to have good future performance prospects, particularly with respect to job stability; thus discrimination is seen to be a factor governing the access of workers to primary employment. Many female candidates who possess the requisite behaviour characteristics for primary sector employment are excluded from it. Since wage differences are seen as due to the way in which the market is structured, women's lower earnings are attributed to their supposed secondary sector characteristics – such as lower attachment to the labour force – rather than to their exclusion from primary sector occupations.

In order to examine the extent to which the arguments mentioned above can shed some light on women's working situation within the 'dual labour market' context of the library, interviews were carried out with twenty-seven per cent of the women working in the library, 15 per cent being in the 'primary' sector and 85 per cent in the 'secondary' sector [2]. The sample was self-selecting in that the women were informed of the study and could, if they wished, volunteer to be interviewed. Of the twenty-seven women interviewed, 34 per cent were full-time and 66 per cent part-time. Approximately 52 per cent of the sample worked part-year, particularly during the university terms.

Dual labour market theory postulates that occupations in the secondary sector require low levels of skill relative to occupations in the primary sector, so that workers in the secondary sector are paid correspondingly

Maura Luck

lower wages. The survey showed that the standard of educational and professional qualifications of the women in the secondary sector who were interviewed was high: only 8 per cent had no educational qualifications; 13 per cent had one to five 'O' levels; 69 per cent had between five and ten 'O' levels; and 10 per cent had more than ten 'O' levels. Forty-seven per cent of the women in the secondary sector had 'A' level qualifications; 36 per cent had between one and three 'A' levels; 6 per cent had four 'A' levels; and 5 per cent had five 'A' levels. All of the women who had acquired 'A' levels were also graduates.

The qualifications of the women in the secondary sector compared very favourably with those of the women in the 'primary' sector who were interviewed. Of the latter, 25 per cent had no qualifications; 50 per cent had between five and ten 'O' levels and 25 per cent had more than ten 'O' levels; 50 per cent had between one and three 'A' levels; 25 per cent had four 'A' levels; and 75 per cent of those interviewed were graduates; 67 per cent had professional qualifications which included librarianship qualifications, secretarial qualifications, management qualifications, and qualifications in teaching. What was also interesting was the extent of the commitment of the women to obtaining more educational qualifications, with 37 per cent expecting to obtain a further qualification in the next two years. These included degrees in history, librarianship and English, management qualifications, and a higher degree.

The results indicate that women's inferior position in the library workforce cannot be explained on the basis of a low level of qualifications. Hence it is possible that recognition is not given to the skills – abilities or qualifications – which the women bring to their jobs. As Cockburn (1983) has pointed out, skill can be defined in three ways: in the person, in the job, and as politically acquired skill. Skills in the person are those abilities and knowledge which the individual has acquired over a period of time. There is also the skill which is demanded by a particular job. Political skill is that skill which workers grouped together into trade unions can defend against the challenge of employers and, indeed, other workers. Thus, an individual may have a skill which is not required by the job and a political definition of skill would result where the power of the union was such that it could lay claim to 'new' skills in jobs and through bargaining produce a compromise skill definition. Skill, therefore, is a much more complex concept than at first appears the case. Further, skill should not only be seen as a class weapon; it is also a sex/gender weapon which plays an important part in the power relations between women and men. The existence of a sexual division of labour means that women and men do different work and:

the classification of women's jobs as unskilled and men's jobs as skilled or semi-skilled frequently bears little relation to the actual amount of training and ability required for them. Skill definitions are saturated with sexual bias. The work of women is often deemed inferior simply because it is women who do it. Women workers carry into the workplace their status as subordinate individuals and this status comes to define the value of the work they do. Far from being an objective economic fact, skill is often an ideological category imposed on certain types of work by virtue of the sex and power of the workers who perform it.

(Phillips and Taylor 1980: 79)

Evidence of this can be seen in the way part-time work, work which is often the only option open to women with children, is usually classified as unskilled, often regardless of the degree of skill in either the job or the worker. Unions in this model are seen as frequently reinforcing the gap between men's and women's skills and related pay and conditions. Hence, the role of men organizing through trade unions to define skills in ways which have devalued women's work, creating hierarchies of skill and excluding women from certain areas of skilled work, is of major importance.

Cockburn's analysis shows that skills which are embodied in the person and are required in order to carry out the job often fail to correspond to the political definition of skills which are incorporated within a job grading structure. A grading system is not an unbiased system, for it can fail to include factors which are viewed as 'natural' to women, such as an ability to deal with people or an aptitude for monotonous or repetitive tasks, or it can give weight to factors which disadvantage women. For instance, giving factors such as part-time work a high negative weight can perpetuate the undervaluation of some jobs so that other factors, such as education or expertise in the job, are of relatively small importance.

The women in the library not only brought a high level of skill to their jobs, but felt that their abilities and qualifications were necessary in order to enable them to perform the jobs efficiently. Sixty-seven per cent of the sample thought that they had qualifications and/or experience which, though necessary, were not an official requirement of the job. This expertise included a knowledge of languages, a high level of literacy, ability to organize, communication skills, a trained and educated mind, numeracy, and experience of dealing with people. Most of the women also stated that they did not believe that gaining more formal qualifications would enhance their own chances of obtaining promotion and better pay in the library. Many saw the differentials between the earnings of staff on professional grades and those on clerical grades as 'phenomenal' compared with the differences between

Maura Luck

the tasks involved, and felt that not enough recognition was given to experience.

The fact that many well qualified and experienced women were employed on low grades did not result from a characteristic frequently attributed to members of the 'secondary' sector of the labour force: instability of employment. The women in the sample constituted a highly stable labour force, the average number of years of service being 6.8, with 80 per cent of the sample having completed over 4 years of service. There instead appeared to be a number of structural barriers to promotion. When asked if they expected to be promoted in the coming year 96 per cent of the sample said 'no'. When asked the reason why, the most frequently cited reason was that in order to gain promotion they would have to work full-time as there were no part-time jobs at grades 3, 4 or 5. Evening and weekend workers would have to move to daytime work in order to obtain a higher grade, often for carrying out the same work. The gender bias of this type of structural constraint has not been considered by dual labour market theorists and yet the way in which work is structured across the day and week has enormous implications for women. Grading systems which incorporate part-time work in a negative way are, ultimately, biased evaluations in which women are penalized because of familial constraints which limit their participation in full-time work.

The failure of dual labour market theory to provide an adequate explanation of women's position in the labour force results from its lack of acknowledgement that the differences between women's and men's positions are gender- as well as work-related. Cockburn's (1983, 1985) work goes some way towards compensating for this deficiency and feminists such as Hartmann (1979), Mackintosh (1981) and Rubery (1978) have provided additional relevant contributions. Heidi Hartmann's analysis emphasizes the role of men in creating and reproducing job segregation in the labour market, thereby maintaining men's dominance in both the labour market and the home:

Job segregation by sex . . . is the primary mechanism in capitalist society that maintains the superiority of men over women, because it enforces lower wages for women in the labour market. Low wages keep women dependent on men because they encourage women to marry. Married women must perform domestic chores for their husbands. Men benefit, then, from both higher wages and the domestic division of labour. This domestic division of labour, in turn, acts to weaken women's position in the labour market. Thus the hierarchical domestic division of labour is perpetuated by the labour market and vice versa.

Hartmann 1979: 139)

A major problem with Hartmann's analysis of occupational segregation originates from her failure to apply a materialist perspective to the study of women's work. In arguing that the domination of women by men exists apart from any particular economic system, but always in concert with whatever system of production accompanies it (whereby regardless of the system of production, men are, on the whole, accorded public roles that bring them material as well as psychological success while women continue to be relegated to the separate and unequal sphere of domesticity), Hartmann has reduced theories of patriarchy to biologism.

Mackintosh (1981), in contrast, explicitly incorporates a materialist perspective within her analysis of the sexual division of labour (more appropriately termed the gender division of labour). Mackintosh examines the relationship between economic production and the reproduction of labour, arguing that the allocation of the major responsibility of domestic tasks, and especially childcare, to women effectively weakens women's position within the labour market by contributing to the segregation of work by gender, part-time work for married women, and consequently lower pay for women. The existence of the sexual division of labour has meant that women and men cannot be seen to have a common interest within the labour market because men's greater earning power and career achievements have been predicated on women's disadvantage and a relationship that allows men to evade most, if not all, domestic labour and childcare. Women are constrained in their participation in the labour market by the need to accommodate domestic commitments and the care of others.

To what extent were the women in the library constrained by domestic responsibilities such as the need to care for children or to give prime importance to their male partner's job? Seventy per cent of the women in the sample had not worked continuously since finishing their full-time education, the main reason given being domestic or family responsibilities. Of those who had experienced a break in employment, the return to the workforce was also constrained by domestic responsibilities. When asked about their most important considerations when they were thinking about starting their job in the library the most often quoted factors were the availability of part-time work and interesting work, mentioned by 98 per cent of the sample. The next most often mentioned factor was flexible hours, i.e. hours to fit in with school hours or childcare, followed closely by work near home, and good working conditions. However, once the women were at work a shift in priorities appeared to occur and 89 per cent of the women interviewed said that they did not organize their work around their domestic commitments, but rather the other way round.

Seventy-eight per cent of the sample were married or living with

33

someone and 95 per cent of their partners were in employment. Most of the sample said that their partners were in favour of them working. The reasons given as to why partners held this opinion were the need for more money, or the psychological benefits the women obtained from their work, in that some partners felt their wives were more 'interesting' if they were at work. Could such a high level of support mean that marriage is becoming an egalitarian relationship? Is there fairer sharing out of the work in the home? Only 1 per cent of the sample said that their husbands did not approve because they considered that the man should be the breadwinner and the woman should not work; however, they were forced to 'put up with it' because of the need for extra money. Seventy-six per cent of the sample said that they felt that their husband's work did not affect their work in any way, the most commonly cited reason being that even if their husband was at home all day 'he wouldn't do any more in the house'. Of the 31 per cent who said that their husband's job did affect theirs, most said that their husband already had a flexible job and was taking more responsibility in the home as a consequence. However, the organization and responsibility for the running and care of the household was taken by almost all (98 per cent) of the women interviewed.

An important way in which women can be constrained in their participation in the paid workforce is in the responsibility which they are allocated for the care of children or ageing or disabled relatives. Although 78 per cent of the total sample had children, only approximately 14 per cent had children under 7 years of age; 47 per cent had children over the age of 14 (classified by age of the youngest child) and the remainder had children between the ages of 7 and 14 years. Only 3 per cent of the sample were responsible, at the time of interviewing, for an ageing or disabled relative. The combination of the opportunity to work part-time and during the university terms only, meant that most women could combine childcare and paid work without undue difficulties. Forty-three per cent of the sample said that their husbands had regularly looked after the children while they were at work, although this often occurred when the women worked during the evenings or at weekends. Seventy-six per cent of the sample said that their husbands had never taken time off work to look after their children. The availability of part-time work and time off during the vacations was therefore seen as extremely important by the women, as was the library management's flexibility in allowing the women to take time off to care for sick children and to make it up at a later date.

In spite of the fact that the major responsibility for childcare and domestic arrangements was borne by the women, 67 per cent of the sample said that women should be able to work even if it inconvenienced their family, and 48 per cent said that their work was as important as their family or social life. Many women said that it was not good for the family if the woman put them first all the time, nor was it good for the woman to be burdened with the total responsibility for the care of the family. Many felt that the family, as well as the woman benefited from the woman going out to work. Although 33 per cent said that they did not think it right that women should work if it inconvenienced the family, many of these women qualified their answer by adding that some women do not have the choice as they may well be the breadwinner in the family. When asked if they thought it was more important for their husband/partner than for them to have a good job, 55 per cent said 'yes'. However, 74 per cent of the sample said that given their time again, they would choose a different career. Many of the careers chosen involved considerable responsibility, education, and investment of time. Full-time work was not seen as an important goal.

Rubery (1978) criticizes dual labour market theory for failing to include an analysis of the role of trade unions. She suggests that in viewing the development of the labour market structure solely from one perspective – through the motivations and actions of individual capitalists – insufficient attention has been paid to the ways in which maintaining a divided workforce may be of advantage to some male workers. While broadly accepting Braverman's (1974) assertion that the development of monopoly capitalism involves the destruction of old skills, she goes on to argue that this process also involves the creation of new ones. It is the process of the recomposition of skills which has given rise to defensive attempts on the part of trade unions to maintain old skill divisions within the labour market. An example of this is in the printing industry where the craft printing unions organized vigorously in an attempt to prevent their skills from being undermined by new technology. Rubery argues that the basis of labour market segmentation lies, therefore, in the way in which the introduction of both new technology and new workers by the employer could lead to lower wages within a given occupation and reduced employment opportunities for men. In the struggle to maintain wage rates in such occupations, trade union strategy has been to attempt to confine women to a particular sector of the labour force, through such mechanisms as apprenticeship schemes and promotion lines based on strict seniority provisions. The role of trade unions, then, is seen as crucially important in maintaining labour market segmentation, and in some cases this has involved attempts to restrict the access of women to skilled jobs.

Given the high percentage of women working in the library it could be hypothesized that the women would display a high level of interest in trade unions, owing to the important role which unions can play in determining wages and conditions of work. It could also be expected that the national increase in the number of women in the labour market would tend to make unions more sensitive to the needs and demands of women in the labour force and to make women an increasing target for recruitment as members.

The two unions which represent the library staff are the AUT (Association of University Teachers) which is responsible for the workers on the professional grades IIA to IV, and NALGO (National Association of Local Government Officers) which covers the clerical grades 1–5 and IB. Although 85 per cent of the women sampled knew that a union operated in the library, only 45 per cent knew the names of both the major unions, while 22 per cent did not know the name of either union. Only 29 per cent of those interviewed were members of a union. As predicted by dual labour market theory, union activity was notably higher for members of the 'primary' sector, where all of the women on professional grades who were interviewed were members of the AUT, than for members of the 'secondary' sector, where only 21 per cent of the women on clerical grades were members of NALGO. When asked why they were members of a union, the main reason the women gave was that union membership was important to ensure good working conditions and protection for jobs. Of the women who were not members of a union, 15 per cent said that they had resigned from the union because the union had asked them to go on strike and they were against striking in principle, and 21 per cent said that they would not belong to a union because they disagreed with militant unions. However, the main reason given by the remaining 64 per cent who were not members of a union was that part-timers could not join the union (although membership of NALGO by part-time workers is, in fact, possible).

An important reason why people join unions is that they see them as being effective in achieving gains for the membership. Seventy-eight per cent of the sample felt that the unions in the library were weak, although a small percentage of the sample distinguished between NALGO and the AUT and saw the AUT as being strong relative to NALGO. The AUT's ability to protect the jobs and pay of professional staff was said to be obvious from the enormous differential in pay and status that existed between professional staff and other staff in the library. Those who saw the AUT as strong explained its strength in terms of its high membership level and the support of its members. The most frequently mentioned reason for NALGO's weakness was the lack of membership in the library. This was believed to result from a lack of commitment on the part of the union to seek to increase membership by recruiting women part-time workers, accompanied by a lack of interest on the part of the women in the library.

Women often have specific problems in the workplace, as was also pointed out by the Turkish women interviewed by Yildiz Ecevit in

Chapter 4. If unions are aware of such problems this can be extremely important, not only for women but also for increasing the membership of the union. The main issues for women in the library included health and safety because there was a considerable degree of lifting associated with some jobs, wages, job security, and opportunities for promotion. Opportunity for training was also an important issue, particularly for part-time workers in the 'secondary' sector, who felt that as part-time workers they were denied the funding or opportunity to take time off for training, even if related to their jobs. Seventy-four per cent of the sample did not know what the unions' positions, if any, were on these issues. Only 37 per cent saw the union as obtaining benefits for them in terms of pay and believed that the union had been instrumental in the ungrading of some staff members. Many women felt that more regular meetings including part-time day, evening and weekend staff, as well as professional staff, could be held so that there would be a better flow of information between all the staff. This, it was felt, would help to alleviate the feeling among many part-time day, evening and weekend staff that they were 'left out' and that they were not as important as the professional staff, thereby helping to reduce the 'them and us' situation.

In spite of the lack of opportunity for promotion the workforce appeared to be remarkably stable, 85 per cent of the sample saying that, for the foreseeable future, they intended to remain in their present jobs in the library. The reasons for this varied but, in general, the convenience of the job and the way it fitted in with home commitments were of major importance, as was the satisfaction which was derived from the job itself, 81 per cent saying that they would definitely not be happier if they stayed at home. When asked if they would apply for a job of a higher grade if one became available, 78 per cent of the sample replied that they would, although a considerable number also said that the job would have to be more interesting than their present job and also that it would have to be part-time. The women were aware of the low value attached to part-time work and that they were disadvantaged by it; 89 per cent of the sample thought that part-time women workers had less opportunity for promotion than full-time women workers. A majority of the sample said that this was because women who worked part-time were seen as 'pin money people', or that part-time workers were seen as both cheap and expendable labour.

Although the women saw part-time work as a major disadvantage and barrier to promotion, they did not relate it to the division of labour between the sexes. When asked if they thought equal opportunities were present within the library, 52 per cent said that women had the same opportunities as men for promotion. The reason given was that as almost all women were employed on grades 1–5, there was no competition with men at the lower grades, but that if men were employed on these grades, there would be equal opportunity. It was felt that at the professional level there were equal opportunities for women and men. However, the women overlooked the fact that it is the segregation of work itself which is indicative of inequality. Women library workers do virtually all the jobs which are defined as part-time and of low value. Even at the profession- al grades, women had not progressed beyond the lowest professional grade in the library. The fact that almost all the men employed in the library were on the higher grades appeared to make it difficult for the women to see themselves as being in competition with men, and so to ascertain whether or not they had equal opportunities for promotion. In this respect, segregation of work into jobs carried out by males and females seems to be an extremely effective way of limiting awareness of inequalities between the sexes; it also makes it more difficult to challenge.

Conclusion

The data which emerged from the study showed that the library could be said to be divided in approximate accordance with dual labour market theory; that is into a primary sector where workers were predominantly full-time, had relatively high wage rates, were acknowledged to have high skill levels, good career prospects, and were represented by a relatively strong trade union, and a secondary sector characterized by part-time work, lower wages and status, little provision for career development, and relatively weak trade union representation. The workers employed in the primary sector were predominantly male and those in the secondary sector were almost all female. The actual structure of employment in the library was, however, more complex in that the secondary sector consisted of two broad categories: the part-time day staff who were allocated to the grade 2 pay scale; and the part-time evening and weekend staff who, although performing the same jobs as the former, were classified on the lower grade 1 scale. The case study showed that the characteristics of the women in the secondary sector of the library did not generally coincide with those which dual labour market theorists attribute to workers in the secondary sector: such as, low commitment to work, the lack of intention to remain in their jobs, and an absence of desire for responsibility. What was obvious was that domestic commitments, responsibility for childcare, and the prioritization of their partners' jobs made it necessary for the women to seek part-time work.

Part-time work not only played an important part in women's lives, but was seen to play an important part in the organization and efficient running of the library. It is far from an unstable or unskilled source of employment, and appears to be undervalued in the workplace (see also

Beechey and Perkins 1987). Work which is part-time appears to be defined almost entirely in terms of the hours of work, so that the educational level, skill and experience, and productivity of women who do part-time work receive virtually no formal recognition. The undervaluation of part-time work may well be related to the way in which it is perceived as an extension of domestic labour, as is indicated by the way in which it is often referred to as 'work which women do to fit in with their domestic commitments'.

Women who worked part-time appeared to have little access to promotion and a major barrier (although not the only one) is that jobs above a certain grade are defined mainly as full-time work, so that women who work only part-time are excluded. It is also clear that women themselves saw this as a major barrier; 89 per cent of the sample saw part-time workers as having less opportunity for promotion than full-time working men. The way in which domestic commitments constrain women's participation in the labour force can be seen in the reasons why the women chose and stayed in their jobs. The burden of domestic commitments is further illustrated by the fact that most of the partners of the women in the sample did not appear to carry out an equal share of domestic tasks and certainly did not appear to share the responsibility for such tasks, in spite of their stated support for the women's paid work.

The women seemed to have a very positive attitude to work and felt that they had a right to work, although this was not reflected in membership of the relevant unions, about which the part-time women workers had very little knowledge. Unions must take at least part of the blame for this, in that, despite the high numbers of women in the labour force, they have usually failed to involve themselves in the problems and difficulties which women experience in the workplace. They have also failed to press for opportunities for promotion for women to be increased by continually arguing the case for training for part-time (and full-time) women workers, by seeking to have the jobs of all or most grades opened up as job-share posts and by arguing for a change in the criteria used for grading the different jobs carried out in the library, in order to prevent the grading system from continuing to reinforce the existing pattern of job segregation. Until they do so, women will not see unions as 'acting in their interests'.[3]

Overall, what is clear is that the place of women and men in the library is intimately related to the gender division of labour in the home – a division of labour whereby large numbers of women engage in part-time paid employment. Whereas the decisions most men make about their careers and the opportunities which are open to them are predicated on a lack of major responsibility for domestic tasks and childcare, for the majority of women, restricted career decisions and

39

Maura Luck

limited opportunities are related to the rigidity with which family tasks are allocated to them. It is the absence of major responsibility for such tasks which allows men to be seen as more rational, because they are usually able to make decisions about work which are not constrained by domestic commitments. Even women who do not have domestic responsibilities are constrained in the workplace by the perception of them as 'future' or 'natural' wives and mothers. Thus, all women are constrained by a gender division of labour which affects the type of work they do and creates patterns of participation in paid work which disadvantage them in terms of pay and opportunities for promotion.

Notes

1 The table gives the numbers of workers employed on different grades and should be interpreted with care, since a number of employees are employed on more than one grade or are employed for both day and evening and weekend work and, though classified as having a part-time job, may actually work the same or a similar number of hours per week as a full-time worker.
2 The interviews involved the use of a questionnaire; further information about the sample and the questionnaire are given in Luck (1986).
3 Between August 1986, when the study was carried out, and August 1988, NALGO succeeded in achieving promotions for both part-time and full-time library workers. Four part-time and eight full-time women workers were upgraded, although none of the women was an evening or weekend worker.

References

Becker, G.S. (1957) *The Economics of Discrimination*, Chicago: University of Chicago Press.
Beechy, V. and Perkins, T. (1987) *A Matter of Hours*, Cambridge: Polity Press.
Braverman, H. (1974) *Labour and Monopoly Capital*, London and New York: Monthly Review Press.
Cockburn, C. (1983) *Brothers. Male Dominance and Technological Change*, London: Pluto Press.
——(1985) *Machinery of Dominance. Women, Men and Technological Know-how*, London: Pluto Press.
Doeringer, P.B. and Piore, M.J. (1971) *Internal Labor Markets and Manpower Analysis*, Lexington, Massachusetts: D.C. Heath.
Hartmann, H. (1979) 'Capitalism, patriarchy and job segregation by sex', in Z.R. Eisenstein (ed.) *Capitalist Patriarchy and the Case for Socialist Feminism*, London and New York: Monthly Review Press.
Luck, M. (1986) *The Female/Male Wage Differential, Occupational Segregation and the Sexual Division of Labour*, MA Dissertation in Women's Studies, University of Kent.

Mackintosh, M. (1981) 'Gender and economics. The sexual division of labour and the subordination of women', in K. Young, C. Wolkowitz, and R. McCullagh (eds) *Of Marriage and the Market. Women's Subordination Internationally and its Lessons*, London: CSE Books.

Phelps, E.S. (1972) 'The statistical theory of racism and sexism', *American Economic Review* 62 (4): 659–661.

Phillips, A. and Taylor, B. (1980) 'Sex and skill: notes towards a feminist economics', *Feminist Review* 6: 79–88.

Rubery, J. (1978) 'Structured labour markets, worker organisation and low pay', *Cambridge Journal of Economics* 2(1): 17–36.

Chapter three

Images and goods

Women in retailing

Adelina Broadbridge

Introduction

Most shop workers are women. Shop work is hierarchically organized,
with the highest positions traditionally being filled by men and the lower
positions being occupied by women. Over two million workers were
employed in retail distribution in March 1988 (one-tenth of the
employed population), of whom 36 per cent were men and 64 per cent
were women, with 38 per cent of women working on a part-time basis
and 25 per cent working full-time (DOE 1988). Many male jobs are
managerial and traditionally defined as skilled jobs, while most women
work as sales assistants and clerks, 83 per cent of sales assistants being
female (OPCS 1984). This is reinforced by the high proportion of
female jobs that are part-time, while managerial jobs are almost
invariably full-time. The increasing opportunities for part-time work in
retailing are accompanied by the introduction of new technology and
result, in many instances, from tight wage budgets and longer trading
hours. The trend towards using more part-time labour is likely to
continue, and much of this labour will be supplied by married women
with childcare responsibilities, who have difficulty in finding suitable
alternative employment.

Retailing has become far more marketing oriented. Businesses now
understand the importance of providing what the consumer wants, not
only as far as the products are concerned, but also in terms of the
package of experiences offered by the store. Women provide part of this
package. They have been conditioned to provide a particular service to
their customers, involving characteristics such as efficiency, patience,
submissiveness, and pleasantness. The expectation of that behaviour is
upheld by their general working conditions. This study will show how
the department store takes on and perpetuates these stereotypes.

Having worked in several London department stores for approximately five years I undertook the study from which this chapter is
drawn (Broadbridge 1986) in order to examine female sales assistants'

perceptions of their work, their experience of pay and working conditions, and prevalent assumptions about skill and expected behaviour. The major sample consisted of forty-three female sales assistants in a number of department stores located in central London. Ten managerial female staff and ten male staff were additionally interviewed as control groups. Wherever possible interviews were conducted during the respondent's own time, outside the working environment. The interviews followed a semi-structured questionnaire format and the information gained from respondents included their general retail background and personal characteristics, their reasons for choosing their job, the aspects of the job they liked and disliked, general staff and customer relationships, how the employees rated their jobs, and the changes they would like to see implemented. Some of the key issues raised by the questionnaire responses are discussed in this chapter. First it will be useful to give a brief historical account of the nature of retailing in order to understand the present day position.

Historical background

The historical literature is divided about the role of women in retailing. Some (Oakley 1974; Alexander 1976) claim that women played a prominent role in pre-industrial British retailing, while others (Clark 1982) suggest that a woman's role was that of her husband's helpmate. The form of retailing was, of course, different from that of today, with much of the working class community being served by door-to-door vendors and street sellers, while the middle classes used the small scale family business traders and skilled craftsmen. Holcombe (1973) argues that there was an absence of women in retailing in Victorian Britain. She describes how most traditional retail traders were craftsmen, their work demanding a variety of skills involving product knowledge, buying, storage, and the processing of large quantities of goods. This entailed an apprenticeship system which largely excluded women, mainly due to parents' refusal to pay for their daughters to be apprenticed, since apprentices earned low, if any, wages. The apprenticeship system gave rise to little demand for shop assistants, and because apprentices were so cheap there was no need to substitute cheap female labour.

As capitalism developed the nature of retailing changed. Jefferys (1954) suggests that between the last quarter of the nineteenth century and the beginning of the First World War there was a major transformation within the distributive trades. This transformation helped to undermine the skilled nature of the work. For example, many traditional craft skills were passed over to wholesalers and manufacturers and retailing concentrated on the sale of finished goods only.

The expanding market resulted in an increase in the number and size of shops, as both working class, and particularly middle class demands accelerated. Jefferys argues that high class multiples and department stores developed to meet this middle class demand. This, in turn, created the need for shop assistants who were now unskilled as their craft traditions had declined and who, as Holcombe argues, did little more than keep the stock tidy, show merchandise, and receive payment. As a consequence the apprenticeship system declined and so it was easier to obtain a retail job. With the decline in skills, came the belief that female assistants appreciated customers' needs better than men, which masked another major reason: women could be paid half the wages of men. Women, therefore, began to enter the retail trade in greater numbers. Holcombe claims, however, that the nature of retail work was highly segregated by sex. Women appeared to be employed only where minimal training was necessary; where the work was considered light; in departments where the customer was likely to be female; and where the wage bill was highly important to the shopkeeper. Men continued to be employed in departments where the work was considered skilled and required training (e.g. chemists); where the stock was considered more important than the wage bill (e.g. jewellery, wine, books); where the work was thought to be too rough and heavy for women (e.g. furniture, butchery); and where there was a predominantly male clientele (e.g. tailoring). This sex segregation persists today.

At this time of increasing competition (1875–1914), retail establishments needed to attract customers to their stores. This meant providing a complete marketing package for the client. Retailers did this via the service offered to the customer in the form of the behaviour and appearance of employees and the layout of the store, which was designed for the customers' pleasure and luxury. Most department stores began to provide restaurants and tea rooms for their customers, as well as providing sumptuous displays and grand stairways. Some of the larger stores even supplied rest and writing rooms. An emphasis on total customer service began to be attached to the concept of the department store. This was further extended by the introduction of lifts and escalators for customer use, the first escalator being installed in England in 1898 at Harrods (Dale 1981). Hence shopping for the middle classes was intended also to be an afternoon out. Winstanley (1983) argues that shopping was no longer a chore but a pleasurable social activity, and although the department store was originally intended to appeal to all social groups, most stores realized that their clientele largely comprised the middle classes who were concerned with convenience, comfort and quality.

In order to complete this kind of shopping experience it was necessary for a particular kind of service to be provided by the staff.

Unfortunately this was often at the expense of the shop assistants' working conditions. Holcombe (1973) and Bondfield (1899) describe shopworkers' appalling conditions which included extremely long hours of work, involving standing all day, with minimal rest and meal breaks. They received very little pay, out of which they were expected to dress as well as their customers. Linked to the poor pay system was the living-in system which, in many instances, could be likened to a workhouse (Holcombe 1973). In addition, fines were payable for various disciplinary misdemeanours including talking, sitting down, or making business errors. Job security was minimal, with dismissal threatening assistants for what today may seem bizarre events such as allowing a customer to leave the store without making a purchase (Whitaker 1973). The customers were also given a sense of superiority when they visited the store; they looked down upon the assistants and felt they could treat them accordingly, expecting servility and submissiveness.

The consumer package

Many consumers still expect convenience, comfort, and quality from their shopping expedition. Following Lancaster's (1966) approach to consumer theory, which argues that each market good embodies various characteristics that ultimately yield utility, it is possible to argue that consumers, in purchasing a product, are purchasing a bundle of characteristics. These vary according to the kind of purchase required, and the type of establishment from which the consumers choose to make their purchase. At one end of the continuum is the department store where, in addition to the characteristics of the product itself, the package which the consumer is purchasing may include comfort, elegance, quality, exclusivity, and service. At the other end of the continuum, say at the self-service supermarket, the package offered to the consumer is somewhat different. Here low prices, freshness, convenience, and car parking facilities may be ranked as more important characteristics. Customers are increasingly expecting better and improved service levels from the supermarket employee, but of a somewhat different nature from that of the department store employee. Major supermarket employee attributes may be the speed and efficiency of service and cleanliness. All retail employees are expected to provide a certain degree of service to their customers. This is particularly relevant currently as retail businesses are adopting methods of competition other than price, including service competition, in order to maintain or increase their market share. The service expected from a department store employee traditionally embodies more characteristics than other forms of retail service. For example, included in the list of attributes consumers expect from department store sales assistants are good quality personal service, which may also embody product knowledge, efficiency, patience, submissiveness, pleasantness, friendliness, and an attractive appearance.

Shop assistants are expected to possess these characteristics in order to provide the customer with a specific kind of experience. Some of these have direct consequences for staff; others are more concealed. In the stores under study the shop assistants were expected to dress in a 'business like' manner. Management policy stipulates that a good standard of appearance and grooming is very important for representing the store image and selling the merchandise. Female assistants are expected to wear sombre colours such as black, navy, and grey, and put on their make-up in a particular manner. Perhaps the worst expectations are those placed upon assistants in cosmetics departments. Just in case the message was not firmly conveyed, one store provided a booklet to all employees explaining exactly how a woman should prepare for work. Female sales assistants were told to try to get up a little earlier each morning to ensure that their hair was neat and tidy; to leave enough time to apply make-up carefully in good natural lighting – as there is nothing worse than racing to work and having to make-up on arrival; to decide on their outfit the night before – as decisions on accessories and ironing of clothes would be much better done when they were not in a tearing hurry.

Equally patronizing was its advice to men, reminding them to wash their hands a couple of times during the day! The aim is to create the stereotyped image of a saleswoman, aptly described by Game and Pringle (1983) as having hair up high, rings on fingers, heavily made up, and dressed in a smart casual suit. The situation is a direct overspill from the past, when sales assistants were inspected each morning by their department manager, and sent home or threatened with dismissal if not properly dressed.

It was also clear that both management and customers require a particular behavioural pattern from the sales assistant. For example, submissiveness is a characteristic which is expected of sales assistants, especially females. Customers have a preconceived idea of the way in which they believe assistants should behave. If the assistant does not react in the way the customer wants, she may be open to criticism. Sales assistants are expected to be immediately at hand, pleasant, helpful, efficient, courteous, patient, enthusiastic, and imaginative at all times. If customers wish to fire abuse at the assistant they can do so freely. The sales assistant is always expected to accept abuse without retaliation. Even in instances where the assistant is carrying out store policy, if the customer decides to complain further the assistant is seldom backed up by senior management. The store gives way to the customer, in order to show goodwill. This leaves the assistant in an utterly submissive role.

A sexual element also characterizes relationships between shop assistants and customers, customer behaviour towards assistants, and the responses which are expected from them, varying considerably between female and male assistants. Customers may be more hostile to female assistants than to males. Because men appear to be in more responsible departments, and can exert their skill and knowledge to a higher degree, they are often given more credibility and respect. Women are regarded as there to serve, please, and be humiliated, and they are treated accordingly. Sexual harassment of female assistants by male customers was, for example, a problem noted by several respondents. The assistants felt that they were unable to take control of the situation, but had to grin and bear it.

The modern department store is designed to provide its clientele with a comfortable and appealing environment. In a handbook about one of the stores in the study, given to all new employees, management described the store as 'a showpiece' with 'comfort, elegance, space, a modern appearance', and stressed that all customers must find shopping in the store a 'totally satisfactory experience'. However, the moment one walks through the doors into the areas not designated for customer use, the stark contrast between the enticing appearance of the shop floor and the drabness of the non-customer areas is apparent. One female sales assistant's description of non-customer areas was 'disgraceful, dirty, smelly, and tatty'. This very often extends to the employees' facilities which are usually basic and inadequate to meet the needs of all the employees. Staff canteens often have very poor facilities, are dirty and very cramped and noisy, not allowing for the proper rest most assistants feel they need at lunchtime. Rest rooms, if provided at all, are also usually sparsely furnished and not conducive to relaxing. Most respondents complained bitterly about meal break facilities and were left with the belief that management feel 'staff can put up with it'.

The meal break system conceals another indirect method by which sales assistants are controlled in order to meet their customers' every demand. Meal breaks rotas are drawn up by management and breaks are staggered in order to retain as many staff on the sales floor as possible. Hence, a regular meal or tea break routine is never established. This ensures that the customers receive the service they require and it also maintains the impersonal relationship between assistant and manager, first introduced during the Victorian era. In fact, management staff are warned in their training not to become too friendly with ordinary staff either in or out of shop hours!

Similar conditions are imposed concerning days off and holiday arrangements. Many employees had no set day off per week, but were merely told the previous week which was to be their day off for the following week. There are also severe restrictions on when holidays may be taken, with certain times of the year such as Christmas being totally prohibited. During the permitted times, staff have to stagger holidays. As Saturday is the major trading day few staff are allowed their day off on this day. There is increasing evidence of stores opening on bank holidays. Most employees are obliged to work these extra days and refusal to do so could cost them their job. For the employee, then, retail work is largely anti-social. The whole concept of working hours again shows how customer service is paramount to the business.

Such poor conditions of work bring into question the role of the shopworkers' union, USDAW (Union of Shop, Distributive, and Allied Workers). It was found that 60 per cent of the female assistants felt that the union had no influence in improving work conditions for the staff. Many only saw the union's role as negotiating the annual pay rise and, like the Turkish women factory workers studied by Yildiz Ecevit in Chapter 4, cited no examples of union recognition of issues of specific importance to women.

Gender differences in skill and pay

It is important to outline how male and female sales assistants are perceived to be different by the customer in terms of definitions of skill, and how this, in turn, affects the fundamental differences between male and female sales assistants on issues such as pay levels. The issue of skill definitions is extremely contentious, with origins firmly entrenched in history. Jefferys argues that the decline in skill historically depends on the nature of the trade. This is important considering the gender segregated nature of the retail trade. Even today men are associated with those jobs which command a high degree of human capital, and require a knowledge of the product. The characteristics which are associated with male sales assistants' jobs are, as will be seen, different from those associated with female assistants' jobs.

It has become far more noticeable that departments which are recognized as those requiring socially defined skills and knowledge to sell the merchandise are those dominated by male sales assistants, while those not requiring any formally recognized skills are predominantly female departments. Men are associated with the possession of certain socially defined skills; women are not. The customer is also conditioned to approach male assistants in preference to female assistants in the former kind of departments, based on the assumption that male assistants are more authoritative than female assistants, the set of requirements expected from male assistants being different from that expected from female assistants. The sale of a carpet is considered to involve certain skills, whereas the sale of hosiery is not. Men predominate in carpet departments; women in hosiery.

Selling hosiery does require a skill. It simply goes unrecognized. The assistants in both kinds of departments require detailed knowledge of the merchandise they are selling. Within a good-sized hosiery department it takes about a month to command perfect knowledge of all the stock, the suitability of a particular product to customer requirements such as size, occasion, co-ordination with the outfit, and the price range. Given a particular situation the assistant has to assess the customer's needs and suggest suitable products and alternatives. In a department where high volumes of individual sales and/or staff shortages restrict the assistant's ability to spend much time with individual customers, the assistant must be able to provide such product knowledge immediately. She thus has to know her exact stock and its location without referring to the product information (unlike assistants in less busy departments). Moreover, information about small items may not be as readily available as information about larger items, so that the assistant often has to do more information hunting herself in order to be able to advise her customer correctly. It is not impossible for such a sales assistant to be serving several customers at once, all at various stages of purchase. This would never happen in a carpet department where service is strictly on a one-to-one basis.

The different characteristics possessed by male and female sales assistants may be further highlighted within the store, where men and women work in different departments, many of which mirror Holcombe's earlier findings of men being in departments where more skill and 'knowledge' is presumed. General examination of the department stores under survey provides support for these traits. Departments such as heavy electrical goods, furnishings and carpets tend to employ more male assistants, while departments in which low cost, high volume items are sold tend to employ more female staff. There are some areas in which the traditional sex segregated nature of departments has become rather blurred, with women being represented in some areas which, traditionally, were designated as male-only preserves. Game and Pringle (1983) attribute this to the 1930s when there was a move towards increasing the number of departments in which women could work, because women were cheaper to employ. Sex segregation according to the nature of the department shows how work is organized around gender, and how gender itself is constructed at work. It maintains the barriers between men and women over issues of pay, conditions of work, and job status which, in turn, affect the employee's job perception. Such occupational segregation has been shown to have similar effects in a variety of different contexts such as library work in Britain, studied by Maura Luck in Chapter 2, and factory work in Turkey, examined by Yildiz Ecevit in Chapter 4.

A major area which came under criticism by the female shop assistants was the issue of pay, which is related to issues of skill definitions and gender linked departments. Shop assistants are notoriously badly paid (Department of Employment 1987) and the survey showed that of the younger female assistants many were forced to continue to live with their parents because the low level of their wages prevented them from living away from home. Some employees may negotiate their basic wage, but employers try to maximize their profits by keeping basic rates as low as possible. The pay system is not very different from the days when Whiteley's employees were asked 'What is the lowest wage you will work for?' To corroborate how low the basic sales assistant's wage rate was, an USDAW branch newsletter from one of the survey stores provided data from its own survey, in which staff members had been asked about their month's expenses. It revealed that basic living requirements amounted to 99 per cent of the average shopworker's monthly wage. These findings added support to the author's own findings from the questionnaire. It should also be noted that this particular store paid better basic wages than the other stores examined. A staff discount was given to all permanent staff in the stores. For many stores the percentage given increased according to rank, with sales assistants receiving the minimum amount of discount. Staff discount could be seen as a saving to the employers on the basic rate which they paid. Many employees could not afford to take much advantage of the discount owing to the high prices of the goods sold in the store.

What is interesting, however, is that only one man (a trainee) complained about his rate of pay. The others seemed fairly satisfied with their salaries. Although basic rates may be similar for men and women, real earnings are different. The New Earnings Survey placed female sales assistants' pay at only 70 per cent of men's in 1986 (DOE 1987). Much of the difference in rates of pay between men and women stems from the amount earned in overtime or commission payments. This was demonstrated by the results of the survey. Commission was found to relate to certain departments – not every department's employees received commission or premiums. Some departments provided premiums for selling certain products, while others provided opportunities to earn commission on everything. Interestingly it was the predominantly male departments which paid the full commission, and the female departments where little or no commission was paid. The whole issue of pay was invidious in that senior management could use it at their whim to encourage some assistants but not others. Since basic pay levels were minimal, the opportunity to earn commission or premiums was the method used as an incentive, the main incentives thus being available almost exclusively to male employees.

Many assistants and managers earned different levels of commission without their colleagues knowing about it. One example was found in the furniture department where the male assistants were employed directly by the store and received 1 per cent commission on the retail price of everything they sold. The female assistants in the department were employed by the manufacturing firms and they received 1 per cent commission on the cost price (approximately half the retail price) of their firms' products. Furthermore, when a woman sold an item of furniture, she had to assign the name of a male employee from the store to the bill, which entitled the man to receive additional commission from the sale carried out by the woman. Hence, the men had the opportunity to earn approximately four times as much commission as the women in the same department. Put another way, when a woman sold an item of furniture, a man received twice as much commission for doing nothing! So although women were represented in a typically male dominated department, they were nowhere near parity with their male counterparts.

The male assistants did not, on the whole, complain about their rates of pay, whereas pay was a major issue on the list of female assistants' grievances. This implies that men's pay is inextricably linked with commission. One male assistant claimed that he was reluctant to change departments because his pay and commission were closely related to his length of service in the department. To change departments, he would have to accept a cut in real wages and it would take time to raise his take-home pay to the amount he presently received. In contrast, many women expressed a desire to change departments for various reasons, pay obviously not being a determining factor in keeping them in a particular location. Formalized definitions of skill and what is perceived to be a superior level of service from the customer viewpoint are clearly of fundamental importance in determining men's higher earnings levels. The shopworkers' union did not appear to have challenged such definitions.

Attitudes towards shop work

The conditions according to which the department store sales assistants are expected to work ensure that a certain type of service is provided to the customer. It is part of the total product with which the customer is provided when shopping. But how do shop assistants perceive their work and what is their level of job satisfaction? The respondents were asked their reasons for choosing retailing as a job. Several female assistants specifically said that they only chose the job for pecuniary reasons (despite wage rates being so low). Others argued that because they lacked educational qualifications, shop work was one of the very few jobs open to them. It was regarded as preferable to factory work. Various respondents provided particular reasons for choosing this type of retail outlet rather than any other. They believed that working in a department store would be more prestigious, more exciting, and less boring then other forms of retailing. Few maintained these beliefs once they had actually experienced the work.

In trying to ascertain how female sales assistants felt about their jobs they were encouraged to speak freely about their likes and dislikes. Many found difficulty in thinking of any aspects of their jobs that they enjoyed. Of the responses given, many were not specific to retailing. For example, this question elicited responses such as work colleagues, the social life it generates, working in central London. None of these criteria pertain to retailing alone. In addition, 'going home' was another positive aspect, together with 'skiving'. Only 19 per cent of female assistants actually enjoyed dealing with customers, while only 12 per cent liked serving and selling, the main component of the job. Furthermore, assistants only enjoyed serving some customers. They placed greater emphasis upon 'awkward' customers.

This is an important issue to explore further, given that the customer expects a particular behaviour pattern from the sales assistant. To do so it is relevant to consider how the staff perceive the way in which the customers treat the female sales assistant. Of the descriptions given of customers by female assistants, those used most frequently were 'ignorant, rude, obstinate, arrogant, bad-tempered, patronising, and demanding'. Many assistants felt they were being treated like servants and comments such as 'customers look down on you – sales assistants are nothing' were made frequently. Assistants often felt they were not treated like human beings, but had no means of redress. Instead they had to 'bottle up your frustrations – you can't let them out'. The prevailing attitude was that the assistants are there to 'bow and scrape'. The younger respondents complained that customers very often would not respect their advice, preferring to be served by an older member of staff.

Some women sales assistants were angry about sexual harassment by male customers and all respondents talked of the extreme frustrations of dealing with awkward customers. The aim of introducing name tags to be worn by sales assistants in one or two of the stores was vehemently opposed by the respondents, who felt that it could result in further harassment from customers, as well as being an invasion of their privacy. Some said that they were overpolite to the awkward customer, their way of embarrassing the customer into being polite in return. Others tried to win the customer over, seeing the situation as a challenge, and found it rewarding if they could manage to obtain a sale. The attitude adopted by customers has a direct effect on the sales assistants' enjoyment of their jobs.

It was found that female assistants felt more overall dissatisfaction with their jobs than the male assistants and female managers interviewed. This would suggest that it is women who make up most of the voluntary staff turnover figures (rated at 48 per cent per annum in the store in which most of the interviews took place). Less than 5 per cent of the female sales assistants interviewed felt their job to be totally rewarding, compared with 26 per cent who considered it totally unrewarding. Over half the female assistants were discontented with their job, compared with only 20 per cent of female managers and 20 per cent of male assistants; 80 per cent of both female managers and men considered their work as relatively or totally rewarding. It is interesting to compare the findings concerning the assistants' expectations and actual enjoyment of their work. For female sales assistants, their expectation of enjoying their work (67 per cent) was much greater than their actual enjoyment (40 per cent). The male assistants, on the other hand, actually enjoyed their work (80 per cent) more than they had expected to (70 per cent). Men's greater enjoyment is likely to be related to the benefits which they receive from the formal recognition of their skills, which alters the way customers treat them and which is certainly reflected in their superior pay levels.

The survey revealed that given the relevant opportunities, the majority of female workers, nearly 75 per cent, would like to stop work or change jobs, which suggests that women may remain in their jobs due to factors beyond their control. Factors preventing women from leaving their current employment included the lack of availability of another job, lack of relevant qualifications/experience in other fields, and lack of money. Over 80 per cent of female respondents said that if they could relive the last ten years, they would plan their lives differently, as Maura Luck also found for 74 per cent of the female library workers she interviewed. An overall impression gained was that men do not regret having entered retailing whereas women do. Commenting on the future, 70 per cent of female sales assistants said that they foresaw, or would like to see their future out of retailing altogether.

Conclusion

Many retailing practices have their roots in history, but the sales assistant's job no longer carries the status it held at the beginning of the twentieth century. The occupation has become associated with a female workforce as skill labels have been stripped away. The minority of male shop assistants are found in sex segregated departments which, in contrast to those in which women are employed, are characterized by socially defined skills, and their average earnings are considerably higher than those of female assistants. Although many assistants are dissatisfied with their job content and conditions of work, men, because of the higher prestige associated with their jobs, find it easier to over-look the more unsatisfactory aspects of their work and can perceive their jobs as enjoyable. Female sales assistants have a considerably higher sense of dissatisfaction with their work than male sales assistants or women in managerial positions. Ideally, many would like to leave their employment, but materially they do not have the opportunity to do so.

The future for females shop assistants is also bleak. For instance, a growing proportion of workers are being engaged on a part-time basis resulting, in part, from the introduction of new technology which will result in the department store shop assistant's job becoming even more 'deskilled'. Martin and Roberts (1984) claim that women who work part-time tend to trade off aspects of a job such as good pay, security, and the opportunities to use their abilities, in favour of convenient hours. This may be applicable to retailing, especially as the interviews revealed that one-third of female sales assistants did not expect to enjoy their work in the first place.

Although the union is pressing for legislative protection for part-time workers, British retailers have strongly opposed proposals to bring Britain into line with the rest of the EC, allowing part-time workers employment rights in line with those of full-time workers. The current position sounds almost like a return to Victorian Britain, with cheap labour, long trading hours, and little legal protection. Many Victorian practices have never been eroded – especially those which maintain the particular female sales assistant/customer relationship of patience and submissiveness. As the study showed, these characteristics are funda-mental in the construction of female shop assistants as an essential ingredient of the consumer package.

Acknowledgements

I should like to thank Thea Sinclair for advice and encouragement in writing this chapter; also the many retail workers, who gave up much free time to let me interview them, especially Debbie Symonds who showed much enthusiasm in the research.

References

Alexander, S. (1976) 'Women's work in nineteenth century London; a study of the years 1820–50', in J. Mitchell and A. Oakley (eds) *The Rights and Wrongs of Women*, Harmondsworth: Penguin.

Bondfield, M. (1899) 'Conditions under which shop assistants work', *The Economic Journal* 9: 227–286.

Broadbridge, A. (1986) *Are You Being Served? A Study of Women and Retailing*, MA Dissertation in Women's Studies, University of Kent.

Clark, A. (1982) *Working Life of Women in the Seventeenth Century*, London: Routledge & Kegan Paul.

Dale, T. (1981) *Harrods. The Store and the Legend*, London: Pan.

Department of Employment (1988) *Employment Gazette* 96(8): 514, London: HMSO.

——(1987) *New Earnings Survey 1986*, Part D Analyses by Occupation, London: HMSO.

Game, A. and Pringle, R. (1983) *Gender at Work*, Hemel Hempstead: George Allen & Unwin.

Holcombe, L. (1973) *Victorian Ladies at Work*, Newton Abbott: David & Charles.

Jefferys, J.B. (1954) *Retail Trading in Britain 1850–1950*, Cambridge: Cambridge University Press.

Lancaster, K. (1966) 'Change and innovation in the technology of consumption', *American Economic Review, Papers and Proceedings* 56(2): 14–23.

Martin, J. and Roberts, C. (1984) *Women and Employment. A Lifetime Perspective*, London: Department of Employment, OPCS, HMSO.

Oakley, A. (1974) *Housewife*, London: Allen Lane.

OPCS (1984) *Population Census 1981*, Economic Activity Tables, Great Britain, Table 4B.

Whitaker, W.B. (1973) *Victorian and Edwardian Shopworkers: The Struggle to Obtain Better Conditions and a Half-Holiday*, Newton Abbot: David & Charles.

Winstanley, M.J. (1983) *The Shopkeeper's World 1830–1914*, Manchester: Manchester University Press.

Chapter four

Shop floor control

The ideological construction of Turkish women factory workers

Yildiz Ecevit

Introduction

In the 1970s and 1980s women's employment has been one of the most widely discussed issues within feminist discourse. A major reason for this has been the supposed relationship between women's participation in the labour market and their emancipation. Although women have long been engaged in many kinds of productive activities, their involvement in the labour market as wage labourers has been seen as particularly significant, offering an alternative to their restriction within the domestic domain as reproducers, nurturers, and subsistence producers. Participation in social production and control of income have been seen as crucial elements in increasing women's autonomy and power.

In spite of the proliferation of theoretical and empirical analyses of the extent and nature of women's participation in the labour markets of industrialized countries, there has been a general absence of studies of women's labour market participation in urban areas of the 'South'. When the literature on women in the 'South' is examined, it can be seen that the main focus of attention has been, on the one hand, rural women's economic activities and, on the other, women's role in export processing zones. The information which is available about urban women is usually limited to census reports which fail to capture the full range of women's economic activity; what types of jobs urban women hold, their conditions of employment, and the wages they earn have received relatively little attention. This study will attempt to compensate for the general neglect of women's work in urban areas by providing a case study of women workers in Turkish factories. In particular, it will examine the conditions of women's participation in social production and their motives for work; the variety of ways in which women are controlled and supervised on the shop floor; their relations with trade unions; and the mechanisms through which existing forms of gender subordination are reproduced in the factory.

Women's employment in the Turkish province of Bursa

Nine major provinces account for almost 90 per cent of the industrial workforce in Turkey. Bursa, located in the Marmara region, is one of these provinces. The province consists of a provincial city centre and ten districts. It had a population of one million two hundred thousand inhabitants in 1980 and, with an area of 11,027 km², is the fifth largest province in Turkey. The annual population growth rate was 36 per cent and population density is high, with seventy-seven people per km² in 1970, increasing to eighty-seven in 1975 and 104 in 1980.

The study was conducted in the central city, which had a population of around 670,000 in 1980. The reasons for choosing Bursa were that, first, the city has a long tradition of female employment. Women have been working in the textile factories since the Ottoman period. Second, almost all branches of manufacturing industry which are known to be heavily reliant on female labour can be found there. Third, the co-existence of traditional, small factories and large, modern factories is a common characteristic of urban industrial structures in developing countries (Roberts 1978) and this feature is very apparent in Bursa. The city contains both types of factory, providing an opportunity to compare women's work in the two contexts. Finally, manufacturing industry does not only consist of private enterprises. There are also two major state enterprises which rely heavily on women's labour, permitting a comparison of women's work in state and private firms.

Interviews were conducted with twenty-three female workers in the largest state factory in the city, producing woollen yarn, fabric, and clothing; with twenty-two workers in two private textile factories producing dyed and woven synthetic fabric; with twenty-one workers in two private food factories producing canned food, jam, and fruit juice; and with thirteen workers in a private factory which produced electrical components for cars. The latter was a recently established, sub-branch of the car industry and was thus a non-traditional source of employment for Bursa women. Fourteen workers were interviewed in the state tobacco sorting and grading workshop.

The factories were relatively large, employing between 300 and 3,000 workers. The numbers of female workers employed varied between 100 and 1,000. Interviews were also conducted with women workers in seven small, traditional textile factories employing between ten and fifteen workers. In total, 100 women factory workers were interviewed.

Although female employment in Bursa has not been as high as male employment, women have been extensively employed in manufacturing industry. In 1970, 64.7 per cent of the total female active population was employed in manufacturing (Koray 1975:214), and the number of women in the manufacturing sector was higher than in any other Turkish province. Despite this high involvement in manufacturing industry, women workers are heavily concentrated in certain branches. In 1980, 72 per cent of women workers in Bursa were employed in textile, clothing, and leather industries, and 16 per cent worked in the food, beverage, and tobacco industries. All other industries employed less than 15 per cent of the total number of women who were employed in manufacturing. Sexual segregation is not unique to the manufacturing industry in Bursa. It is also the most visible characteristic of female employment in Turkish manufacturing industry as a whole, with 51 per cent of women being employed in the textile, clothing and leather industries and 18 per cent in the food, beverage, and tobacco industries in 1980.

Women's proper place: ideology and material motivation

According to familial ideology in Turkey, the proper place for a woman is in the home, attending to housework and the children, while her husband is the breadwinner. Although this view of women's proper place is extremely deep-rooted in Turkish society, in reality it is mainly upper class women who conform to the stereotype. Working class women in Bursa have a long tradition of participation in production. According to historical data, in Bursa, and in many towns in Turkey, women were engaged in handicrafts such as spinning and weaving long before industrialization. However, they did not sell or distribute their products themselves, but relied on various intermediaries, usually Jewish and Armenian women. The making of silk textiles in Bursa was also an exclusively female activity. Before the establishment of silk-reeling factories, women raised silkworms, produced cocoons and extracted and reeled silk in their homes (Erder 1976).

When production outside the home began, women were the best candidates for employment in the textile, food, and related factories, since they used the same skills and did almost exactly the same jobs in the factory as they were used to doing in the home. The sexual division of labour in industry in the early phases of industrialization was thus largely predetermined by the sexual division of labour in the pre-industrial family and household. Social disapproval of the first women who worked in the factories was, however, very much evident, in spite of the fact that the women worked in areas separate from those of men and did not interact with men outside the network of kin, family, and household unit.

Since women's work drew such disapproval, it spread very slowly and was confined to the activities which were seen as 'suitable for women'. Customs regarding male and female work practices and the confinement of women to certain industrial activities were very power-ful. Not only parents, but employers too, tried hard to allocate women into 'appropriate' places. 'Appropriateness', according to employers, implied two things. First, a male job was not appropriate for women because women *could not* do it owing to their physical weakness and/or lack of knowledge. Second, it was not appropriate because women *must not* do it for moral reasons. As long as employers saw the work they offered as compatible with the work which they thought was suitable for women, they did not hesitate to employ them. But in traditional male industries, even though women were cheaper and available for work, they were not employed.

The mixing of the two sexes gradually took place when large, modern factories were established. For example, the State Woollen Mill in Bursa employed hundreds of workers and greatly modified existing views about 'factory work'. Before its establishment, young girls who had been working in the factories were called 'company girls', which implied promiscuity, loss of respect, and moral degradation. For many women other obstacles to engaging in paid work still remain, such as the objections put forward by male members of the household and responsibilities for children. Many Turkish men from the lower class find themselves in a dilemma. On the one hand, they are often out of work or have casual jobs with which they are unable to support their family. If their wives had a job, their financial position would improve. Yet, at the same time, they are heavily influenced by social values which do not approve of women, especially married women, working. They think that if their wives work, they will lose respect; allowing a wife to work is to confess publicly to not being a man. Interviews with women factory workers disclosed that most opposition to women's participation in paid employment came from male members of the household; 40 per cent of the women who met opposition said it came from their husbands and 40 per cent said it came from their fathers, while only 20 per cent said they met opposition from other members of the family and acquaintances.

Although women are influenced by the same values and beliefs as men, many are able to overcome the objections which arise when starting work. Given the nature of the work that the Turkish women factory workers do, it would be wrong to expect that they work for reasons such as personal fulfilment. Why, then, do the women undertake factory work? The question seemed absurd to many of the respondents because, for them, there could be no reason for taking an outside job except economic necessity, 83 per cent of the women citing this as their motive. As one woman put it, 'Never mind what people think about you. What really matters is to bring bread home at the end of the day'. It is possible that the financial motive may be a blanket term which covers many other considerations that in an environment more tolerant of women's work might be declared more easily. However, many of the women explained what they meant by economic necessity. Their answers clearly show that women do not work for extras or to earn pin money as is frequently argued (Huang 1984:257). They work for reasons such as insufficient family income, husband's unemployment, death and illness in the family, and to have a house. There is no doubt that the earnings of women constitute a significant part of many household budgets: 35 per cent of the wives in the study earned as much as their husbands and 16 per cent earned more.

Having entered the paid labour market, how strong is women's attachment to it? It has been argued that women's turnover rate is higher than that of men and that women's attachment to work is lower; as women frequently change their work they lose the chance of better jobs or promotion and remain marginal to the labour market. In the case of Turkey it is also argued that a female household member is not principally responsible for the upkeep of the household; rather she works to keep the household supplied with non-essentials. Therefore, 'when she works in an unskilled job or is unqualified, she can easily give up work when the family's need for her work ceases' (Topcuoglu 1978). Employers believe that there is greater job turnover among women than among men. This is usually explained with the view that women are less in need of work and more free to give up work or to change their jobs. Zaim (1956) argued that women give up work because of familial reasons such as marriage and children.

Detailed information was collected about the work histories of the women who were interviewed during the study. Of the respondents who had previously worked in other jobs, 33 per cent said that they had interrupted their working life between jobs. Three main reasons had caused such interruptions. The first relates to marriage. The expectations of most of the young girls who work in factories are centred upon marriage and wherever they turn these are reinforced. They are so eager to become socially accepted that they rarely think what their life will be like after marriage. They do not question too deeply whether they can afford to give up their earnings and are reluctant to consider what will happen if they do not get on well with their husband, if they are divorced, or if their husband leaves them. About half the single girls among the respondents gave affirmative answers when asked if they would give up work when they got married.

Despite the traditional idea that women should give up work when they marry, more and more young women are staying in their job when they marry or, if they do give up work upon marriage, are later returning to work. This trend is particularly important among low income families, and the study showed that this resulted almost entirely from financial motives. It is interesting to note that having a child was not cited as a major reason for leaving work by the women in the study. Nor was their participation in the labour market facilitated by the availability of part-time work. In Turkey, women's part-time work is very rare. Working people usually work a minimum of eight hours a day in both industrial and service jobs. Even domestic cleaners are expected to work eight hours and most factories work on a shift system involving at least eight hours. In spite of the lack of part-time work and childcare facilities in Turkey, the presence of young children did not act as a constraint on women's participation in paid work. This contrasts with the findings of studies concerning the effects of children on the labour market participation of women in industrialized countries, which argue that the presence of young children induces women to interrupt their working lives (Chiplin and Sloane 1974; Hein 1984).

When marriage and childbirth are considered together, they amount to only 29 per cent of all the reasons for leaving work given by the women in the study. In the light of these findings, the argument that familial influences result in a fragmentary work history for women seems unconvincing, at least in the case of Turkish factory workers. However, the assumptions about women's low attachment to their work, not only in terms of leaving the labour force upon marriage or childbirth, but also in terms of changing jobs, still prevail. Employers often relate turnover among female employees to changes in family circumstances. For instance, a woman is said to be more likely to change her job if it involves shift work because she cannot spare enough time for her family. However, the other two main reasons for leaving their jobs which were given by the women in the survey were not related to family circumstances: 29 per cent of the women had interrupted their working lives for reasons to do with their working conditions and workplace. Some had been dissatisfied with their conditions of work or their wages, while others had lost their jobs involuntarily as the factory was closed or the worker had been dismissed. Migration came third among the reasons which caused women to interrupt their working lives, with 21 per cent of the respondents citing it as the reason for having left their previous job. Each of the last two reasons could easily have been given also by male workers. Both male and female workers want to improve their working conditions, obtain more satisfactory jobs, and earn better wages, and both may migrate in order to do so. Economic rather than family considerations appear to be of primary importance in structuring the labour market participation of the women factory workers, and turnover is related to the insecurity of their status as employees, rather than to individual characteristics.

Yildiz Ecevit

Job segregation on the basis of gender and skill

Women's and men's work in Turkish factories is divided both horizontally and vertically. Horizontal segregation refers to the concentration of women in some occupations and men in others. For example,
the spinning sections of every yarn manufacturing factory are a female
domain, whereas the dyeing sections are a male domain. Vertical segregation relates to the positions of male and female workers within the
factory hierarchy. Women factory workers in Turkey are almost invariably concentrated at the bottom of the factory hierarchy and are
called *duz isci* or *vasifsiz isci*, both of which mean unskilled worker.

Men work as skilled or semi-skilled workers as well as unskilled
workers and their distribution through these grades is relatively even.
Furthermore, they hold responsible positions in both the shop floor and
management hierarchies. Women are hardly ever found in supervisory
positions. The most they can become is a group leader and this position
is only attained when the group consists entirely of women. Even this
results in reservations on the part of the management, because of their
view that workers do not obey a woman group leader. This sexual
segregation is not unique to factories in Turkey. It has been clearly
demonstrated that women do most of the unskilled, low grade jobs in
factories, whether they are in Germany (Herzog 1980), England (Pollert
1981; Armstrong 1982; Westwood 1984), Malaysia (Heyzer 1982),
Morocco (Joekes 1982), or in many other countries (Elson and Pearson
1981).

Innate capacities and gender attributes

The allocation of the sexes to different jobs is usually carried out
according to characteristics which are attributed to the jobs and to the
workers. According to shop floor terminology, jobs have certain
characteristics such as 'easy and light', 'difficult and heavy', 'requiring
patience and dexterity', 'requiring skill or experience', or 'requiring
mechanical knowledge and technical ability'. Like jobs, certain
characteristics are attributed to workers, as Adelina Broadbridge in
Chapter 3 also shows in the case of shop assistants. It is believed that
passivity, patience, dexterity, and accuracy are typical female attributes,
so that women are better suited to sedentary, monotonous, 'fiddly', and
repetitive jobs. On the other hand, typical male attributes include a high
level of activity, physical strength, and technical ability, which are said
to make men suitable for jobs requiring mobility, strength, and technical
knowledge.

In Turkey, patience is considered a feminine attribute and women are
believed to be naturally good at routine 'fiddly' work. Thus, in the fruit

62

juice factory for example, women sat for eight hours in front of a screen, watching the bottles on the conveyor belt to see if they had any defects. According to a machine engineer in an electrical components factory, only women were found suitable for repetitive work: 'men could not stand long, routine work. If they did it they would get bored.' The manager in the tobacco shop expressed a similar view about leaf gradings: 'This job needs patience, it is certainly women's work, because women are *naturally* (my emphasis) more patient than men. Men cannot do monotonous jobs.'

Certain jobs are regarded as 'heavy' and are given to men. 'Heavy job' has two meanings. First, it requires lifting and carrying heavy material. In one factory, fabric cutting was designated as heavy (as well as skilled) work on the grounds that fabric rolls were heavy, and women could not carry, roll, and handle them easily. This was also the case in lifting the full beam of material. Women beamers tended the beam, but when the beam was full they called male workers to replace the full beam with an empty beam. Second, it implies that the job is tiring. In this sense it involves not only lifting, but using the muscular strength which women are thought to lack.

Since women are considered to be physically weaker than men they are employed in 'light jobs'. 'Light job' also has two meanings. First, it is believed to be easy to learn and perform. Second, it is said not to be exhausting. By giving light work to women, managers thought that they were protecting women and doing them a favour. The irony is that most of the women workers in the factories had village backgrounds and had previously performed arduous work such as working in the fields and carrying water. Some of them still had to carry water from the communal tap when they returned from the factory.

The employers' belief that women are only suitable for light work and men for heavy work also has influence among the workers. Women talked about their work in terms of these distinctions. As one woman put it: 'This is light work; men cannot do it. They should do heavy work.' She did not mean that men were physically less able, but believed that men were not socialized to do light work; accordingly, it would have been a waste to employ men in light jobs. Often the distinctions rest not on the inherent quality of the work itself, but on the meaning given to it in a particular context.

The majority of male workers are in jobs that involve the operation and maintenance of machinery. A corollary of this is the employment of women in manual jobs or jobs requiring the handling of only simple tools. Even when women are employed in machine based jobs their task is to 'watch' the machine rather than to operate it. The case of card tenders in the yarn section of textile factories is an example. Sometimes the division between women's work and men's work is based entirely on this distinction. In the fruit juice factory, jobs are separated into two groups, 'mechanical' and 'manual', the former being given to men while the latter are given to women.

It has been argued that in the processes in which manual dexterity is needed women workers are ideal. When asked, employers gave the following reasons for the employment of women in particular jobs.

In a silk yarn factory: 'Young girls are indispensable for us. They have soft and smooth hands. Only they can reel the silk without doing the material any harm.'

In the auto electrical components factory: 'Women are more productive than men in assembling parts since they are used to the activities requiring manual dexterity, such as embroidery.'

In the woollen factory's clothing department: 'Ever since we employed women, our production capacity has increased. They are speedy in stitching.'

Similar reasons were given by other factory personnel who also emphasized the view that women were good at jobs requiring dexterity.

Despite the recognition that women are good at most delicate jobs and carry them out quickly, their proficiency has usually been evaluated as a natural characteristic rather than an acquired one. Elson and Pearson challenge this view by arguing that women achieve high speed because of the early training they have received: 'The famous nimble fingers . . . are the result of the training they have received from their mothers and other female kin since early infancy in the tasks socially appropriate to women's role' (Elson and Pearson 1981).

But when the early training which many women have received in their homes is socially unrecognized and their dexterity is taken for granted, women are attributed neither training nor skill. When they become wage workers, the jobs which make use of this training are classified as unskilled or semi-skilled.

Skilled work and education

The classification of women's work as unskilled and the concentration of women in low grade jobs in manufacturing industry is invariably explained by citing women's level of educational attainment. It is argued that since women are barely educated, they do not have the skill and training which 'skilled jobs' require. Men, on the other hand, are better educated and therefore able to use machines or to learn their use quickly. 'Better educated' means having a diploma higher than a primary school diploma. Often it means secondary schooling. It may also mean high school graduation, since more people with high school diplomas have taken factory work in recent years.

Explaining the grade and skill differences between men and women by their educational attainment is quite widespread among the managers because, since the level of education is an objective criterion, its use is believed to support the view that there is no discrimination based on subjective criteria and sex. To what extent do women and men in the factories differ in terms of educational attainment? At the national level there is a considerable difference between men's and women's levels of schooling and men are given better educational opportunities. It is therefore to be expected that large differences regarding education continue on the shop floor. However, there were many instances in which women in the Bursa factories, despite their better education, were working in low grade jobs, whereas men with the same level of education occupied higher positions. Two examples illustrate the types of situation which occur. In the clothing department of a textile factory, graduates of a girls' technical craft school who had been taught a high level of dressmaking were employed as machine operators. In the auto electrical components factory, girls who had graduated from the electrical department of technical school were employed as assembly operators, while their male school-mates were employed as higher grade production workers and supervisors. Neither group of women was recognized as skilled, paid higher wages, or upgraded according to their training. As can be seen from these examples, as in the case of library workers studied by Maura Luck in Chapter 2, the supposed association of skill with education rests on shaky ground. This gives rise to the suspicion that the classification of some workers as skilled and others as unskilled may not be based upon objective criteria.

Designation of skilled work

This suspicion increases when certain tasks which are carried out in the factories are examined and compared. For example, in a food processing factory, cans were produced by hand. The factory had been established in 1958 and was using backward technology. Fifty of the 250 women worked in the tin producing section. In this section, two men cut the tin plates according to size and women carried out the remaining processes by using non-electrical soldering machines. It was not a simple job, women were exposed to gas and unpleasant smells and it took a considerable time to finish each can. Every day a fixed number of cans had to be produced, and the women had to work hard to do this. Despite the fact that the job needed skill and experience, it was not defined as skilled. In another modern food factory cans were produced by automatic machines. Men were employed as machine operators and the job was defined as skilled. In the same factory, peas had formerly been podded by hand by women. The management decided to install a new machine which podded both peas and green beans. Here too, men were employed and the job defined as skilled.

These examples illustrate a phenomenon which was common to the Bursa factories. Skill is associated with machine operating and machine work is given to male workers rather than female workers since women are considered to be less capable of using machines, despite the fact that the actual work involved decreases. When new machines are installed, even though neither men nor women know how to operate them, men are trained and given the responsibility. This association of men with capital-intensive machines is very widespread. Similar examples substantiate this association. Craig *et al.* (1980) found that women who produced cardboard boxes by hand-fed machines were classified and paid as unskilled workers, while men who produced cartons using a more automated process which required less individual concentration were classified at a higher level of skill. Armstrong's (1982) study revealed the fact that men tend to monopolize both craftwork and capital-intensive processes, whatever the level of skill involved in the latter. Conversely, women's work tends to be of a labour-intensive kind and not to be recognized as skilled, whatever the actual levels of skill involved.

So far three points regarding skill definitions in the factories have been identified. First, the employers' association of skill with education and their assignment of men to skilled tasks on this ground is not convincing, since women with a similar level of schooling are not given skilled status. Second, skill definitions are arbitrary and variations between these definitions are quite striking. Third, skilled work is usually associated with the use of machines and with the male monopoly of machine work. When women are employed in machine-related jobs, it is as 'tenders' or 'overseers' and not as operators.

One final, very important point must be included in this analysis. To be defined as skilled is often a condition for achieving a higher position in the factory hierarchy; for instance, foremen are invariably defined as skilled. Hence, being skilled and possessing authority are interrelated. Employers are reluctant to appoint women as supervisors for two reasons. If the production unit consists of both female and male workers and the supervisor is a woman, it would not be appropriate for men to take orders from her; many employers argued that 'men would not accept orders from a woman supervisor and would not behave respectfully.' As Elson and Pearson argue: 'Typically the giving of orders in the capitalist labour process is defined as a male prerogative while the role of women is defined as the carrying out of orders' (Elson and Pearson 1981: 98).

Second, in seeking reasons for the concentration of female workers in low grade jobs, it is impossible to ignore prevailing ideas concerning women's role in the family. Whenever I asked why women were not upgraded or given responsible positions, their being home-bound figured strongly in the answers. It has been argued that women, because of their domestic responsibilities, are not as reliable as male workers. The argument has been put forward on two grounds: that women are absent more than men; and that the likelihood of women giving up their work is more than that of men.

Here too, reality and assumption intermix in such a way that it is hard to know to what extent women's family responsibilities really affect their work. To what extent are women really absent more than men? Employers hold different views about the absenteeism, turnover, and the productivity of female and male workers. Views not only vary between employers, but also vary according to the context in which the issue is discussed. In cases where women's and men's reliability is discussed, most of the employers express the view that women are more conscientious and responsible. In another context, when asked why women are not found in supervisory positions, they reply that women are absent more often, are more concerned with their family problems, and are more likely to leave work and that it is therefore not worth training women for higher positions or giving them supervisory jobs. As far as the factories in Bursa are concerned, there are no data regarding women's and men's absenteeism and turnover rates, and the views expressed were usually based on preconceived notions about men and women. Thus, women's lower chances of being promoted to supervisory positions are related to employer stereotypes concerning women.

It has been argued that the allocation of the sexes to certain activities in the labour process is usually carried out according to gender attributes which are both psychological and social. Women are assigned to labour-intensive jobs because they are seen as suitable for these jobs. The 'suitability' of women for certain activities has strong legitimacy as it is not only assumed by employers but is also accepted by society as a whole, often without questioning. But how functional are these attributes? What role do they play in the labour process in concrete situations? These questions will now be examined.

Control: technical or patriarchal?

Much of Turkish factory production is labour-intensive. Two characteristics of the workforce are therefore of particular concern to employers. The first is the cost of labour; the lower the wage rate, the higher the level of profits. Ideas influencing the relative wages of women and men are as important as other factors. They are particularly important in those societies where women's status is determined mainly by custom,

67

tradition, and religion. To Turkish employers, women's main role is as homemaker, whereas men are the breadwinners. This view of the appropriate roles for women and men influences the relative wages paid to women and men. As one employer said: 'Well, it is obvious that my male workers must earn more than my female workers. They are the head of their families and the breadwinners, aren't they? Women and girls can rely on their husbands and fathers.' The low level of wages paid to women is therefore justified by women's assumed dependency on men. It is argued that the male members of their families will support them, so women do not need to earn as much as men.

This assumption of dependency prevails in spite of the fact that the man's income is often insufficient to maintain the family, so that the wage earned by the male worker is rarely a 'family wage'. Apart from those working in unionized factories, the bulk of the industrial workforce earn minimum wages. In theory, the minimum wage is supposed to be sufficient to maintain a man and his family; in practice it is very low and insufficient for a family. It is based on the needs of one adult man and 30 per cent of this amount is added for the needs of a wife and children. It is highly questionable whether a wife and children can be maintained with 30 per cent of the amount which is sufficient for an adult man. Even if the minimum wage had been a 'family wage' this would not make much difference because in 1980 only 42 per cent of all 'heads of household' in Turkey and 44 per cent of those in Bursa were working (SIS 1984a, 1984b). Moreover, many men earn wages below the minimum wage level. Those working in the informal sector, in particular, cannot even earn the minimum wages of their counterparts in the formal sector. In spite of the fact that the ideology of the family wage does not correspond to the reality of most Turkish workers, it is particularly useful to employers who are keen to define women as dependent, marginal workers as a justification for continuing to pay them low wages.

The second point concerns the control of labour. In labour-intensive processes, the control of labour is particularly important as it can increase the productivity of the workers and the quality of the work. Therefore, labour policy in labour-intensive factories is not just concerned with cost *per se*, but with control as well. Gender identity is crucial here too. The docility and submissiveness of women is highly valued; they are meek, patient, and willing to accept tough work discipline. Men are described as being more restless and rebellious than women, more willing to unionize and less inclined to accept exhausting work rates. In so far as women demonstrate typically feminine attributes, they can only be in the position of taking orders, not giving them.

Responsibility for exercising control over the workers lies with two groups of people: supervisors and foremen. Managerial personnel are more influential than supervisors in top level decision-making and in determining the general policy of the firm, but as far as the workers are concerned they are invisible and play no direct role in the daily work experience. Each of the different departments within the factory is headed by a supervisor who usually works within the department, in a glass-walled room which enables him to observe the workers and the production process without difficulty. The foreman is directly responsible for a group of about ten to twelve workers and is expected to have knowledge of all aspects of the work done in the department. He gets orders from the supervisor and directs the workers accordingly. When new employees are taken on, the foreman is responsible for their instruction. He usually has more direct contact with the workers than the supervisor and when a problem arises, deals with it immediately or calls the supervisor.

Control over workers employed in factories with capital-intensive production processes takes a different form from that which occurs in factories with labour-intensive processes. In the former the workers respond to, rather than set the pace at which the machines are operated. The work situations are often fairly far apart and the workers have little chance of varying the work pace. Since women workers are not allowed to leave the machines they attend, they are unable to communicate with other people. In the textile factories even those who work close to each other are unable to converse, due to the extremely loud noise of the machines.

Workers in factories based mainly on manual or very simple machine work potentially have relatively flexible conditions of work. For example, women using sewing machines work separately, can work at differing speeds, and stop while others continue to work. Since the speed of work cannot be controlled by the assembly line itself, the foreman's role increases and the workers are strictly supervised so that they cannot impose their own rhythms of work. The foreman not only determines the pace of the production process, but is the principal person to evaluate the worker's performance. According to his report, the supervisor may reward, punish, or fire the worker. Since evaluation is usually carried out on the basis of subjective opinions, the foreman is a very important person in the worker's eyes.

The extent of the foreman's and supervisor's power in evaluating the worker's performance and determining her stay in work varies greatly among different types of factories. First, it varies according to whether the firm is a small or a large establishment. Foremen and supervisors have the most power in small firms. Workers in small factories are vulnerable and unprotected. A word from the foreman is sufficient for a woman to be fired. There is no mechanism to protect her from a foreman's malice.

In relatively large firms the foreman, though still playing a very important role, is dependent on the supervisor's decision. Action is taken by the supervisor rather than the foreman. Shop floor rules are very strict and must be obeyed. If the rules are overlooked, the supervisor is fully authorized to penalize the worker. In Bursa, at least, supervisory personnel in state run factories appear to exercise control less strictly and to identify with the workers to a greater extent than supervisors in private factories.

With few exceptions, supervisory staff are men. This is so even in those factories where the number of women workers is high. The recruitment of men to supervisory positions is a very important means of controlling women workers. The commonest fear among women was to 'hear a word from the foreman', and they really tried hard not to be subjected to the foreman's reprimand. One of the spinning workers said that the women kept themselves busy even when their machine worked well and they did not have anything to do except wait for the bobbins. She said: 'I, at least, dust and clean my machine to pretend to be working.'

It became obvious during the course of the interviews that management and personnel officers showed great preference for taking on female workers, with the objective of maintaining a passive workforce. They invariably argued that women workers are easy to manage, easy to subject to factory rules, and that it is easy to make them work hard. Far from being troublemakers, they behaved just as the management wanted; that is, they were passive, submissive, docile and obedient. In a synthetic yarn plant, the personnel director explained the tendency to employ more women by saying that: '*Naturally* (my emphasis) they are timid. That makes them easy to manage. They are more responsible towards their work than men.'

A chemical engineer in a food processing factory alluded to the women's need to protect their sexual reputation, saying: 'It is easy to make them work. When you raise your voice a little, they work like bees. They are also docile. They do not talk back to their supervisors. Men talk back to you, walk about on the shop floor and pay visits to their friends in other parts of the factory. Women cannot do that, because they are deadly afraid of rumours.'

A small textile factory owner touched on the same point: 'A woman worker is always alert and does not leave her work. She thinks that if she walks around she will be subject to men's sexual harassment. Men ignore their work often to smoke cigarettes and if I am not around they even go to the coffee shop on the corner.'

The men thus had considerably more freedom than the women. Jobs such as loading and carrying are exclusively carried out by men on the grounds that carrying heavy loads is 'men's work'. They are also engaged in the repair of broken machines. As they walk round the factory floor they can easily slip out of the foreman's control, can have a short break, and talk to other workers. The foremen themselves are more tolerant towards the subterfuges of the male workers.

The women in contrast, are almost as locked in place as the machinery and are subject to a specific form of gender subordination which may be termed patriarchal control. Patriarchal control is the situation where men and women work in the same department, the relations between the two sexes do not resemble a relationship between workmates, but those of a family. Men behaved towards women as if they were their fathers or husbands. What is more, this behaviour was exhibited not only by the male foremen and supervisors, but also by the other male employees.

The exercise of traditional forms of patriarchal power by the supervisory personnel is understandable; what is surprising is that the same relations are generated among all the male workers. They, too, behave according to a patriarchal code which already exists in society and puts women into subordinate positions. They treat women as if they were their daughters or wives and, what is more interesting, the women did not oppose this. They conformed, without question, to the traditional stereotypes of feminine behaviour. Existing forms of gender subordination are reproduced in the factory. The argument that women's subordinate positions stem from a lack of job opportunities and can be ended by the provision of sufficient jobs does not hold true as long as women cannot free themselves from this subordination.

Capitalist production is not merely a technical process involving the interaction of a number of factors of production, one of which is human labour power; it is also and ultimately a social process in which the human element, labour, must be made to work. Recruiting men to the supervisory roles serves this purpose very well. From the perspective of women workers, it perpetuates patriarchal control, and the secondary status arising from women's subordination as a gender continues in the factory.

In almost all factories the same pattern is observed. Women work exclusively at the bottom of the hierarchy and the upper levels of the hierarchy are invariably occupied by men. Only in a few factories is it possible to find women in supervisory roles and then only when the department or group which is to be supervised consists exclusively of women. If the workers are male, women are recruited neither as foremen nor as supervisors. Supervision of men by women is considered to be an insult to men and would result in male workers' resistance. If, on a rare occasion, the management decides to give a supervisory role to a woman, they prefer to choose a mature and educated woman so that she can exercise authority over the employees.

The interviews with women workers, managers, and employers revealed that they would not favour women as supervisors, and that women employees were not eager to accept such positions. Employers stated that women with demanding home commitments are not able to give whole-hearted attention to their work and are therefore reluctant to accept responsibility. They also argued that women are naturally too 'soft'. This trait was said to be inconsistent with the most important function of a supervisor: the maintenance of discipline. Supervisory positions were said to demand a more authoritarian style. Furthermore, supervisory roles require close contact with male supervisors and administrative and managerial staff. Women do not want to enter such relationships as they are thought to threaten their femininity and their relations with family members.

All these factors have considerable significance when the incentive for women to work is taken into account. Women usually work in factories to meet their immediate needs. They come from traditional peasant households where men's authority is still unquestioned. Therefore, women feel that they are not suited to exercising authority over other people. The main obstacle hindering women's recruitment to supervisory positions is therefore men's undeniably higher position, both at home and in the factory. Nothing could be more unthinkable in Turkey than a situation in which women are authorized to control a group in which men are present.

Women workers and the trade unions

Hartmann (1976) and Rubery (1980) have emphasized the role which workers' organizations have played in maintaining the sexual segregation in paid work. Has this been the case in Turkish industry? In the Ottoman period guilds were the principal organizations of craftsmen and artisans. They were so powerful that it was almost impossible for anyone to practise a trade outside the guilds and they were completely closed to women. However, entirely the reverse is true of the more recently established trade unions. The main focus of union energy has been on the problems of organization, stability, and unity. One of the initial aims of the unions was to increase their membership, to represent as many workers as possible, and to be recognized as a bargaining agent by employers. Therefore, rather than restricting women's involvement, they encouraged the membership of both sexes. Furthermore, due to the very low proportion of women workers in industry, women at no time became a real threat to men in the job market.

Women working in the large factories where interviews were conducted tended to be trade union members, whereas women working in the smaller factories tended not to be union members. One of the reasons for this was that according to the Collective Labour Agreements, Strikes and Lockouts Law, unions that represent the majority of the workers in any particular industry were allowed to negotiate with employers on behalf of the workforce. Therefore, unions concentrated their recruiting efforts on the larger rather than smaller factories. Another reason was the paternalistic and anti-union attitudes of employers in small factories.

Most of the interviews with unionized women were carried out in the larger factories. They showed that women's membership of trade unions was only formal, being limited to the payment of union dues which were automatically deducted from their wages. They participated very little in union activities and did not usually identify themselves as workers or develop trade union consciousness. Moreover, the local union officials in Bursa paid little attention to the women workers. There were several possible reasons for this. The first was the political climate of the 1970s. Particularly between 1975 and 1980 all unions devoted themselves to political struggles. The wealth and well-being of workers was viewed as of secondary importance. Involvement with political issues decreased the significance of the material conditions of the workers. Issues like improvements in work conditions, housing, and crèches had become unimportant in the eyes of the union officials.

The second reason relates to the social background of the local union representatives and shop stewards. Almost all of them came from families of rural origin and the few who did not were the sons of factory workers. Their attitudes towards women's work were very similar to the attitudes shared by other men. For instance, they did not see the sexual division of labour in workplaces or differences in wages between the sexes as problematic. For them, women were not a special category with different problems from other groups within the working class. Many union representatives held the view that, ideally, women in Turkish society should stay at home while their husbands went out to work to support their family. When women worked, they regarded this as a temporary phenomenon in women's lives and thought that they worked for pin money. As a consequence, they saw the woman's wage as a supplement to the man's wage. They seemed to assume that all women in society lived with a man, either their husband or their father. It was therefore hardly surprising that women's low pay was not seen as problematic by the unions.

It might be expected that some unions with a relatively high proportion of female members (in textile and food factories) would concentrate more on the specific needs of their female members and make every attempt to integrate them into the organization. Yet, far from being integrated, women workers were ignored by the unions. Unions did not attempt to provide the women with knowledge and information about workers' rights and unionism. Rather, they concentrated their efforts on obtaining improved wages and fringe benefits. No particular attention was paid to issues such as training courses for women, opportunities for promotion, apprenticeship schemes for girls, improved work conditions, or health facilities. Nor did they take serious steps to obtain assistance for the particular needs of women. For example, women's requests for nursing rooms or crèches in their workplaces would have been relatively easy to meet, because the requirement for firms to provide these facilities was already included in the labour law, yet the unions took no action in demanding this provision.

Women workers, in general, have not approached the unions enthusiastically. The union, like many other things in the factory, just happened to be there. It was not something they had even thought about, let alone fought for. They acquired knowledge about the unions by listening to others; no formal information was provided. Those who had male factory workers in their family were more informed since they could discuss matters related to unions at home. One woman described the union as 'something which protects our rights'; another said 'it increases our wages'; a third worker talked about it as being 'an organization which protects the workers from the bosses'. Usually a woman worker knew that in every large factory a union existed and that its primary goal was to increase wages and provide more benefits for the workers. They also knew that they had to pay union dues, and that they should participate in union elections.

In terms of interest in unions and relations with them, it was possible to divide the women workers into two or three groups. Those who were married and had children had no leisure to allow them to take an active role in the union. The burden of running a family was so heavy that after a day's work in a factory they could hardly find the time or energy to carry out union activities. The combination of work at home owing to childcare and other family responsibilities with the women's factory work meant that they were frequently physically exhausted. The virtually unaltered distribution of household responsibilities offered no incentive to participate in union activities. In addition, these women were affected by social pressure to stay within their family circle.

The group least involved with unions and union activities were divorced and widowed women. The majority were heads of households and often expressed fear of losing their jobs. Their family roles remained central in their lives and they hardly ever participated in union activities. These women expressed no open dissatisfaction with wages and working conditions. On the contrary, many adopted a favourable attitude towards the employers. One old widowed woman prayed for the employers: 'God bless them.'

The group of women which was most enthusiastic towards the unions was the younger age group. They were relatively highly educated, most were unmarried and, like the women who were most active in NALGO, interviewed by Jenny Walton in Chapter 8, few had young children. They discussed union matters among themselves, attended some of the local union meetings, became involved in strikes, and participated in picket lines. However, they also said that they felt great social pressure being put on them by their families and people in their neighbourhood. Some said that they had been much more active before, but as a result of this pressure had become less involved in union issues. Many others who were formerly active became less active after they married because of their husband's disapproval and social and familial pressures.

Most criticism of the unions came from the young women. They criticized the unions for their ineffectiveness and practices towards women. They criticized them on two counts in particular: first, some unions worked too much with management; and second, they mainly protected male workers' interests and made little effort to understand issues of importance to women. In the tobacco processing workshop women criticized the union and the workers. They told me that they paid visits in small groups to the local union office to talk about the crèche problems, but the union representatives would not meet them. They also tried to discuss the health problems arising from the extreme humidity in the spinning departments, but union officials made no attempt to improve the conditions. Another group of women had asked the union to attempt to negotiate their night-shifts, but the union had made no effort to help them.

Most women, regardless of the factories they worked in or the unions they belonged to, thought that the unions did not provide enough back-up information for them. A general criticism made by many women referred to union rivalries. They were in favour of fewer unions being represented in the plant, because this would eliminate the unnecessary inter-union rivalry and would also increase their bargaining strength. A woman expressed her anger with union officials: 'They are quarrelling with each other, forgetting us and our problems. Their immediate task is to be concerned with us, not to argue about the issue of the majority. When they spend all their energy in this way they do not have time to deal with our problems.'

It seemed that the woman workers' attitudes towards their unions depended greatly on the attitudes of the shop steward. He was the key man because, for nearly all female workers, he represented the union itself. They often judged the union according to the attitudes of the shop stewards. In almost all the factories shop stewards were men; there were only two women shop stewards, one of whom had been a steward for some time, the other having been elected recently. It was evident from the interviews that women workers wanted to have women shop stewards rather than men. They thought that communication with men was difficult, both because they found it hard to explain the problems they faced at work, and because men did not pay much attention to these problems.

In many instances, the stewards themselves did not believe in issues such as equal pay or opportunity, and did not realize that women's experiences of work were different from those of men. This was partly as a result of the job segregation between men and women. Men did not usually work in the same jobs as women and therefore lacked direct experience of the nature of these jobs. Furthermore, because the traditional sexual division of labour continued at home, men, as husbands or fathers, did not feel the pressure of household responsibilities as women did. Therefore, the special requirements of women such as short leaves without pay or the right for time off to care for children, were not widely appreciated by the male shop stewards. When women did bring their problems or requests to the union meetings, these problems were overlooked. This lack of concern then resulted in women being indifferent towards, or mistrustful of the unions.

Conclusion

The material changes which are occurring in Turkey are bringing about some changes in the sexual division of labour in Turkish industry. For example, the car industry is a fairly new industrial activity in Bursa, having been established in the 1960s. Both women and men are employed in the factory sections which produce subsidiary products such as electrical parts and upholstery. The mixing of women and men on the shop floor of these factories shows that such material changes weaken seclusion and exclusion patterns, and that stigmatizing social norms are not as effective as they were in the past and do not prevent women's employment in newly opened factories. However, the ideologies of domesticity and motherhood inhibit women's full access to all sectors of the labour market on the same terms as men. In so far as women workers are concerned, the secondary status arising from women's subordination as a gender determines their place in the factory. There, women's gender-ascribed characteristics and supposed personality traits play a significant role in their allocation to certain jobs and in their being subject to patriarchal control. Management and employers deliberately promote naturalistic assumptions about women's docility and submissiveness which reinforce the idea of patriarchal control: the more women are subject to control, the more the firm will benefit.

Although they sometimes participate in industrial activity, women workers' relations with unions are weak, since few women see the union as a relevant channel for voicing their demands about working conditions. Nevertheless, married women factory workers in Bursa have gained a considerable degree of power over decision-making in their families as the result of their employment. Over half the married women who were interviewed reported that they and their husbands took decisions together and often consulted each other. However, women's domestic work and childcare is less open to change when women are employed. Caring for children, the sick, and the elderly is still seen as the responsibility of women, as is their role in housework and the provision of meals. Women workers, influenced by the ideologies of caring and nurturing, try to carry out housework and childcare, even under the most difficult conditions, without asking for help from their husbands; men take for granted that these are provided by their wives. Therefore, while decision-making and financial control are seen as an area in which women have growing autonomy, the sexual division of labour at home is still governed by ideologies of appropriate behaviour which are strongly resistant to change.

References

Armstrong, P. (1982) 'If it's only women it doesn't matter so much', in J. West (ed.) *Work, Women and the Labour Market*, London: Routledge & Kegan Paul.

Chiplin, B. and Sloane, P.J (1974) 'Sexual discrimination in the labour market', *British Journal of Industrial Relations* 12(3): 371–402.

Craig, C., Rubery, J., Tarling, R., and Wilkinson, F. (1980) *Abolition and After: The Paper Box Wages Council*, Research Paper by the Labour Studies Group, Department of Employment.

Ecevit, Y. (1986) *Gender and Wage Work: A Case Study of Turkish Women in Manufacturing Industry*, PhD Thesis in Sociology and Social Anthropology, University of Kent.

Elson, D. and Pearson, R. (1981) 'Nimble fingers make cheap workers: an analysis of women's employment in Third World export manufacturing', *Feminist Review* 7: 87–107.

Erder, L. (1976) *The Making of Industrial Bursa: Economic Activity and Population in a Turkish City, 1835–1975*, PhD Dissertation in Philosophy, Princeton University.

Hartmann, H. (1976) 'Capitalism, patriarchy and job segregation by sex', in M. Blaxall and B. Reagan (eds) *Women and the Workplace: The Implications of Occupational Segregation*, Chicago: The University of Chicago Press.

Hein, C. (1984) 'Jobs for the girls: export manufacturing in Mauritius', *International Labour Review* 132 (2).

Herzog, M. (1980) *From Hand to Mouth*, Harmondsworth: Penguin.

Heyzer, N. (1982) 'From rural subsistence to an industrial peripheral work force: an examination of female Malaysian migrants and capital accumulation in Singapore', in L. Beneria (ed.) *Women and Development: The Sexual Division of Labour in Rural Societies*, New York: Praeger.

Huang, N.C. (1984) 'The migration of rural women to Taipei', in J.T. Fawcett, S-E. Khoo and P.C. Smith (eds) *Women in the Cities of Asia*, Boulder: Westview Press.

Joekes, S. (1982) *Female-led Industrialisation. Women's Jobs in Third World Export Manufacturing: The Case of the Moroccan Clothing Industry*, Institute of Development Studies Research Report Rr. 15, University of Sussex.

Koray, T. (1975) *Working Women: A Study of Female Labour Force and Determinants of Participation in Six Large Cities of Turkey*, PhD Thesis in Demography, University of Pennsylvania.

Pollert, A. (1981) *Girls, Wives, Factory Lives*, London: Macmillan.

Roberts, B. (1978) *Cities of Peasants. The Political Economy of Urbanisation in the Third World*, London: Edward Arnold.

Rubery, J. (1980) 'Structured labour markets, worker organisation and low pay', in A. Amsden (ed.) *The Economics of Women and Work*, Harmondsworth: Penguin.

State Institute of Statistics (1984a) *Census of Population. Social and Economic Characteristics: Turkey*, Ankara: State Institute of Statistics.

——(1984b) *Census of Population. Social and Economic Characteristics: Bursa*, Ankara: State Institute of Statistics.

Topcuoglu, H. (1978) 'Turk Toplumunda Kadinin Statusu', in Turkiye Universiteli Kadinlar Dernegi (ed.) *Turkiye Kadin Yili Kongresi*. Ankara: Yayin No. 1.

Westwood, S. (1984) *All Day Every Day: Factory and Family in the Making of Women's Lives*, London: Pluto.

Zaim, S. (1956) *Istanbul Mensucat Sanayiinin Bunyesi ve Ucretler*, Istanbul Universitesi Yayinlari 655, Iktisat Fukultesi Yayini 83, Istanbul: Sermet Matbaasi.

Chapter five

Prostitution and tourism in South-East Asia

Wendy Lee

Introduction

In the 1960s Franz Fanon warned the poor nations not to become the 'brothels of Europe'. His warning has taken on new relevance for South-East Asian countries where an important incentive for tourism is the availability of women, either openly as prostitutes in brothels or performers in sex shows, or less obviously as bar or hospitality girls, massage and bath attendants, hostesses in hotels, and waitresses in nightclubs and cocktail lounges. It is in Thailand, South Korea, and the Philippines where the most blatant and systematic organization of sex tourism is to be found. Here prostitution has developed on an unprecedented scale: it is women's bodies which underpin the balance of payments. Studies of the issue sometimes give the impression that it is the product of specifically Asian practices and attitudes, something over which the governments of South-East Asian countries have relatively little control. This chapter will question that interpretation, by examining the material and ideological factors which maintain prostitution as in integral aspect of South-East Asian development.

In Thailand, the increase in prostitution began in the nineteenth century when commercialization of the rice trade led to a large-scale influx of Chinese migrants. The Sampeng area behind the port of Bangkok became a red light district and prostitution expanded. Later, in 1962, the American military arrived and many acquired Thai mistresses called *mia chao* or 'rented wives'. In 1966 American servicemen began arriving on one week rest and recreation visits from South Vietnam. During the twelve years of US military 'occupation' there was a massive growth in the number of prostitutes in bars, nightclubs, and brothels in Bangkok and around the bases in the North-East. At the Udon base alone, the number of 'special job workers', masseuses, and entertainers increased from 1, 246 in 1966 to over 7,000 in 1974 (Thitsa 1980:15).

Throughout this period, thousands of girls were employed to help the estimated 700,000 American troops 'unwind'. After the soldiers left, the industries did not decline as expected, but expanded as the tourists came, males outnumbering females two to one (Phongpaichit 1982:5). Of the Japanese tourists arriving in 1977, for example, 81.7 per cent were male (Thitsa 1980:13). The majority of visitors however, were Americans and Germans (Lenze 1979: 8).

In 1970, the Bangkok-Thon Buri agglomeration, with a population of three million, was estimated to have 20,000 prostitutes. By 1977 the figure was 100,000 (65,000 full-time female prostitutes, 35,000 part-timers, and 10,000 male prostitutes). By 1981 it was estimated that there were 200,000 in Bangkok alone and between 500,000 and 700,000 in the whole country, that is, about 10 per cent of the females aged between 14 and 24 (Thanh-Dam 1983:543; Phongpaichit 1982:7; Hantrakul 1983:27). A Mahidol University study carried out by Thepanom, cited in Phongpaichit (1982), indicates that in Bangkok there were 119 massage parlours, 119 barber-cum-massage and tea houses, 97 nightclubs, 248 disguised brothels and 394 disco-cum-restaurants which all provided similar services for males (Phongpaichit 1982:9).

The succession of wars and the presence of foreign military personnel in Asia during recent decades had a similar effect on South Korea and the Philippines. During the Korean war the presence of huge numbers of Americans facilitated the establishment of mass prostitution, especially in Seoul. During the 1970s, the rapid growth of Japanese tourism also acted as a stimulus to the new forms of prostitution (prostitution was outlawed in Japan in 1958). By 1978 tourism was earning the country US$408.3 million annually, two-thirds of the visitors being Japanese (FEER 1980a:70). However, by 1981, in response to negative criticisms, the Government claimed to be 'seeking to attract a different type of tourist' and declared that new policies would 'give emphasis to propagating Korea's unique culture and folklore . . . rather than offering entertainment to them as in the past' (Reditt 1981: IV).

In the Philippines American bases were established as early as 1901 and during the 1960s huge numbers of servicemen visited on leave from South Vietnam. By 1976 the number of soldiers had dropped but sex tours increased, two out of three tourists being men. Of 250,000 Japanese tourists, 84 per cent were men and of 30,000 Germans, 72 per cent were men (Villariba 1982:10). By 1983 in Olongapo City, population 200,000 (where the Subic Bay Naval Base is situated), it was estimated that 16,000 women were registered at the 'social hygiene' clinics (Golley 1983:32). Lucina Alday, Director of the Philippines Bureau of Women and Minors, Ministry of Labour and Employment, estimated that there were 100,000 licensed women in the hospitality industry in Metro Manila, but this may be an underestimate as there are many illegal workers such as call girls, brothel workers, and street walkers who do not obtain Government permits (Neumann 1979:13).

Thus, the initial expansion of facilities originally developed for local men and foreign residents occurred mainly to serve the American military. After the US withdrawal new markets were built up to maintain what had become big business. Budget air transport, cheap accommodation, and package tours, together with increased incomes and more leisure in industrialized nations, led to mass tourism which in turn is linked to the mass production of prostitution. Tourism and prostitution are now a 'packaged commodity' marketed on an international scale.

The nature of prostitution

Any discussion of the character of, and reasons for, mass prostitution must wrestle with the problem of definitions. Gagnon (1968:592) defines prostitution narrowly as:

> the granting of sexual access on a relatively indiscriminate basis
> for payment either in money or goods . . . . Payment is
> acknowledged to be for a specific sexual performance. . . .Payment
> for the specific act is what distinguishes the prostitute from the
> mistress or from females who accept a range of gifts while having
> sexual contact with a male.

But this is hardly adequate for the situation in Thailand, for example, where, as Cohen points out, Thai bar girls' relationships with *farangs* (foreign men) are often incompletely commercialized. Many dealings are not solely economic but also social exchanges which may last for some time (1982:411).

A variety of traditional sexual relationships do not entirely fit the Gagnon definition either. For example, in Thailand marriage was a kind of purchase where rights to a girl were transferred from her parents to her husband. Men paid silver to their future in-laws as compensation for the parents' expenses in bringing up a girl. Thai wives were divided into three ranks: the principal wife (*mia klong muang*) given to a man by his parents; the secondary or minor wife (*mia klang nok*) who brought no property with her; and the slave wife or concubine (*mia klang thasi*) who was a bought woman.

> Under parts of the 1805 'Three Seals' Law Code . . . the husband
> could at any time sell, pawn or give away his wives, could
> administer bodily punishment to them in proportion to their
> 'misdeeds' and could moreover kill an adulterous wife and her
> lover if they were caught in the act . . . Wives were thus seen as

items of commercial exchange – chattels, or in the stated legal term, *khwai* (water buffalo).

(Thitsa 1980:5)

The rights of parents to sell their children and of a husband to sell his wives were abolished as late as 1905 (Hantrakul 1983:27). In the past only members of the *sakdina* (feudal élite) could afford to practise polygyny, but in the late nineteenth century with an expanding economy, more and more men acquired concubines and prostitution also spread. Polygyny and the number of concubines became the measure of a man's status, power, and wealth (Phongpaichit 1982:4). While concubines might be socially mobile, women in brothels were bought as slaves, subject to moral disapproval, and received no return for their labour beyond food and lodging. They might also be subject to repeated exchange as an item of trade (Thanh-Dam:535).

Truong Thanh-Dam (1983:536) has identified five current forms of prostitution in Thailand. The first type is the bonded girl, a new version of the traditional concubine, now illegal and fairly uncommon. The second is the freelancer whose main occupation may be a government or factory job, but who supplements her income by prostitution. These women may work in massage parlours, or clubs and bars. The third type, call girls, however, are professionals who work through intermediaries. Then there are chartered prostitutes who work on the basis of a time-charter negotiated with the client for the length of his sojourn in an area. Lastly are the mail-order brides who work through agencies which sell catalogues with their photographs and histories to men in search of wives.

Taking an international perspective and eschewing any ethnocentric beliefs about western women's supposed advantages in the equality stakes, it seems that the position of women in industrialized societies is not, in fact, as different from that of women in eastern societies as we might imagine. Harold Barnett (1976) has argued that in a western context, women are legally and socially perceived as property, men having the right to claim their services. Women's capacity to act as fully adult subjects in relation to rights in people is always more circumscribed than that of men. Laws on divorce, rape, child custody, alimony, and employment reinforce this view since women's rights tend to be determined by male property interests. Most importantly, a woman's right to claim her body as her own has not been established in law: many have no legal right to abortion or even to decide whether or not to bear a child. This pervasive view of people as property has meant that women either become the property of an individual man, or else they are considered common property and forfeit many rights such as protection in the case of rape (Barnett 1976). In this context the prostitute cannot, therefore, claim to be selling her own sexual property, since a woman's ownership of her body is not legally recognized. It follows logically that it is the prostitute who is usually prosecuted, while the purchaser of her services is left untouched; she is denied the moral right to claim the returns from her labour since her body is not hers to sell. In South-East Asian societies it could be further argued that official control of prostitution makes prostitutes not just common property, but state property whose bodies serve state interests. Although the incidence of polygyny and traditional brothels has declined, new institutions supported by the state have arisen.

To take account of the wide variety of forms which sexual relations take, it is therefore necessary to widen Gagnon's definition of prostitution. At one end of the continuum, legal marriage and polygyny can be seen as 'undercover' prostitution where a 'woman contracts to sell her sexual and other services to an individual man in exchange for economic security and/or protection from other men' (Lindsey 1979:4). At the other extreme, professional prostitution may be seen as the 'supply of sexual services on a relatively indiscriminate basis in a manner similar to the sale of any commodity' (Thanh-Dam 1983:535). A wider definition would also need to acknowledge that men and boys also sell sexual favours, although data on male prostitution in South-East Asia are hard to come by and are outside the scope of this chapter.

Why do women enter prostitution?

Kate Millett (writing of western societies) says that 'the causes of female prostitution lie in the economic position of women, together with the psychological damage inflicted upon them through the system of sex-role conditioning in patriarchal society' (1975:50). Prostitution has both a material and ideological basis. The cultural subordination of women takes different forms in different societies, creating a climate where the sexual exploitation of women is not only tolerated, but very often promoted. Some investigators such as Cohen (1982:406) claim that in the case of Thailand there are specific features which encourage permissiveness and legitimize promiscuity, and that prostitution grows out of traditional cultural practices. However, others, such as Phongpaichit (1982:47), question this view. While it would be wrong to overemphasize the ideological factors influencing women's recruitment into prostitution, an examination of the historical and cultural background is important in understanding the overall context in which South-East Asian prostitution takes place. This examination must take account of both the individual level, that is from the standpoint of the women involved, and the collective or institutional basis of prostitution.

In the Philippines, the 'Madonna-whore' values of Catholicism and its emphasis on virginity, have led jilted or raped women to become prostitutes, feeling that they have nothing to lose. In Korean villages, it may not be guilt which drives women into prostitution, yet the traditional Confucian values which demand that women show respect and obedience to their husband and all members of his household are just as oppressive to women. As in the case of Greek women in rural areas discussed by Mary Castelberg-Koulma in Chapter 10, a wife is surrounded by prohibitions which must be observed if she is not to bring discredit to the family:

> The Confucian tradition in Korea has a puritanical aspect that emphasizes strict rules of physical modesty and reticence regarding sexual matters. Such values are linked to the subordinate role of women and the emphasis on deference and obligation rather than emotion in personal relations.
>
> (Brandt 1971:133)

Because traditional family systems exert such rigid control over young women, giving them few choices, for example, in marriage, some wish to escape the restrictions of family and the constraints of village life for the bright city lights. Rejection of traditional norms is thought to play a role in female migration to cities. Women who have been drawn into the food and drink business find that the majority of customers are male, a fact which reinforces the pattern of men being served and women serving. Moreover, in the tea rooms and drinking places, the waitresses frequently provide not only nourishment but also sexual services and companionship. 'As a consequence, once a woman begins to earn her living by serving food or drink, she finds it very hard to move into another business – both because she thinks of herself as a 'fallen woman' and because other prospective employers regard her in the same way' (Chang-Michell 1985:23).

Thai women have always taken an active economic role in trading, marketing, and agriculture, while men have traditionally dominated the bureaucracy, the professions, and the religious domain (Thitsa 1980:15). Despite the fact that there are three times as many women as men in business and trade, women are debarred from real influence by male monopoly of the network of power relations between the Buddhist order, the monarchy, and the military. The Buddhist belief in the transience of wordly things and the dangers of desire has particular implications for women. Karma (the sum of your actions in past lifetimes; a kind of balance sheet of religious merits and demerits) is believed to determine gender: being born a woman indicates an insufficient store of merit. Women, more worldly beings than men, 'may engage in types of activity . . . which might pose threats for men in their merit accumulation, for if women sin, it is only to be expected and the consequences are less' (Kirsch 1975:185). Prostitution in this context signifies not a rejection of traditional customs nor an attempt to escape family ties, but an alternative means for women to fulfil their obligations as breadwinners. Girls are sometimes pressured by parents to help buy back agricultural land, pay medical expenses and school fees for siblings, or to provide payment for hired labour during the harvest season, and despite customary disapproval of promiscuity, public opinion has shifted somewhat. Since young women are supporting the needs of the family, prostitution is becoming socially validated and accepted as an economic necessity (Phongpaichit 1982:71).

The new forms which prostitution takes are related to the process of capitalist development and 'modernization'. When, in 1905, the King of Thailand abolished slavery, the peasantry were freed of service obligations to the king and state, the agricultural economy became oriented to the market rather than to subsistence use, and land grew scarce. Under these conditions poorer landless peasants had few options. Some entered bondage in client relationship with others who were wealthier. 'Debts were frequently discharged by selling oneself or, not uncommonly at least, some of one's children into slavery' (Piker 1975:307). There are still some cases of parents selling a daughter into bondage to pay debts, but this is a measure of their desperation and certainly no longer a socially desired practice. Agents may advance cash to poor peasants and when they are unable to repay the debt, they are forced to sign a promissory note engaging to send a daughter to Bangkok to work as a domestic servant or waitress. On arrival, the girl may be forced to receive clients. It is estimated that about 10 per cent of prostitutes in Thailand are deceived or forced into the profession (Hantrakul 1983:29). But, more commonly, families act as agents of recruitment. Most prostitutes get their jobs through aunts, sisters, or cousins already in the trade. They are socialized into the job by their peers through informal networks.

Phongpaichit does, however, mention a growing band of middle-men and agents developing, and even where prostitution is technically illegal, it is often officially sanctioned; frequently the brokers are government officials (Ong 1985:5). The 1928 Law on the Traffic in Women and Girls and the 1960 Prostitution Prohibition Act officially banned prostitution in Thailand, but in reality allowed massage parlours and tea houses to be used as fronts for the sale of sex. The 1950s saw some token campaigns against the import of 'western permissiveness', but the legislation relating to prostitution was never implemented. This was because the élite still associated power with the amassing of wives and consorts so that their private lives bore little relationship to their public utterances. Former Prime Minister, Field Marshal Sarit Thanarat who had over a hundred wives, was not seen as being in the least inconsistent when he condemned prostitution for corrupting and threatening the family institution (Hantrakul 1983:28).

In the Philippines, too, women's entry into prostitution is facilitated by an officially endorsed system. Despite an anti-streetwalking ordinance which makes soliciting punishable, prostitution inside clubs is legal, and in cities, employees in the 'entertainment' business are issued with a Mayor's Permit or ID card which licenses them for work. South Korea enacted a Law Prohibiting Decadent Acts in 1962, which provides for penalties on both parties involved, yet prostitutes (*kisaeng*) are still issued special ID cards by the Seoul Tourist Association that permit them to engage in business, and Korean embassies list the telephone numbers of *kisaeng* houses in their official tourist pamphlets.

There are few long-term professionals among South-East Asian prostitutes; most are amateurs drifting in and out of prostitution depending on need, and their numbers are replenished by a continual stream of girls and women (mostly aged between 15 and 24) migrating from the countryside. The development policies pursued by Thailand, the Philippines, and South Korea have opened a huge gap between the incomes and opportunities available in the city and those in rural areas. In the Philippines the women who come to the military bases or to Manila are fleeing from the economically depressed provinces of Leyte, Samar, and Cebu, areas where the government has done little for agricultural development or land reform (Neumann 1979:15). In Thailand they come from the North and North-East, areas notorious for their poverty and high rates of out-migration. There, land is poor, there are frequent droughts, the per capita GDP is less than half that of the Central Plain area, and up to one-third of families have no land at all, and depend on tenancy or casual labour to survive (Phongpaichit 1982:27–30).

Once in the cities, what choices do women have? Finding any kind of job is difficult and for unskilled, poorly educated women, prostitution offers some advantages over petty trading, domestic service or work in large world market factories, all of which are associated with low wages and poor working conditions. Even if women do opt for factory work, they may eventually be forced to prostitute themselves:

> If a woman loses her job in a world market factory after she has re-shaped her life on the basis of a wage income, the only way she may have of surviving, is by selling her body. There are reports from South Korea, for instance, that many former electronics workers have no alternative but to become prostitutes.
>
> (Grossman, quoted in Elson and Pearson 1981:101)

For some forms of prostitution, there are big financial incentives. Dr Pawadee Tongudai's 1982 study found that Thai women migrants working in nightclubs and massage parlours earned a monthly average of about £125 (1982 figures), while most female migrants in other occupations earned less than £21 per month (Hantrakul 1983:28) (although there is a wide disparity between girls working in high class establishments and those who are bonded to poor owners). Neumann has estimated that prostitutes in the Philippines earn six to ten times as much as sales clerks or factory workers (1979:15). These figures help to explain the attraction of prostitution for some women, although it should be remembered that while these jobs appear lucrative, prostitutes have a short working life with declining earning power and their health costs may be high. They also retain only a small proportion of their gross income. For example, reports from Thailand found that agents who procure girls aged between 12 and 14 from poor families and take them to Bangkok, receive US $150 from customers paying 'to break them in', while the girls themselves receive only US$15 (Barry 1984:37). Because commercial sex is technically illegal and women working in the street are liable to be arrested, they are forced to use hotels, bars or other distribution outlets which allows others (bar owners, pimps, and police) to receive a share of their receipts – a kind of market rent (Thanh-Dam 1983:541). Nevertheless, prostitutes do retain some of the proceeds of their labour, and send home to impoverished parents between one-third and one-half of their earnings (Phongpaichit 1982:23).

Apart from poverty, there are other reasons which may lead women into prostitution. Some research shows that many prostitutes were abandoned by husbands, have a history of unhappy relationships, or were raped. It is not clear to what extent youthful prostitution is precipitated by sexual abuse, but there is evidence from the child prostitutes in Olongapo that rape (by policemen) was one of the reasons for their recruitment into the profession (Ocampo 1983:34; Golley 1983:32). Barry (1984:29) notes that: 'Trafficking children into prostitution and providing them for pornography is a highly profitable market for pimps and procurers.' Although none of the women researchers of this subject appear to concur, Cohen claims that there are additional 'positive' recruitment factors. Bangkok bar girls, he says, profess an aversion to Thai men because of past experiences and the women serving tourists are drawn by the excitement of meeting 'strange and often attractive foreigners with a respected status and cultural background' (1982:412).

Some accounts of prostitution do point to other advantages. The flexible working hours are important to single mothers and some prostitutes may enjoy greater autonomy in their personal and sexual lives than middle class women who are repressed by conservative double standards (Hantrakul 1983:28). A similar case arguing the advantages of not being dependent on any one man is made by the western prostitutes interviewed by Kate Millett (1975:31): 'If one of them gives you trouble, you can just say "fuck you". But you can't do that if you're married and you can't do that if you're being kept.' In another variation of this argument, some defenders of prostitution justify it as a form of work which, unlike unpaid domestic work, at least gives women some return for their labour and freedom from sexual commitment. According to this view, all women are subject to sexual harassment so prostitution is no more exploitative than other forms of work. Certainly there are reports from the free export zones in South Korea of Japanese supervisors sexually abusing women employees with impunity and many domestic servants suffer the same fate (Elson and Pearson 1981:100).

If sexual exploitation is possible within marriage and in other jobs, can it be argued that prostitution really offers greater freedom? And are women exercising 'free choice' in choosing to become prostitutes? I think not. Avoiding certain personal relations with men and working for oneself may give women the illusion of freedom from economic control, but more probably the prostitutes of South-East Asia have merely exchanged the domination of fathers, brothers, and husbands for that of male managers, pimps, and police. 'The apparent independence of women can be misleading: while women may not be directly subordinate to a particular member of their male kin, they are none the less, subject to an overall culture of male dominance' (Phillips, in Elson and Pearson 1981:95).

There have been far reaching changes in female labour patterns in South-East Asia and with the erosion of kin relations of production, patriarchal control over women's mobility and labour has been somewhat reduced (Thanh-Dam 1983:536). However, the penetration of capital and extension of capitalist relations of production have tended to reproduce and reinforce the subordination of women as sexual services have become commoditized in a similar fashion to other forms of labour power. New gender divisions are grafted on to, and make use of existing forms of female subordination so that, as Bryceson (1985:151) points out, women's new 'choices' really amount to non-choices: 'The working-class woman prostitute represents the epitome of 'freedom' under capitalism. She is 'free' to sell her labour power and her sexuality, but in reality she is forced to do either or both to secure her subsistence.'

People in the north of Thailand interviewed by Phongpaichit (1982:49) said that 'they admired the girls for the loyalty they showed towards their parents. They appreciated that the girls were not running away, but rather were showing a proper filial responsibility for looking after their parents in old age.' Thus, they become prostitutes for both economic and non-economic reasons. However, to explain prostitution we must also ask where the clients come from and what leads men to patronize prostitutes.

Who are the customers and what are they buying?

Kathleen Barry makes the general observation that:

> The demand for sexual service is most significant where men congregate in large groups separated from home and family.
> The sexual demands of military men, travelling businessmen or sailors and immigrant laborers create a major market for women's bodies.

> (Barry 1979:59)

As well as the short-term concentrations of foreign military personnel associated with the wars in Indo-China, there are permanent American bases in South-East Asia such as Olongapo (home of the US Seventh Fleet) and Clark Air Force Base in the Philippines. This is coupled with increasing militarization generally, as insecure élites become obsessed with 'national security'. Susan Brownmiller (1975:94) describes prostitution during wars as 'the unspoken military theory of women's bodies as not only a reward of war but as a necessary provision like soda pop and ice cream, to keep our boys healthy and happy'.

After a war, women were recycled from the military market to the major cities of Manila, Bangkok, and Seoul which, with the intensification of capital, have become important business centres providing bases for many multinational companies. Business travel interrupts established relationships between men and women, and prostitution flourishes. Urban drift creates a local demand from young male migrants separated from village kinfolk and too poor to afford marriage. In South-East Asia the prostitute's customers are American troops, European (notably German and Dutch), Japanese, Australian, British and American businessmen, tourists from all corners of the globe, Singaporean and Malaysian neighbours (especially visiting the southern Thai towns of Hadyai and Sugnai Kolok), and local indigenous men.

What they are buying is a more complicated question. The argument that men have natural irrepressible sexual urges while women do not, making it impossible to eliminate prostitution, is a familiar one (Davis 1976:249). Davis and many others uncritically accept the ideology of male sexual 'needs', the idea that men have innate cravings or desires which go beyond monogamy and which women somehow lack. However, Davis also makes the more interesting suggestion that:

> The demand for the prostitute's services arises out of the regulation of sex itself and the limited liability of the commercial relationship.

If the customer has the money, he can obtain satisfaction with no further obligations. He does not become enmeshed in 'courtship', 'friendship' or 'marriage'.

Davis (1976:247)

Money is very important to the transaction, for when men pay, it frees them from guilt. Men are buying not just a service, but a particular type of unsanctioned sex which entails a lack of engagement. Barbara Ehrenreich (1983:12) suggests that this avoidance of commitment became widespread in America in the 1960s. She sees it as a form of male rebellion against traditional cultural expectations of husbands as breadwinners. There has developed a new hedonistic consumer ethic where the man 'who postpones marriage even into middle age, who avoids women who are likely to become financial dependants, who is dedicated to his own pleasures, is likely to be found not suspiciously deviant, but "healthy"' (Ehrenreich 1983:12). She sees *Playboy* and other sex magazines as feeding a new kind of extra-marital consumerism. 'The message, squeezed between luscious full-color photos and punctuated with female nipples, was simple: You can buy sex on a fee-for-service basis, so don't get caught up in a long-term contract' (1983:46). The use of prostitutes becomes proof of masculinity.

That men want impersonal sex is not a new idea. One might well ask, why are they travelling to South-East Asia for it? Kate Millett gives a clue when she suggests that the purchaser is not buying sexuality at all, but power over another human being: 'It is not sex the prostitute is really made to sell: it's degradation' (Millett 1975:56). If sex is no longer scarce, then maybe something else is. With an increasingly active global feminist movement, male-controlled sexuality (or female passivity) appears to be a scarcer resource. The travel advertisements are quite explicit about what is for sale: docility and submission. Travel promoters offer European men a deeply racist mythology of Asian women when they speak of them as 'without desire for emancipation but full of warm sensuality and the softness of velvet' (Lenze 1979:6). Even in Japan, sex tours have been blamed on non-compliant Japanese women (Awanohara 1975:6). The Rosie Reizen travel advertisements put great emphasis on the women's compliance:

Thailand is a world full of extremes and possibilities are unlimited. Anything goes in this exotic country. Especially when it comes to girls . . . the coffee shop is full of willing girls . . . .

Men will live like kings in Bangkok . . . with the most beautiful women of the east at their side. And their future Thai partners are not especially particular, so that no European need fear going to Bangkok for nothing. The man who has difficulty in establishing

relationships here . . . in Bangkok can choose among hundreds of
young women who for a tiny amount will make him feel like a
great Don Juan.

(ISIS 1979:9)

Japanese travel agents sell a similar line, stressing the girls' subser-
vience:

men are attracted to the stories of *kisaeng* girls . . . waiting on men
at parties and even putting food into the customer's mouth for him.
It is advertised that the *kisaeng* spirit is so self-sacrificing and
dedicated that when a man brings a *kisaeng* girl back to his hotel,
she will even do his laundry if he will leave her a big tip.

(Matsui 1977:27)

The attraction is power and the relationship one of master/slave.
Racist stereotypes of the exotic, sexually licentious oriental woman fuel
the sex tourist industry in South-East Asia. It is partly 'the subconscious
feelings of sexual and racial superiority of Japanese males', former
colonizers of South Korea, which account for Korea's popularity as a
tourist destination (Kikue 1979: 23). Racism also plays a part in
explaining why Japanese wives rarely protest about their husbands'
engagement in sex tourism. Takazato (1980:23) claims that they prefer
their husbands to use prostitutes overseas and that they find it easier to
accept an Asian rather than a Japanese prostitute because 'Third World'
women are looked down on, thereby confirming them in their racist
feelings of superiority. The double standard present in Japan (and
elsewhere) separates women into categories of 'pure' or 'fallen'. In the
case of sex tourism these become reinforced by attitudes towards race.

Pheterson identifies a similar racism in Europe through her analysis
of language and the way in which the word 'whore' is connected to
'unchaste': 'one definition of unchaste is impure. Impure is defined as
"dirty", mixed with foreign matter, adulterated, mixed with another
colour . . . such a definition activates associations of racial and ethnic
diversity wherein only white, non-foreign people are chaste' (1987:
215).

Tourists' expectations are created by images offered to them before
they leave home. Airline advertising using photographs of traditionally-
dressed women frequently markets racist stereotypes, particularly the
idea of the superior sexuality of oriental women. The idea that Asians
are superior in the realm of the physical carries with it the implication
that this is the Asian woman's proper sphere. Tourism often has the
effect of turning people into objects, seen merely as part of the scenery
or as servants existing only to make life more comfortable for the visitor.
But racist dehumanization of prostitutes is particularly offensive, with

girls in brothels numbered for selection like goods in a supermarket. As individual human beings they cease to exist and unlike the situation in the Greek agro-tourist co-operatives described by Mary Castelberg-Koulma, there is no way for the male visitor to be drawn into the women's real world in such an exploitative environment. He returns home, his racist, chauvinist views confirmed.

But if docile eastern women are still too threatening to men's masculinity, they can go one stage further and buy someone very young, even a child. Girls as young as 12 can be found working in the massage parlours of Bangkok (Phongpaichit 1982:14) and in 1983, Olongapo became the focus of a national scandal when widespread child prostitution was reported. The girls, aged 9 to 14 years, came to public attention when one complained of genital sores to nuns at the local community centre. It transpired that many had sold their virginity to American servicemen for US$25–60. Subsequently, they earned US$13–20 a visit (Ocampo 1983:34). Youthful sex is another commodity explicitly marketed by the travel magazines:

> No, it it not an exaggeration to say that South Korea fully deserves its reputation as a 'male paradise' . . . those Korean girls are young . . . and very ripe. Most South Korean girls also have tight 'purses'. What man wouldn't want to experience one of those?
> (*Jitsuwa* magazine, quoted in ISIS 1979:22)

What men are buying does not stop there: Asian women are also bought as docile wives. Bureaux exist in Hong Kong, Singapore, Germany, and the Netherlands for those who want to pick out a wife from a catalogue of eligible women. There are overtones of the slave trade in the advertising of these brides: the women are numbered, and can be 'ordered' to specification and 'returned' if they do not suit a man's requirements. Prices range from US$5,000 to US$8,000, none of which goes to the woman. 'Her payment is the acquisition of a "faithful, understanding" husband' and the dubious pleasure of life in the west (Claire and Cottingham 1983:210). Not surprisingly, the result of these marriages is often misery for the bride, cut off from relatives, unable to speak the language or get a job, and no longer indulged by a generous holiday-maker now constrained by everyday economic pressures. Some of these 'wives' find themselves put to work as prostitutes. In the Philippines Australian men who own many of the disco/dance parlours are known to marry brides from the Philippines in order to circumvent the national property laws. Husbands in these mail-order or convenience marriages may be in for a few surprises too. The image of wide-eyed docility suggested in the advertisements may be sharply contradicted by the sophisticated opportunism of some of the new spouses (*The*

Economist 1977, 263:76). But if clients are not always satisfied, others do reap substantial benefits from prostitution.

Promotion and profits

The legacy of the US military was an infrastructure – airports, road networks, telecommunications systems, and accommodation – which has been used by the tourist industry and which has enabled sex tourism to become big business. But to facilitate the link between the supply of rural poor and the demand of foreign clients state policies of actively promoting tourism were also important. The end of the Vietnam war in 1975 coincided with big cut-backs in employment in multinational factories, and the whole edifice of airlines, hotels, taxis, bars, tourist guides, dope-sellers, restaurants, and other service industries looked ready to collapse at a time when employment opportunities were shrinking. Pimps, agents, owners, and entrepreneurs were desperate for business; it was state-promoted tourism which rescued them. Developing countries have not, however, simply stumbled on tourism as a promising way to earn foreign exchange. The UN General Assembly designated 1967 as 'International Tourist Year' and passed a unanimous resolution that: 'tourism is a basic and most desirable human activity deserving the praise and encouragement of all peoples and governments' (Wood 1980:561). South-East Asian governments have received a steady stream of advice from the US Department of Commerce, the Pacific Area Travel Association, the World Bank, the Asian Development Bank, and others (Wood 1981:4).

The links tourism creates between local and international structures, and between the national and world economy, involve a greatly expanded role of the state in, for example, visa policy, foreign exchange controls, and generally in promoting and financing mass tourism (Wood 1980:569). States play an active part in defining and co-ordinating tourist policy, and are thereby involved in prostitution, albeit in a covert way. Truong Thanh-Dam explains the relationship between prostitution and tourism as 'one between a legally marginalized form of commoditization (sexual services) within a national industry (entertainment), essentially dependent on, but with a dynamic function in, an international industry (leisure travel)' (1983:544). Sex tourism is highly organized, not only in the host countries, but also in the tourists' home countries. Much of the travel to Korea, for example, consists of packaged complimentary tours sponsored by businesses as rest and recreation for the company employees, as a work incentive for outstanding managers and salesmen, or as a morale booster for members.

In the 1960s, it was widely believed that tourism would bring general prosperity by acting as a stimulus to modernization, providing employment, encouraging cottage industries, attracting foreign exchange, and reducing balance of payments deficits. The decision to opt for capital-intensive, international standard hotels in South-East Asia has, in fact, necessitated enormous loans and provided little local employment in the formal sector, thus bringing into question the alleged net social benefits of tourism (Chib 1980:290). The mammoth Pomum Tourist Resort Project near Kyongju in South Korea needed a World Bank loan of US$25 million while in 1976–7, the Marcos Government built four-teen new hotels in the Philippines at a cost of US$510 million (most of the money coming from the Development Bank of the Philippines which is loaned money by the World Bank for 'development' projects). By way of contrast, in the same two-year period, only US$13 million was spent on public housing in the entire country (Wood 1981:9–11). The extravagance of this policy is evident. Apart from the initial outlay costs (hotel construction, publicity, and promotion) tourism itself has foreign exchange costs or 'leakage'. The amount which host countries spend on importing goods intended for tourists can reduce or even cancel out the positive gains from tourism when all costs and benefits are taken into account. Leakages occur through government incentives to foreign companies: for example, low interest loans to investors, tax exemptions, and duty-free imports of equipment. Other costs are not so easy to quantify, but would include the wages of the foreign workers who are recruited for hotel management with the consequent loss of employment for locals, roads widened for tourist comfort rather than for marketing of rural produce, and power generated for filtered swimming pools instead of for local consumption. In the Philippines the Ministry of Local Government and Community Development issued a directive to local governments requiring them to establish tourist boards and to spend their budgets on beautification projects and local festivals (Wood 1981:6). Additional disadvantages of tourism are that when growing numbers take jobs in tourist service industries, 'agriculture is neglected and the tourist-intruded society becomes increasingly dependent on imported food . . . and therefore increasingly tied to international cycles of inflation' (Turner and Ash 1975:198). Tourism does little to create a skilled labour force which could contribute to other sectors of the economy, and may actually stunt development in other sectors by com-peting for scarce resources. The high degree of foreign ownership characteristic of tourism tends to consolidate dependent class relations.

There are alternative routes to national development. With so many dubious benefits, why have South-East Asian countries lavished so much of their scarce wealth on tourism? While a country as a whole may not benefit from tourism, individuals do. This is borne out in Thailand, for instance, where the ruling élite of generals, air marshals, and admirals and their wives are frequently 'sleeping partners' in business ventures. New companies in the tourist business take the precaution of inviting military officers in the ruling clique to become directors, thus creating alliances between local ruling classes and multinationals (FEER 1980b:44). While many of the infrastructural costs of tourism are paid from taxation, the benefits accrue to a limited number of individuals. Some leaders are quite open about their support of prostitution: at a national conference of provincial governors in 1980, Thailand's Deputy Prime Minister exhorted governors to help the national tourist effort by encouraging 'certain entertainment activities which some of you may find disgusting and embarrassing because they are related to sexual pleasures' (quoted in Mingmongkol 1981:24). The head of the Government tourist organization in Thailand has also admitted that tourism fosters prostitution 'but since it creates employment, the advantages outweigh the disadvantages' (quoted in Lenze 1979:8).

Benefits are derived at all levels of the social scale. Local police receive protection fees from massage parlour and brothel owners, while unprotected streetwalkers must pay police unofficial 'bail' money apart from their fines (Phongpaichit 1982:11; Hantrakul 1983:30). In the Philippines the Anti-streetwalking Ordinance assures business operators the various fees involved in selling women; for example, to gain access to a woman in a bar clients must pay intermediary 'ladies drinks' (the price of her company), or 'bar fines' (the price of taking her out of the club). Women in hotels report having to pay US$1.80 each evening for police protection. But these profits are only a fraction of the money generated by the sale of women to tourists. Most hotels in the Philippines operate a 'joiner pass' system where guests pay extra to bring women to their rooms. (One hotel claimed to make 40 per cent of its gross income from the 'joiner' system.) In South Korea, while it is the Tourist Association which officially issues ID cards to prostitutes, licences are also sold on the black market. But of course, even though profits are spread widely from hotel managers, to tour operators, police, and pimps (with even the hotel bell boy demanding his cut), the really large profits from sex tourism are cleared by the tourist agencies abroad, the airlines, and the local élite who have invested in the industry.

While there is widespread official acceptance and promotion of sex tourism, the politically powerful will go to great lengths to conceal the links between prostitution and the profits made from drug dealing or the abuse of children. When the Olongapo child prostitution scandal broke in 1982, the city mayor first denied that the children were prostitutes and then attempted to deport the priest who publicized the case. He placed the girls in 'the custody of the mayor's office' and tried various methods to silence them. *We Forum*, one of the newspapers which published details, was closed down by the Marcos Government (Ocampo-Kalfors 1983:34). At the 1984 Groningen Women's Studies Conference, Sister

Mary Soledad Perpinan, well-known for her research into sexual slavery, reported that prostitution is often a front for drug trafficking, although data are notoriously difficult to obtain.

Apart from the profits siphoned off by the local élites, tourism also serves wider political purposes. For example, plans for 'The New Society' launched by President Marcos with his declaration of martial law in 1972, included both land reform and tourism, but equitable redistribution of land, which might have brought real development to the poor, was largely sidestepped in a spending spree on massive hotels. Marcos had to ensure that martial law did not jeopardize the flow of foreign capital investment and he used tourism to promote 'a façade of normality', to give his regime legitimacy in what Linda Richter (1980) has described as a political rather than purely economic programme, implemented with total disregard for the costs. Martial law would, Marcos explained, make the society safe for tourists and protect it from internal subversion. To establish his case, he invited travel agents and tour operators from all over the world to the place 'Where Asia Wears a Smile', and built the huge Folk Arts Theatre to host the 1974 Miss Universe contest. It was, of course, convenient that roads and airports constructed in the southern Philippines and elsewhere, ostensibly for tourism, could be used by the military in their war against Muslim secessionists and the communist New People's Army. President Aquino continued this dual policy of support for tourism and neglect of land reform for much the same reasons.

President Park Chung Hee's repressive rule, held together by American military protection, benefited in a similar way from the emphasis on tourism, the hosting of the 1988 Olympics in Seoul being an attempt to lend credibility to the regime in South Korea. Such authoritarian regimes are not slow to use military force to protect the interests of transnational corporations and to limit the rights of workers, including those in the tourism industry, on the pretext that popular protests will damage their 'tourist image' and promote communist power in the region. Providing 'a stable climate for foreign investment' and keeping labour cheap to maintain competitiveness goes hand-in-hand with the repression of workers' organizations, the banning of strikes and the arrest of leaders (Sudworth 1983:5). Marcos decreed that hotels in the Philippines were industries 'vital' to the national interest and all strikes were therefore illegal (Wood 1981:9). But this is just one of the many factors constraining women's ability to challenge their lack of economic opportunities, poor pay, and working conditions.

Tourism and its associated prostitution is therefore an unlikely path to development or to greater economic or political equality for women. Tourists are, on the whole, prosperous, conservative, and apolitical; they 'cannot or will not see any causal link between the wealth of their class and the prevailing poverty of the countries they visit' (Turner and Ash 1975:291). When young girls are the resources to be exploited for the sake of the economy, it is easy to see tourism as a malign force, 'a new form of colonialism in which the rich of the world fan out through the poorer countries looking for areas to colonise which are pleasanter than their existing homes' (Turner and Ash 1975:249). The sex tourism industry derives its profits from gender inequalities and economic disparities within and between nations, and allows the rich (with leisure) to visit the poor (with 'atmosphere') for cheap sex.

Responses

The issue of sex tourism is related to problems which are fundamental to women's role in the workforce in an international context: women's lack of economic and educational opportunity, their neglect in rural development or land reform schemes, their subjugation within the family, their domestic burdens and family responsibilities, and their exploitation in new forms of factory work. The oppressive character of customary values and much family and employment legislation, together with women's location within the labour process generally, mean that prostitution becomes a means of survival in a patriarchal world. However, there are forms of resistance, both individual and collective. Individually, many young women retain their self-respect even when working at jobs of which they are ashamed, by emphasizing their self-sufficiency and their ways of contributing to the sustenance of their families. Most use prostitution as a temporary means of livelihood and many eventually return to the village.

There are moralists who urge governments to curb 'undesirable activities', who accuse the women of sinning against religious values, or alternatively, those who blame them for upholding patriarchy to the detriment of all women. Campaigns based on these approaches are, like the Victorian ones that preceded them, liable not only to fail but to be counterproductive (Taylor 1981:17). One outcome of the moralizing stance is the institution of the reformatory such as those in Thailand where monks provide prostitutes with 'moral training' and try to make them feel suitably guilty. Similar institutions, often run by Christian charities dedicated to refurbishing moral character, can be found in the Philippines and South Korea. Prostitutes who, by and large, have made a rational economic choice, largely reject such organizations. As Sukanya Hantrakul has noted, the reformatories merely serve to control women's sexuality while leaving unquestioned the unequal moral standard applied to men and women (1983:35). However, there are more practical institutions which provide health services for the women, act as refuges, run drug and alcohol rehabilitation centres, offer vocational training, and try to help women out of trouble (Phongpaichit 1983:76). One of the most successful of these organizations is EMPOWER (Education Means Protection of Women Engaged in Re-Creation) based in Patpong, Thailand which runs English classes, a school of drama, counselling services, health education programmes (focusing on prevention of Aids), and workshops on women's rights for prostitutes.

Other collective responses in both 'North' and 'South' have focused on public awareness campaigns in an attempt to make the problem visible and to expose the underlying ideological context upon which international prostitution is based. These campaigns have challenged traditional marriage practices and religious beliefs, denounced sexist and racist airline advertisements and beauty contests, and organized demonstrations against tourist agencies, airlines and governments which promote sex tourism. When Japanese feminists learned of sex tours in 1973, they launched a series of protests which included greeting Japanese men at the airport on their return. The South Korean Church Women United and the Christian Council of Japan have joined others in publishing research papers and making slide shows to publicize the issue. In 1977 different groups came together to form the Asian Women's Association which publishes a regular magazine. Perhaps the most dramatic impact was made at an International Workshop on Tourism held in Manila in 1980 when there were massive demonstrations against Premier Suzuki of Japan on his tour of the region. Asian women co-ordinated their protests so that at each stop on the tour, Suzuki was met by angry protests which are credited with causing a significant decrease in Japanese tourism (Barry 1984:44). Letters went to Reagan, Marcos, and the Pope, while at the same time, the American Society of Travel Agents' convention in Manila was bombed, causing its cancellation (Claire and Cottingham 1983:212; Southeast Asia Chronicle 1981). The concerted action became known as the Third World Movement Against the Exploitation of Women (TW–MAE–W) based in the Philippines, while in Thailand, the Friends of Women group was organized. These groups have had considerable success in raising public awareness. Even Japan's major labour unions have appealed to the Prime Minister for the prohibition of group sex tours as they found themselves embarrassed and 'losing face' at regional workers' conferences. Other collective efforts have centred on the international links, with European feminists and church groups such as the Ecumenical Coalition on Third World Tourism attempting to expose both ends of the traffic in women, particularly the plight of mail order brides and migrant workers (Holden *et al.* 1985:3).

However, almost all those fighting sex tourism concede that these actions, despite their publicity value, have limited effect and address the symptoms, not the main causes of the problem. There is the danger that condemnation will merely deprive impoverished women of their means of livelihood: 'No amount of agitation is likely to change things while the cost incentives remain the same, and the opportunities for alternative employment are so limited' (Phongpaichit 1982:76). For this reason, the International Feminist Network Against Female Sexual Slavery, set up in 1983, emphasized the need to rethink national development strategies and to create alternative worthwhile, non-exploitative jobs for women. It also sought to develop strategies that would oppose the institution of prostitution, but not penalize the individual women in prostitution. Decriminalization of prostitution would mean that legal action would focus on procurers and other exploiters of women, rather than on the victims of this exploitation. The network urges other legal reforms to remove customary and civil laws which reinforce and perpetuate double standards of morality and maintain the subordination of women in society. The 1949 United Nations Convention for the Suppression of the Traffic in Persons and of the Exploitation of the Prostitution of Others, and the 1981 UN Convention for the Elimination of Discrimination against Women could provide the basis for these changes (Barry *et al.* 1984:50).

There are also more extreme responses to sex tourism. 'Kill a sex tourist a day' was the slogan of one of the Philippine guerrilla movements (Gott 1985). It is significant that large-scale prostitution in cities, the legacy of an imperialist system, has preceded revolutions in many parts of the world, examples being Shanghai, Saigon, Aden, Maputo, and Havana (Molyneux 1981:5). Revolutionary governments have been much more zealous in tackling the problem than capitalist states. Vietnam's solutions may offer some insights to South-East Asian women. In 1975, at the time of liberation, there were over 100,000 prostitutes in Saigon (White 1979:3). The new communist regime tried 'on-the-spot' education to reform prostitutes, members of the local women's union being given the job of educating them to quit. But many continued in prostitution and so it was thought necessary to group them into schools which, at first sight, looked suspiciously like reformatories, although there were differences. First they were treated for diseases, then sent on to study politics and education. The emphasis was not on individual moral condemnation, but on the historical framework which allowed women to become oppressed and exploited in serving foreign interests. The women then graduated to a third type of school which taught handicraft and work skills. They could choose to return to their villages or work on state farms as agricultural labourers. The Youth League and residential district committees were given the job of re-educating the clients who buy women. Meetings were held to criticize men in their trade union or workplace. If a man did not reform he could be fired and forced into a study centre. But most importantly, the demand from

Wendy Lee

foreigners was cut off. Even after such a revolution, old attitudes persist. The Vietnamese schools for prostitutes were at first called 'Centres for the Restoration of the Dignity of Women' (implying that they had none before). 'The men who had been soldiers for American dollars, presumably could be considered mercenaries, military prostitutes, but the centres to re-educate them were called 'study' centres (*hoc tap*). The function was the same, to make them see the errors of their past ways and prepare them for a new life' (White 1979). Fortunately, the Vietnamese seem to have realized the double standard implied in this name difference and they re-named the women's centres 'Schools for New Women', a more hopeful attitude (White 1979:2).

It is clear that women's subordination through sex tourism is not just a problem of ideology, and it will take more than propaganda or rehabilitation centres to change the present situation in Manila or Bangkok. While so many profit from the exploitation of women, the limitations of many current feminist strategies are glaringly obvious, though the agro-tourist co-operatives examined by Mary Castelberg-Koulma offer the potential for an alternative form of host-guest interaction. The process by which governments and international agencies have 'integrated' women into development, discussed by Joy Lyon, together with the commercialization of sex in the industrialized capitalist world, frequently make prostitution the only option for poor women. Western feminists cannot pretend to offer solutions on behalf of women from other countries. We cannot harbour any racist notions of superiority in confronting what is a truly international problem for women. As one South-East Asian woman has remarked: 'There's obviously something radically wrong with *your* society when your sex problems have to be exported to the Third World' (Claire and Cottingham 1983:212). The long-term solution to prostitution in South-East Asia involves not only a complete change in the distribution of resources between rural and urban people, but also between rich and poor nations.

References

Apisuk, C, Suraphongchai, C. and McDonnell, E. *Empower Annual Report*, Bangkok: Empower.
Awanohara, S. (1975) 'Protesting the sexual imperialists', *Far Eastern Economic Review* 14 March, 5–6.
Barnett, H. (1976) 'The political economy of rape and prostitution', *The Review of Radical Political Economy* 8(1).
Barry, K. (1979) *Female Sexual Slavery*, New Jersey: Prentice Hall.
Barry, K., Bunch, C. and Castley, S. (1984) *International Feminism: Networking Against Female Sexual Slavery*, New York: IWTC.

Brandt, V. (1971) *A Korean Village: Between Farm and Sea*, Cambridge: Harvard University Press.

Brownmiller, S. (1975) *Against Our Will: Men, Women and Rape*, Toronto: Bantam Books.

Bryceson, D.F. (1985) 'Women's proletarianization and the family wage in Tanzania', in H. Afshar (ed.) *Women, Work and Ideology in the Third World*, London: Tavistock.

Chang-Michell, P. (1985) 'Making a living: South Korean women in commerce', *Southeast Asia Chronicle* 96: 17–24.

Chib, S.N (1980) 'Tourism and the Third World', *Third World Quarterly* 2: 283–294.

Claire, R. and Cottingham, J. (1983) 'Migration and tourism: an overview', in *Women in Development: A Resource Guide for Organization and Action*, Geneva: ISIS.

Cohen, E. (1982) 'Thai girls and farang men: the edge of ambiguity', *Annals of Tourism Research* 9 (3): 403–428.

Davis, K. (1976) 'Sexual behaviour', in R. Merton and R. Nisbet (eds) *Contemporary Social Problems*, New York: Harcourt, Brace Jovanovich.

The Economist (1977) 'Packaged brides', 25 June, 263: 76.

Ehrenreich, B. (1983) *The Hearts of Men: American Dreams and the Flight from Commitment*, London: Pluto Press.

Elson, D. and Pearson, R. (1981) 'Nimble fingers make cheap workers: An analysis of women's employment in Third World export manufacturing', *Feminist Review*: 87–105.

Fanon, F. (1966) *The Wretched of the Earth*, New York: Grove Press.

Far Eastern Economic Review (1976) 'Thailand: what the GIs left behind' 91: 26–28.

—— (1980a) 'Letter from Lake Bomun' February, 107: 70.

—— (1980b) 'The success of Thailand's sleeping partners' April, 108: 44.

Gagnon, J.H. (1968) 'Prostitution', in *International Encyclopedia of the Social Sciences* 12: 592–598.

Golley, L. (1983) 'For sale: girls', *Southeast Asia Chronicle* 89: 32.

Gott, R. (1985) 'Shots in the sex war', *Guardian*, 22 March.

Hantrakul, S. (1983) 'The spirit of a fighter: women and prostitution in Thailand', *Manushi* 3(6): 27–35.

Holden, P., Horlemann, J. and Psäfflin, G.F. (1985) *Tourism, Prostitution, Development: Documentation*, Bangkok: Ecumenical Coalition on Third World Tourism.

Hutchcroft, P. (1982) 'No smear, no work: safeguarding American interests in the Philippines', *Southeast Asia Chronicle* 84: 12–13.

ISIS International Bulletin (1979) 'Tourism and Prostitution' *ISIS International Bulletin* 13: 3–28.

Kikue, T. (1979) 'Kisaeng tourism', *ISIS International Bulletin* 13: 23–25.

Kirsch, A.T (1975) 'Economy, polity and religion in Thailand', in G.W. Skinner and A.T. Kirsch (eds) *Change and Persistence in Thai Society*, Ithaca: Cornell University Press.

Lanfant, M–F. (1980) 'Tourism in the process of internationalization', *International Social Sciences Journal* 32(1): 14–43.

Lenze, I. (1979) 'Tourism prostitution in Asia', *ISIS International Bulletin* 13: 6–8.

Lindsey, K. (1979) 'Madonna or whore?', *ISIS International Bulletin* 13: 4–5.

Matsui, Y. (1977) 'Sexual slavery in Korea', *Frontiers, A Journal of Women's Studies* II 1: 27–28.

—— (1984) 'Why I oppose Kisaeng tours', in K. Barry *et al.* (eds) *International Feminism: Networking Against Female Sexual Slavery*, New York: IWTC.

Millett, K. (1975) *The Prostitution Papers: A Candid Dialogue*, St Albans: Paladin.

Mingmongkol, S. (1981) 'Official blessings for the "Brothel of Asia"', *Southeast Asia Chronicle* 78: 24–25.

Molyneux, M. (1981) 'Socialist societies old and new: progress towards women's emancipation', *Feminist Review* 8: 1–34.

Neumann, A.L. (1979) 'Hospitality girls in the Philippines', *ISIS International Bulletin* 13: 13–16.

Ocampo S. (1980) 'Philippines bases and American guns', *Far Eastern Economic Review* March, 107: 16.

Ocampo-Kalfors, S. (1983) 'The age of innocence lost', *Far Eastern Economic Review* March, 119:34.

Ong, A. (1985) 'Industrialisation and prostitution in South-East Asia', *Southeast Asia Chronicle* 96: 2–6.

Pheterson, G. (1987) 'The social consequences of unchastity', in F. Delacoste and P. Alexander (eds)' *Sex Work*, London: Virago.

Phongpaichit, P. (1982) *From Peasant Girls to Bangkok Masseuses*, Geneva: ILO Women, Work and Development Series, No.2.

Piker, S. (1975) 'The post-peasant village in Central Plain Thai Society', in G.W. Skinner and A.T. Kirsch (eds) *Change and Persistence in Thai Society*, Ithaca: Cornell University Press.

Reditt, J. (1981) 'Travel will take over from titivation', *The Times*, 3 August.

Richter, L. (1980) 'The political uses of tourism: a Philippines case study', *The Journal of Developing Areas* 14: 237–257.

Southeast Asia Chronicle (1981) 'Tourism: selling Southeast Asia' April, 78.

Sudworth, E. (1983) 'Freetrade zones and women workers', Unpublished paper from Women, Aid and Development Workshop, held at the Australian National University Development Studies Centre, Canberra.

Takazato, S. (1980) 'Prostitution tourism: sexual exploitation', *Asian Women's Liberation* April, 2.

Taylor, B. (1981) 'Female vice and feminist virtue', *New Statesman* 101 (2601): 16–17.

Thanh-Dam, T. (1983) 'The dynamics of sex tourism: the case of Southeast Asia', *Development and Change* 14 (4): 533–553.

Thitsa, K. (1980) *Providence and Prostitution: Image and Reality for Women in Buddhist Thailand*, London: Change International Reports.

Tokuhisa, T. (1980) 'Tourism within, from and to Japan', *International Social Science Journal* 32(1): 128–50.

Turner, L. and Ash, J. (1975) *The Golden Hordes: International Tourism and the Pleasure Periphery*, London: Constable.

van der Vleuten, N. Report on the international strategy meeting against the traffic in women, Rotterdam April 1983, *Insisterhood Newsletter* October, 2: 19–24.

Villariba, M. (1982) *The Philippines: Canvasses of Women in Crisis*, London: Change International Reports.

White, C. (1979) 'Visit to the Centre for New Women, Ho Chi Minh City' 19 September, Unpublished notes.

Wideman, B. (1977) 'Overbuilt, underbooked', *Far Eastern Economic Review* 21 January: 72.

Wood, R. (1980) 'International tourism and cultural change in Southeast Asia', *Economic Development and Cultural Change* 28: 561–81.

—— (1981) 'The economics of tourism', *Southeast Asia Chronicle* 78: 3–11.

Chapter six

Return to the veil

Personal strategy and public participation in Egypt

Homa Hoodfar

Introduction

In recent years the western media have revived the image of the veiled
and oppressed Muslim woman. Media coverage has reminded us of the
orientalists' interpretation of the veil as a symbol of the Muslim
woman's subordination and exclusion from all social spheres and even
her loss of control over her own life. Colonial powers once used this
interpretation either implicitly or explicitly to show the backwardness of
Muslim society (Sayigh 1981; Pastner 1978). This newly revived image,
however, is more startling in that it shows the Muslim woman
voluntarily and actively participating in veiling movements and therefore bringing upon herself the evils of oppression and exclusion.

The media show the same Muslim woman, who is supposedly excluded from all social spheres because she is veiled, joining in political
demonstrations and liberation movements and daily moving about in the
crowded cities of the Middle East. This image has not caused observers
to question in any serious way the accuracy of the view that veiling
equals oppression and exclusion. Nor has it prompted a re-examination
of the social norms and the political and economic forces that influence
the persistence of the institution of veiling. As it is no longer possible to
portray woman as victim, she too is presented as 'backward' and, at the
same time, still wrapped in the exoticism and incomprehensibility of
oriental culture. Even less has any attempt been made to differentiate the
varieties of veiling movements in the various Muslim societies.

Veiling has existed and continues to exist in a wide variety of
economic, political, and cultural situations. Although there has been
some commonality of themes, it is an institution that has communicated
different messages in different societies and during different historical
periods. The veil adopted by Iranian women during the anti-Shah
movement conveyed to the world a different message (Tabari 1980;
Tabari and Yeganeh 1982) from the *compulsory* veiling of the Khomeini
regime, which represents authority and the attempt to control women by

the State (Afshar 1982). Both cases, however, represent women's active resistance to the imposed gender role envisaged for women by the state. Voluntary veiling among educated working women in Egypt is the outcome of social processes very different from those in Iran. Even within one society or a single cultural entity the veil may be worn for different reasons by different classes or social groups. The presentation of Muslim women as a single social group, together with a uni-dimensional concept of veiling and seclusion has further served to confuse the issue.

In this chapter the veiling movement among educated Cairene women from a lower income group, most of whom work in government or other public sector offices and workshops, will be examined. Despite the lack of statistical information, Egyptians and outside observers agree that these women form the most visibly veiled social group in Cairo. It will be argued that veiling in the economic and cultural context of modern Egypt is not an exclusionary measure for this group of women. Rather, it is a means by which they protect the gains and possible opportunities that modernization has brought. Veiling has become an instrument through which women publicly dissociate themselves from some of the culturally disapproved traits and characteristics attributed to the stereotype of the modern woman. At the same time, veiling enables these women to safeguard their traditional rights.

The data presented here come from a wider research project on domestic politics and the household economy conducted in Cairo, Egypt between 1983 and 1985 (Hoodfar 1988a). The anthropological approach gives a voice to the women who have opted to wear the veil as they explain their reasons and motivation for veiling. These explanations are put in context by first providing the reader with a short summary of the many meanings of the veil and the many dimensions of the veiling issue, as well as a brief history of deveiling in Egypt.

The veil

The practice of veiling and seclusion originated in non-Arab culture and predates Islam (Keddie and Beck 1978; Nashat 1982). Nevertheless, because of its presumed sanction by the Koran, it is more widely observed among the Muslim community. Contrary to popular belief, however, veiling is nowhere specifically recommended or even discussed in the Koran. At issue, rather, is the interpretation of the two passages concerned with women's clothing in which the Koran says that women should cover their bodies [1]. In any case, strict veiling and seclusion became an accepted ideal and a sign of status among Muslim communities.

In practice, adherence to the ideology of veiling has not always meant the total covering of the body, but it has involved varying degrees and forms of concealment. The traditional covering of the entire body was once common among women of the highest economic strata in Egypt. In contrast, the majority of both urban and rural women of the poor classes, who need to be mobile, wear dresses which, although though long, often do not provide total coverage of the body. Despite variation in the practice, these women view themselves as veiled and strongly support the principle of veiling, but dress in this way so that they can move about and attend to their work. Focusing on the Islamic text (on sexuality) has often been at the cost of overlooking the discrepancy between principle and practice which varies among different social groups.[2]

Clothing is an important means of non-verbal communication in any society; for instance, details of dress can indicate to the observer the origin and social position of the wearer. Veiling in the Middle East, however, is intertwined with the Islamic ethic, making it a highly complex institution. According to Islamic doctrine, a woman should cover her hair and body (except for the face and hands) when in the presence of men who are not members of her family or certain categories of kin. Therefore, when women put on or take off the veil, they publicly define who is family, who is more distantly related and who is an outsider (MacLeod 1987:122). Moreover, since veiling defines sexuality, women, by observing or neglecting the veil, may define who may or may not be considered a 'man' (Pastner 1978). For instance, veiling may not be observed in the presence of low status men or male children. Further, the dropping of the veil in circumstances of conflicts between male and female roles can be used to insult men or dramatize a point. Perhaps most relevant to our discussion, however, is the function of the veil of conveying publicly the message that the wearer is a Muslin woman who adheres to the Islamic rules regulating the relationships, rights, and obligations inherent in the gender roles.

Modernization and the deveiling movement

In the 1920s Egyptian Muslim women were the first in the Arab world to call for the discarding of the veil and for the admission of females to universities (Shaarawi 1986). Significantly, the deveiling movement was organized by women activists without state intervention. This distinguishes it from deveiling in other countries such as Iran and Turkey, where the state introduced and sometimes enforced deveiling through its oppressive apparatus. In 1923, Hoda Shaarawi, Saiza Nabarawi, and Nabawyya Musa dropped their face veils on their return from a feminist meeting in Rome. In the midst of much heated public discussion, they organized a demonstration in which women marched unveiled in the streets of Cairo. By the time of the anti-colonial movement during the 1940s, women's organizations existed among the urban middle classes and had become a visible political feature of urban Egypt (Philipp 1978).

The movement hardly touched rural or lower income urban women, however. This was partly because the movement revolved around many of the limitations which seclusion imposed on upper and middle class women. Seclusion was an issue which did not exist in any meaningful way in the lives of women from the poorer classes, particularly in the Delta region, who traditionally enjoyed freer physical movement and participation in more spheres of the economy. Other issues, such as voting and entering university, were irrelevant to both females and males of these social strata at that time. Even issues such as the revision of the marriage law by restricting the unilateral right of men to divorce or marry a second wife were not of much concern to this group of women. Lack of financial resources, as well as social pressure and the cultural norms of stable communities, were more effective than any legislation in preventing men from exercising these Islamic rights.[3] Therefore, women from the poorer classes had very little reason to become involved in this movement.

Due mainly to the efforts of women activists, many of the nationalist and secular parties felt compelled to set the woman question as one of their top priorities. As a result, furthering the rights and interests of women was officially viewed as an integral part of modernization and development from the time of the 1952 revolution. This policy was manifested in the emphasis that Nasser placed on the changing position of women, particularly after the 1956 revolution. As the state moved more towards socialism, participation of women in the 'economy' came to be seen as essential to the building of a modern socialist society. In order to facilitate their participation, the state gave its political support to the encouragement of education for women.

In the aftermath of the revolution, hopes were high as Egyptian women took the opportunity to make gains in the fields of education and formal employment, gains which were impressive even in comparison with those made by western women. Many women graduated from high school and entered university entirely on merit. Despite a much higher rate of illiteracy among women in general, the ratio of female to male students increased dramatically at the more advanced educational levels, particularly at the university level (el-Guindi 1981:479).[4] It is noteworthy that many women who took advantage of the revolutionary government's free education policies were from modest backgrounds and very often the first literate female generation. The state's guarantee of a job to all high school and university graduates increased the attraction of education for women.

Labour Law 91 of 1954, over and above its guarantee of equal rights and equal wages, made special provisions for married women and mothers. Later, under Sadat, these provisions were expanded to facilitate women's labour market participation (Sullivan 1981). This law was applied primarily in the public and government sectors, which made jobs in these areas particularly attractive to women. As a result the state has become the single most important employer of women.

Urban women have entered the formal labour market as white collar workers in significant numbers. White collar jobs in the public sector offered a good salary which was considered a family wage at a middle class standard. In cases of husband and wife both working in white collar jobs, the households managed to establish themselves as comfortably middle class, regardless of their social origins. In fact, Nasser's era witnessed the highest degree of positive social mobility in the history of modern Egypt. He used the expansion of the state apparatus as a means of creating a new and larger middle class (Abdel-Fadil, 1980).

The percentage of female blue collar workers in the labour force, however, has shrunk continuously since 1970, after an initial expansion in the 1960s. The low wages earned in these jobs do not compensate for the losses resulting from absence from the home (Hoodfar 1988a). Another interesting aspect of female participation in the formal labour market in Egypt is that the percentage of women in professional and managerial positions is much higher than in most other (similar) developing countries; it is even higher than in the UK (Scott 1984).

Undertaking cash-earning activities was not entirely a new phenomenon in the life of urban Egyptian women, particularly those from the Delta. Many women had engaged in a variety of businesses including shoemaking, tailoring, butchering, midwifery, baking, and trading (Tucker 1985; el-Messiri 1978). The women of the middle classes had managed and controlled their property, i.e. money, real estate, workshops, or trading firms. What was new, however, was that women now had to spend long hours in government offices, away from their homes and thus they could not spend as much time on their domestic responsibilities as before.

Viewed as a symbol of oppression and exclusion from public life, the veil had virtually disappeared among the middle classes and white collar workers in Egypt by 1967. Instead, these women wore a modest version of western-style clothing.[5] They considered themselves liberated from the oppressive aspects of traditions and valued their new position in the labour market and in the public sphere. There was, however, little renegotiation of sex roles within the domestic domain. The political ideology which urged women to participate in the labour market took their domestic contribution for granted. The state considered women's domestic responsibility unproblematic, merely an extension of their biological function. Therefore, there was little attempt to facilitate the combining of work and home responsibilities beyond giving women three months' paid maternity leave and up to two years' unpaid leave of absence for the first three children without loss of fringe benefits or grades. This was a beneficial policy which nevertheless still served to reinforce the traditional gender ideology and division of labour.

There is little evidence of women actively trying to challenge traditional sex roles within the domestic domain, which are regulated and justified by Islamic doctrine. In the past, this was because white collar employees earned a good salary, and could easily employ domestic help from the army of rural-urban migrants serving as cheap labour. Moreover, the first female white collar employees generally came from more comfortable backgrounds where domestic help was taken for granted. For women who could not afford or were unwilling to employ domestic help, the availability of help and support from close female kin, especially mothers and younger sisters, who often lived nearby, resolved the contradictions inherent in going to work and attending to domestic responsibilities, especially child care. In this way, middle class women merely contested middle class men's monopoly over jobs in the formal labour market while keeping control over the domestic sphere themselves.[6]

Steady change in socio-economic conditions since the 1970s has effectively eroded the financial advantage of white collar workers, whose real wages and purchasing power have declined considerably as a result of high inflation. Migration to oil-rich Arab countries coupled with the introduction of the open door policy (market economy) [7] has increased wages in the private and informal sectors. Maids and domestic workers now earn as much as, or sometimes more than, government employees. Rising prices and housing shortages are forcing the younger generation to move further away from their original neighbourhoods where they had close friends and relatives. This has robbed women of the valuable childcare support they could get from their kin, or at best has made it difficult to take advantage of this support.

The upper middle class and those from well-connected backgrounds have switched to lucrative jobs in the private sector with salaries that still make it possible for them to employ domestic help. Lower middle class women, however, are forced to take positions in overstaffed government offices, where their salaries and promotions are regulated according to an established system that does not include consideration of performance. Even in the 1980s, the majority of these women were first or second generation urban dwellers, and were often the first generation of educated females in their families.

Men of this social group, for their part, are forced to take a second or even third job in order to make ends meet. In general, women can neither nor want to look for a second job for two main reasons: first, they rarely have the opportunity to find work which is reasonably paid, or that is more interesting than their regular jobs; and second, women themselves attach a high value to caring for their children and homes. Women value their role as mother and wife, *set el-beit*, which despite being devalued in the processes of modernization, still carries much prestige and status in Egyptian society. Further, MacLeod (1987) points out that women enjoy and value their much greater autonomy in the home than in most office jobs. These circumstances have made the household more dependent on the husband's income and have reinforced his role as provider. This process has led effectively to the disappearance of any fertile ground for the renegotiation of sex roles and responsibilities within the domestic domain.

Such circumstances have dashed the hopes of the younger generation of women who studied to gain financial independence by becoming white collar workers. Consequently, they try to protect their traditional rights, such as the wife's unconditional right to her husband's financial support, regardless of her own earning capability. In this context, women do not view a change in gender roles within the home as either possible or desirable because their domestic responsibility is a means of justifying their claim to their husband's financial support (Hoodfar 1988a). By adhering to Islamic principles, women have managed to keep control over the way in which their own wages and material resources are spent.[8] In fact, women have a vested interest in reinforcing the existing sex roles and sexual division of labour, while at the same time trying to minimize the constraints that such ideology places on them.

The economic logic for married women being employed in the government sector has been eroded.[9] When women work away from the home, the cost to the household in terms of both finance and convenience has become so high that in many cases employment is no longer a viable option. Their expenses include the cost of clothing in conformity with middle class expectations, which is considerable in Egypt (Rugh 1986), transport, and miscellaneous items. The household budget suffers considerably because women do not have the time to shop efficiently. Childcare and nursery expenses are a further cost; even when female kin help, the service they do as a favour is often expected to be repaid in the form of gifts. As a result of all these factors, more and more men are demanding that their wives give up their jobs and stay at home. Although men often justify such a demand primarily on the grounds of cost-effectiveness, there are often other unvoiced desires for reinstating or reinforcing their own positions as breadwinner, a role which brought them much prestige and power and which was practically, if not ideologically, contested in the previous generation by the women's equal earning ability. To legitimize their demand, men use their Islamic right to limit their wife's physical mobility, which, in modern Cairo, is popularly interpreted as their right to prevent their wife from 'working'.[10] They can now easily afford to voice this demand without much cost to their household (since the high costs associated with women's paid work can make their net financial gain very small). In fact, many young men attach a condition to their marriage proposal that their prospective wife should not seek employment outside the home.

Women articulate their financial contribution to the household as their main motivation for entering the labour market. Other motives, such as the financial security that formal employment offers, particularly in case of divorce, widowhood, or old age, were given less importance. The prevalence of this attitude was encouraged by the deep-seated ideology of family and expected selflessness of individuals, particularly the mothers, for the collective interest of the family. However, emphasizing a financial contribution to the household made it easier for the wider society, and men in particular, to accept women's absence from their household and neighbourhood. Women, on the other hand, had little reason to object to this line of approach since their self-interest and that of the household generally coincided.

However, recent economic development has reversed the tide and has put into opposition the women's self-interest and that of the household. Now suitors and husbands argue that the high opportunity cost of women's employment makes it more advantageous for the household if the wife/mother stays out of the formal labour market. While women appreciate such logic, they nevertheless find it difficult to give up privileges such as the financial security that formal employment offers them.[11] They have seen many examples of deficiencies in the informal support institutions on which they were traditionally expected to rely in such times of crisis as divorce or widowhood. Women have understood that they cannot depend only on kin support. On the other hand, their meagre wages make it impossible for them to set up independent households, even if the cultural and ideological obstacles were removed. Moreover, working in a dull job can hardly compete with the much appreciated and socially approved occupation of mother and wife. In any case, the women did not expect to have to choose between the two roles any more than men have to choose between being a father, husband, and employee.[12]

This situation has placed women in a dilemma. They want to protect the possibilities and gains (however small) that modernization of the economy has afforded them. At the same time they want to guard against the loss of their traditional rights as mother and wife, particularly in the face of recent economic development. In response to this situation, and to consolidate and retain traditional and modern gains, many women have revived the old institution of veiling. Through this tactic they publicly convey their adherence to the Islamic tradition and avoid some of the inconveniences of going to work in western style clothing, as well as decreasing the cost of clothing. Perhaps, more importantly, veiling reduces some of the husbands' insecurities caused by their wives participating in the formal labour market. Moreover, the veil has afforded women a fundamental challenge to the conventional and more conservative Islamic ideology that has kept women out of public space under the pretext of veiling.

Reveiling

In Egypt's past, as for many other Muslim societies, a manifestation of increased status of a household was often the total veiling and more restrictive seclusion of women – in emulation of upper class traditions. However, in more recent years the upper classes have worn a rather modest version of western type of clothing. Until recently, this practice was closely followed by the middle classes and those inspired by middle class values. The 1980s have, however, witnessed a new phenomenon in that educated and lower middle class women have returned to the veil.

This modern veil is a style of dress very different in appearance from clothing worn by more traditional *balady* (urban lower classes) or *felaheen* (peasant) women. The most popular version of the modern veil is an outfit consisting of a long, western-style dress or skirt worn with a kind of turban or a scarf. Whatever is worn on the head covers the hair and sometimes the shoulders as well (Rugh 1986). This outfit serves to separate the modern educated women from the traditional women whose style of dress carries the implication of 'backwardness' and lack of sophistication.

Reveiling appeared among university students in the early 1970s (Williams, 1979). By the late 1970s, it had become a widespread movement among the lower middle classes, of which the most visible group were white collar workers in the public and government sector. By 1985 the majority of younger women in most government offices were veiled (MacLeod 1987).

This startling picture has evoked a great deal of comment and criticism from both western observers and Egyptians, although little systematic research has been conducted to examine the phenomenon from the perspective of those women who have chosen to veil not merely out of custom.[13] The question is, why should this group of educated and privileged women voluntarily revive the institution from which the preceding generation had struggled to liberate itself? What does the veil do? How does it change the situation to women's advantage? What are the social forces which induce such action? Does the veil offer previously unrecognized privileges to women?

Deprived of the favourable economic situation which had created tremendous possibilities for the acceptance of a new approach to the female role, women have employed veiling as a strategy that enables them to continue to have access to some independent cash income. A review of the circumstances in which some of my informants took up the veil provides some insight on this issue.

Sommayya was in the last year of teacher training when she became engaged to marry a year after graduation. Once she finished and was going to start her teaching career, her fiancé began to object to her 'working'. His mother and eldest sister came to intervene on his behalf when I was present in her home. A summary of a five-hour visit and discussion will help to demonstrate the way in which these questions are examined by the people involved. They calculated that she and her future household would lose more money than she would bring in if she went out to teach. She would have bus fares to pay and on occasions would eat lunch at work and buy cold drinks for her colleagues. She would also have to spend quite a lot on clothes because it is not acceptable for a teacher to go to work in old or cheap clothes. This would account for virtually all the forty Egyptian pounds per month that she would earn. Furthermore, people would talk, and her reputation might be questioned, because who would know where she really spent her time? In overcrowded buses men who have lost their traditional respect for women might molest her and of course this would hurt her pride and dignity as well as that of her husband and brothers.

When her future mother- and sister-in-law left, Sommayya said that she accepted their logic yet she did not want to give up her future job. She explained to me:

'If I wanted to sit at home I could have been married four years ago and by now have had a complete home and family. I studied hard and my mother suffered to provide the money for my education so that I could 'work'. I cannot imagine staying at home all day. I have gone to school every day since I was 7 years old. I never thought I would live the way my mother did. I can be a good wife and mother and yet have a job where I can have contact with other women like myself. Perhaps one day if I had everything I needed and had children, and my housework demanded I stay at home, I would give up my job. But not now. What if my marriage does not work out? Who knows – my husband might die when I still have young children, like my father did. My mother suffered so much bringing us up after my father died. She did everything she could so that I would not suffer her fate.'

I left her then and came again to visit a few weeks later. She was happier and had solved the problem in a way that satisfied both her and her husband. She had gone to the Ministry of Education and demanded her right as a married woman to work near her future home. Her new workplace was a short bus ride away, a distance she could also walk. After discussing the situation with many of her friends and colleagues, she had decided to take up the veil. She had previously declared on many occasions that she would never veil because she did not see it as essential to being a good Muslim. While showing me her new clothes she explained:

> 'I wear a long skirt and this scarf. First, it is not that bad; it suits me better than many other women because my face is small. Second, if I have only two sets of clothes I can look smart at all times because nobody expects *muhaggabat* (the veiled ones) to wear new clothes every day. This will save me a lot of money. It will also prevent people from talking about me or questioning my honour or my husband's. In this way I have solved all the problems, and my husband's family are very happy that he is marrying a *muhaggaba*.'

She continued to explain that none of the women in her fiancé's family was educated or worked in an office. They had felt a little uncomfortable before because they thought that educated and 'working' women generally do not attend to their homes well and do not respect their husbands. Now that they are assured that she is a good Muslim and will respect her husband, they are at ease with her. She said that her fiancé was convinced that the problem had been solved and agreed to her going to work. Of her own accord she had told him that when they had children she would give up her job and stay at home if they did not need her income. Apparently he had taken her willingness to accept his reasoning and compromise as an indication of her being logical and sincere. He did not continue to insist that she should not work.

She arranged to work two shifts until they were married in order to buy the items they would need for their future home. She repeated many times to me: 'A bride with no wealth wins no respect'. After marriage, she would work only one shift, and so that she could continue to work as long as she wished, her mother promised to help with childcare and with shopping and obtaining subsidized food. In order to facilitate this, Sommayya had negotiated and included a condition in the marriage contract that she should reside not far from her mother.

Clearly, veiling saves a lot on clothing expenditure because *muhaggabat* are no longer compared with women wearing western-style clothing, who as a rule are expected to have a colourful wardrobe. But the function of veiling is not only an economic one. The veil communicates loudly and clearly to society at large and to husbands in particular that the wearer is bound by the Islamic idea of her sex role. A veiled woman indicates that despite her unconventional economic activity she respects traditional values and behaviour. By wearing the veil women lessen their husbands' insecurity; they convey to their husbands that, as wives, they are not in competition, but rather in harmony and co-operation with them. Further, wearing the veil puts women in a position to expect and demand that their husbands honour them and recognize their Islamic rights. Husbands should not claim their wives' wages and they should fulfil their duty of providing for the family to the best of their ability.

It is not only young women in the early stages of employment who are forced by conditions in contemporary Cairo to resort to conventional veiling in order to defend their unconventional activities. Sa'diyya was 37 with three children and had worked for thirteen years when I met her in 1983. A few months after that she decided to take up the veil. When I asked her why she had veiled, she replied that she had never imagined that she would. She went on to explain that she always disagreed with veiling, but that living conditions had changed. She continued:

'When I got married I had not yet finished high school. I married against the wishes of my parents, who wanted me to marry someone else. I thought they were old-fashioned. I married and continued to study because my dream was to have a good job, which I managed to get. I wanted to be well-dressed and have a nice family life with a good, understanding husband who would help me with the children, and he did. For a while things were so good it was like a dream. Everyone envied us, but things have changed and the cost of living has forced my husband to search for a second and even a third job. I am left with caring for the children, shopping and cooking. We have rented a flat farther away from my mother and every day I have to bring the children to her on a bus and then get another bus to go to work. Every afternoon I have to come again to collect them. By the time I have finished my housework and fed the children, there is no time to wash and set my hair and to iron my dress like I used to do. And clothes are so expensive now that since we have to buy things for the children, we cannot afford to spend much on our own clothing. In fact, for me to dress well like my female colleagues who are all unmarried, I would have to spend my entire salary on clothes for myself. All the married women in the office are veiled.'

With much nostalgia about the past she continued:

'The last time I had an argument with my husband because he is
never there to at least help me with shopping or to stay with the
children when I shop, he demanded that I give up my job and stay
at home if I could not handle both. In any case he thought I spent
most of my money to buy clothes for myself, and presents for my
parents and sister because they look after the children. I disagreed
and fought with him but the fact is that he is right. My wages have
been spent mostly on these things for the last few years, but I'm not
well-dressed like I used to be, and I have no comfort. All the same,
I don't want to give up the security of my job even at the cost of
divorce. Who would look after me if tomorrow something
happened to him or if he divorced me. My brothers don't even
come to see me, much less look after me and my three children. I
need the security. These days life is difficult. Women need
security. So I decided to follow suit and take up the veil. I'm so
much more comfortable now. I wear a long dress and a turban.
People are more respectful, particularly in the buses and shopping
queues.'

It has been argued that the veil is inconvenient to wear (MacLeod
1987; Williams 1979). Technically it may be, but a look at the cultural
context and the reality of women's daily life explains why they consider
it more convenient and comfortable. It saves time because veiled
women are not expected to be very meticulously or formally dressed or
to follow fashion trends. Also, in the Middle East and the Islamic world,
women's clothing has always been closely associated with the rules and
conventions of sexual behaviour. Western styles of clothing often
implicitly associate women with the 'immoral' behaviour and images of
western women, images that are based on American soap operas such as
Dallas and *Flamingo Road* and not the reality of western life. The veil
indicates that the wearer supports conventional sexual behaviour and is
not attempting to be sexually attractive to men. The relief that the veil
brings to these women, even if it is occasionally less than desired, has
made their physical movements in the crowded streets of Cairo and in
overcrowded public transport considerably easier.

Whatever might be said for or aganst veiling, the veil is nevertheless
a socially sanctioned style of clothing, and most veiled women feel that
the advantages it offers outweigh any inconveniences it may present.
The social meaning of clothing is an important feature over and above
its physical utility. Choice of clothing communicates innumerable
messages including the desire to be seen as part of a particular ethnic
group, social class, culture, religion, ideology, and so on, all of which
can be much more important than physical comfort. Men, as well, traded

physical comfort for social benefits when they gave up their traditional *galabiya*, a long dress-like garment ideal for the Egyptian climate, for the western-style suit and tie (without, curiously enough, attracting much attention from western social scientists). However, it is interesting to note that while men and women both underwent a westernization of clothing for several decades, they now seem to be going in opposite directions along the continuum of traditional versus modern clothing styles, with the women reverting to the more traditional. The social factors which influence these choices of clothing styles are undoubtedly complex and warrant further investigation.

For centuries Egyptian women have been credited with liberal attitudes and strong characters in comparison with women in other Muslim societies (Williams 1979; Tucker 1985; el-Messiri 1978). Unlike their more traditional counterparts, many modern westernized Egyptian women hesitate to be as assertive as they would like to be because such behaviour on the part of westernized women may be interpreted as immoral and immodest. These women feel frustration as they struggle to preserve a good reputation without losing their traditional prerogative of being publicly assertive. This frustration has further encouraged many of them to take up the veil and thus dissociate themselves from any hint of immorality that may be associated with their western clothes.

Halah is a white collar worker married to one of her colleagues. She said the following in explanation of why she had adopted the veil:

> 'I used to dream of the day I would finish my studies and work to earn enough money to buy the nice clothes I never had because we were poor. When finally I had a good wardrobe and managed to look nice after years of waiting, I had to take up the veil. I did it because in the office men teased us women and expected no answering back. If we answered they would start to think we were after an affair or something. That was difficult. All my life I always returned any remark a man made to me without being accused of immorality. In the office, whenever I would do that, my husband would get upset because he would hear what other men said amongst themselves. But my veiled colleagues were always outspoken and joked with our male colleagues, and they were never taken wrong or treated disrespectfully. So I took up the veil. It has made my life easier and I feel freer to answer back, express my opinion, argue or even chit-chat with men. My husband is also much happier.'

Among the lower middle classes it is mostly married working women who have adopted the veil. Many single women, however, who cannot or do not want to lead their lives in a very traditional manner have also veiled. In many cases, the veil has enabled them to diffuse any doubts about their honour, which is very important to them and to their families. Moreover, it sometimes affords them more respect and freedom.

Soheir lost her father when she was a child and worked as a domestic help in different households. Finally she managed to get her school certificate and afterwards she got herself a job as a seamstress. She would leave work to go to evening school and then return to the shop and work late. She had rented a room in a suburb of Cairo and always took the bus as late as 11 o'clock to go home. She said:

> 'So often people treated me badly that I would go home at night and cry. One day when I had gone to Sayida Zeinab (a popular shrine in Cairo) to cry and complain to her (the shrine) a woman started talking to me and suggested that I wear the veil. Then people would know that I am a good woman and that my circumstances have forced me to work late at night.'

She thought about veiling and discussed it with some of her classmates who thought it was a good idea. So she took up the veil. She said: 'Since then I have had more peace than ever before.' People stopped judging her badly and assumed she must have a legitimate reason for being out late or being out all day. She continued: 'I sometimes miss wearing make-up and making myself beautiful, but there is no way I would give up the veil. When I am married and have a husband, I will put make-up on and let my hair loose for him.'

Considering her lack of power to change prevailing attitudes, a change which would require collective efforts and social and political support, she used the social institution at her disposal in order to protect herself. This has enabled her to invest her energy in what she considers her top priority: going to school. She is hoping to become a white collar worker despite the difficulty of studying and working at the same time.

Modernization has changed Egyptian society, but the actual gains it has brought for women have not met their expectations by any means. The high rate of inflation during the 1980s worsened the economic situation and many of the women in lower income groups have lost their actual or potential economic independence. This has made them much more cautious about giving up their traditional rights or jeopardizing their family support and network. Consequently, they find ways to accommodate both modern and traditional ways in order not to give up either.

Many women find themselves in conflict with their families, especially fathers and brothers, as they try to break with tradition. In the Middle East it is the women who endow their families with honour or shame, bearing some similarities to the position of Greek women in rural areas, discussed by Mary Castelberg-Koulma in Chapter 10. This fact entitles women to protection from the family, while at the same time it may limit their choices and freedom. In many instances women are prevented from engaging in activities of which the intended or unintended consequences may be viewed as harmful to their families' honour. Though there are some signs that this ideology of honour and shame is undergoing modification, its disappearance or redefinition would require more time and collective effort. Many women have adopted the veil as a means of disengaging the issue of family honour from the issue of personal freedom to work or continue their education, or simply to move about more freely.

Samiha comes from a better-off household among my informants. Her father migrated to the Gulf in the early 1970s and returned with enough capital to establish a business. Her sisters finished school and got married, but she wanted to continue even after her first degree. The family strongly disagreed and every time she went out her brothers would object and argue with her. She was accused of bringing disgrace to her family. She gave up her studies for some time. Later, however, she went back to university – but this time veiled. She studied and also started to teach privately, something to which her father had objected before because he thought it implied that he could not support his daughter. She explained to me that if she decided to veil and become a good Muslim, her family could not accuse her of disgracing them. She said she was a lot happier since she started wearing the veil and she regretted that she had not done it earlier. She is planning to continue teaching, and her family and neighbours have a lot of respect for her. The family intended to protect her as well as their honour, not to prevent her from continuing to pursue her interests. By adopting the veil she demonstrated that she was committed to protecting her honour. Thus, there was no longer any reason to prevent her from going to university or from teaching, both of which are socially legitimate goals.

Most women are less concerned about what they wear than their freedom to move about freely, to study, and take employment. They see the veil as a way of maintaining their family and social support without giving up their own priorities. Restrictions on style of dress is apparently a cost they consider well worth paying if it saves them from being forced to choose between having the support of society and their family and pursuing their goals.

The women who veil do not necessarily become more religious. My data confirm MacLeod's (1987) findings; none of the women I came to know prayed or read the Koran more after they took up the veil. In fact, few women of the lower income groups practised their religion strictly. Among the veiled women in my sample, only Sommayya prayed, and she had started to pray five times a day four years before she veiled. For the women who live it, Islam is a way of life, a value system and a recognized set of social behaviours.

There are other social reasons which have encouraged educated and working women to take up the veil. When many of the women marry and set up their own households, they are forced by rising prices to move to cheaper neighbourhoods on the outskirts of the city – much to their distaste (MacLeod 1986; Hoodfar 1988a; Shorter 1989). Living in these neighbourhoods, educated women are more inclined to take up the veil. This is because they are eager to distinguish themselves from the *balady* (traditional) and *falaheen* (of peasant origins) women, who are often illiterate and who behave and dress in traditional ways. The educated women thus separate themselves from the other women; yet they are still in good standing as members of the neighbourhood because their behaviour is socially approved. They uphold cohesion of values, but not equality in ranks.

While going to the local *suq*, Hoda explained:

> 'It is terrible that we had to move to this area because we couldn't afford to stay in a better area. After all these years of studying I had to move to an even worse area with all these *falaheen* and illiterate women ... . It is much better that I am veiled because if I wore European clothes to work, they would accuse me of being loose ... . Even in the neighbourhood I would never go out looking the way they do. Wearing the veil makes them respect me and accept that I am not one of them.'

Women take up the veil of their own accord. As the veil becomes more popular, many may adopt it because they see it as a fashionable style of dress. A few may feel that, as a style, it suits them best (MacLeod 1986; Rugh 1986:149–156). For others, it is a question of conformity; when the majority of their colleagues are wearing the veil, they adopt it in order to promote cohesion among their workmates.[14] Veiling can encompass a multidimensional range of goals and reasons.

Women believe that veiling is something a woman must want and decide to do by herself. A husband can object to his wife's working, and this is an issue that should be settled at the time of marriage. Veiling is not an issue that can be agreed upon in such a way. Aza refused to marry a suitor with good credentials because he said that he would like her to veil after marriage. She said that taking up the veil is certainly very good and that she admires the women who decide to do it, but a man who does not understand that a woman must reach this decision independently cannot be a good husband. Such a man would want to rule the woman and no woman likes that. Aza continued:

'I may decide to accommodate all my husband's desires beyond my duty as his wife, but he has to understand that if I do so, it is my decision and I do it by my own will. He should not expect more than what is his right as a husband.'

Conclusion

The current practice of veiling in Egypt is a movement adopted, if not initiated, largely by the educated women of the urban lower income social groups, the majority of whom are white-collar government employees. I have argued that the new veiling is fundamentally different from the old institution, despite some shared characteristics and common messages that they convey.

In the past, veiling practices over and above covering the female body have often been accompanied by the seclusion of women from much of public life. The contemporary urban women of Egypt have readopted the old institution of veiling, and given it new substance and meaning by separating Islamic law from customary practice. The presence of newly veiled Egyptian women in considerable numbers in public, particularly in government offices, openly challenges the messages and practices associated with veiling by religious leaders and western observers. In fact, I have argued that a primary goal of contemporary veiling is to make it easier for women to remain in public life and participate in the formal economy.

The economic situation in recent years has effectively robbed the women of lower income groups of their hopes of financial independence. Moreover, under the new socio-economic conditions, the high cost of employment in the formal sector for women has considerably diminished the economic advantages for married women of being employed in the public sector. This situation has made women more cautious about giving up their traditional rights within marriage and risking the loss of support from their family and their kin. On the other hand, the reduction in economic advantages has made men much less tolerant of the unconventional role of women within the formal labour market and many have demanded that their wives give up their jobs and remain housewives.

Having invested much energy, time, and family resources in acquiring the educational qualifications necessary for entering the formal sector of the economy, women do not wish to give up the financial security, however meagre, which these jobs bring them. This need is accentuated by the fact that men have a unilateral right to end a marriage, after which a wife's claim to her husband's financial support

ends. Furthermore, the development of a cash economy has been con-
current with an undermining of the non-cash contributions to the household, a process women feel is detrimental to their power and position
vis-à-vis their husbands. In an attempt to combine the advantages of
both traditional marriages and modernization, women have returned to
the veil. In this manner they minimize some of the inconvenience of
working away from home as well as diminishing the antagonism of their
menfolk by publicly adhering to Islamic ideology and the gender roles
which are implicit within it. This strategy has made it easier for them to
remain in the public domain and formal economy.

What deveiling did in 1923 was to challenge the ideology that had
excluded women from the public domain and to pave the way for
bringing them more fully into it. The women involved were mostly of
the élite and upper income groups, but at that time they were, as a group,
more removed from the public sphere than the majority of the female
population. The reveiling of today, however, is making it easier for
women of the lower social strata to enter the formal labour market and
other areas of public life.

Notes

1 See E. Warnock-Fernea and Bezirgan (1977: 2–26) for the translation of the
verses of the Koran relevant to women and the veil. Also see Yeganeh and
Keddie (1986).

2 To demonstrate the extent of such discrepancy among my informants I cite
the following story from my field notes.

   While I was visiting Umm Waa'il she invited me to go shopping with her.
I accepted, and since she was in a hurry I made my way to the alleyway,
where I waited ten minutes before she joined me. When I commented on her
delay she explained: 'I could not find my *tarha* (a long see-through black
scarf not wider than half a metre worn loosely on the head) and I could not
come out naked.' Though the *tarha* did not cover her half-length sleeves and
low-cut neckline, it nevertheless symbolized the veil to her and others in the
neighbourhood.

3 In order to protect women from divorce, cross-cousin or kin marriages are
preferred, or a large *mahr* is requested. The *mahr* is an agreed sum of money
or property which the bride can demand from the groom before or after their
marriage.

4 In 1952–3 the ratio of female to male students was 1 to 13.2. By 1975–6 this
had changed to 1.8 to 1.0 (el-Guindi 1981).

5 By law male workers were required to wear western-style clothes, but the
law remained silent on female dress or mentioned it only implicitly.

6 Despite the general assumption, activities in this sphere, which encompass
some activities classified as public in other societies, have traditionally
brought women great power and status (Singerman 1990; Hoodfar 1988a;
MacLeod 1987).

7 The swift socio-economic change from what was referred to as Egyptian socialism to a liberal or market economy has come to be known as the open door policy or *infatah*.

8 Women spend their money mostly on those extras which their husbands are unwilling or unable to buy. They may also buy household goods which, though for communal use, are primarily beneficial to women (Hoodfar 1988a, 1988b).

9 It may still make economic sense for unmarried women to work for the small income obtained from these jobs. Unmarried children, especially daughters, live with their parents and are not expected to contribute much to the family beyond buying things for their own use after marriage.

10 In Egypt, it is not clear that a husband can legally make such demands on his wife. Court cases have been decided both in favour of and against husbands.

11 In the case of divorce, a woman receives only three months of alimony and no share of the wealth except what she owns independently of her husband. Further, she inherits only an insignificant portion of her husband's wealth. If the husband is a government employee, after his death the wife (or wives) receives his salary until she remarries.

12 Clearly, women in Egypt face a contradiction between their different roles which men do not face.

13 For an excellent example of such research, see MacLeod (1987).

14 Now in 1988, the veil has become a new popular fashion and many modern stores are selling ready-made *muhaggabat* clothing; this commercialization was hardly apparent in 1985. This process has been encouraged by the increased number of Egyptians who have adopted an Islamic style of clothing as well as by the fact that Cairo has become a commercial and tourist centre for the other Arab countries. This development has somewhat diminished the economic advantage of this style of clothing.

References

Abdel-Fadil, M. (1980) *The Political Economy of Nasserism: A Study in Employment and Income Distribution Policies in Urban Egypt 1952-1972*, Cambridge, Massachusetts: Cambridge University Press.

Afshar, H. (1982) 'Khomeini's teachings and their implications for women', *Feminist Review* 12.

el-Guindi, F. (1981) 'Veiling *Infitah*, with Muslim ethic: Egypt's contemporary Islamic movement', *Social Problems* 28 (4): 456–487.

Hoodfar, H. (1988a) *Survival Strategies in Low Income Neighbourhoods of Cairo, Egypt*, PhD thesis in Anthropology, University of Kent at Canterbury.

——(1988b) 'Patterns of household budgeting and the management of financial affairs in a lower-income neighbourhood in Cairo', in D.H. Dwyer and J. Bruce (eds) *A Home Divided: Women and Income in the Third World*, Stanford, California: Stanford University Press.

Keddie, N. and Beck, L. (1978) 'Introduction', in N. Keddie and L. Beck (eds) *Women in the Muslim World*, Cambridge, Massachusetts: Harvard University Press.

MacLeod, A. (1987) *Accommodating Protest: Working Women and the New Veiling in Cairo*, PhD thesis in Political Science, Yale University.

——(1986) *Hegemony and women working and re-veiling in Cairo, Egypt*, Paper presented at the North East Political Science Association Annual Meeting, 15 November, mimeo.

el-Messiri, S. (1978) 'Self-images of traditional urban women in Cairo', in L. Beck and N. Keddie (eds) *Women in the Muslim World*, Cambridge, Massachusetts: Harvard University Press.

Nashat, G. (1982) 'Women in pre-revolutionary Iran: a historical overview', in G. Nashat (ed.) *Women and Revolution in Iran*, Boulder, Colorado: Westview Press.

Pastner, C.M. (1978) 'Englishmen in Arabia: encounters with Middle Eastern women', *Signs* 4(2): 309–323.

Philipp, T. (1978) 'Feminism and nationalist politics in Egypt', in L. Beck and N. Keddie (eds) *Women in the Muslim World*, Cambridge, Massachusetts: Harvard University Press.

Rugh, A. (1986) *Reveal and Conceal: Dress in Contemporary Egypt*, Syracuse, New York: Syracuse University Press.

Safiah, K. Mohsen (1985) 'New images, old reflections: working middle-class women in Egypt', in E. Warnock-Fernea (ed.) *Women and the Family in the Middle East: New Voices of Change*, Austin: University of Texas Press.

Sayigh, R. (1981) 'Roles and functions of Arab women: a reappraisal', *Arab Studies Quarterly* 3(3): 258–274.

Scott, A.M. (1984) *Industrialization, gender segregation and stratification theory*, Paper presented to the ESRC Gender and Stratification Conference, University of East Anglia, July, mimeo.

Shaarawi, H. (1986) *Harem Years: Memories of an Egyptian Feminist 1874-1924*, translated and introduced by M. Badran, London: Virago.

Shorter, F.C. (1989) 'Cairo's leap forward: people, households and dwelling space', *Cairo Papers in Social Science*, vol 12, monograph 1, spring.

Singerman, D. (1990) 'Politics at the household level in a popular quarter of Cairo', *Journal of South Asian and Middle Eastern Studies* 13 (4).

Sullivan, E.L. (1981) 'Women and work in Egypt', *Cairo Papers in Social Science* 4(4): 5–29.

Tabari, A. (1980) 'The enigma of veiled Iranian women', *Feminist Review* 5.

Tabari, A. and Yeganeh, N. (eds) (1982) *In the Shadow of Islam: Women's Movement in Iran*, London: Zed Press.

Tucker, J.E. (1985) *Women in Nineteenth Century Egypt*, Cambridge: Cambridge University Press.

Williams, J.A. (1979) 'A return to veil in Egypt', *Middle East Review* 11(3): 49–54.

Warnock–Fernea, E. and Grattan Bezirgan, B. (eds) (1977) *Middle Eastern Muslim Women Speak*, Austin, Texas: University of Texas Press.

Yeganeh, N. and Keddie, N.R. (1986) 'Sexuality and shi'i social protest in Iran', in J.R.I. Cole and N.R. Keddie (eds) *Shi'ism and Social Protest*, New Haven: Yale University Press.

Chapter seven

Women in struggle

A case study in a Kent mining community

Avril Leonard

Introduction

The prominent role of Aylesham women activists in the 1984–5 miners'
strike is the focal point of this chapter, which examines the impact of
that struggle on their class and gender consciousness. A case study of
working class women in struggle is of central importance to theoretical
debates about relationships of class and gender in contemporary
feminism. In drawing attention to the complexities and contradictions
inherent in the lives of working class women by virtue of their, at times,
conflicting loyalties to their class and gender, it is possible to contribute
to an understanding of the mechanics and resolution of this dilemma.

The ideas that women have about their role in class struggle are
related to both the material reality of their place in the family and to their
conception of that reality (Porter 1982). Fundamental to both socialist
and feminist struggles is the question of effecting a change in consciousness which would lead to a concomitant change in attitudes and
behaviour. Marx, unlike the Utopian socialists, believed that this could
not be brought about by a voluntaristic change of will. Instead he argued
that ideas derive from material conditions and change in the process of
confrontation. This chapter constitutes an exploration of that thesis.

The first part of the chapter provides background information about
the strike, the historical position of women in mining communities, and
a portrait of Aylesham as one such community. The aim of this section
is to locate the case study in its general context, both historically and
contemporaneously. The research methodology and process through
which the fieldwork data were collected are discussed in the second
section. The third section presents and analyses the research findings. I
examine women's role during the strike and the factors which motivated
their active involvement. Was that role predominantly supportive of the
men's struggle and confined to those areas which are traditionally
defined as women's work? I am also concerned with the impact of the
women's involvement on family life: the division of labour in the home

(child care and housework) and the marital relationship. Did the women's conception of themselves and their role within the family alter? The women's political views and activities both before and since the strike are further indicators of their changing awareness. What impact, if any, has the politicization process had on the development or extension of a class consciousness? Finally, I explore their views on women's liberation and the women's movement, and the problem of judging what constitutes feminist action from a middle class standpoint. What is the relationship between class struggle and women's liberation? Can working class women fight (and win) on two fronts, or must the struggles be separate? Has the experience of class struggle provoked a consciousness of the specific oppression of women in a class society?

Studies of working class women are not new (cf. Westwood 1984; Wacjman 1983; Cavendish 1982; Porter 1982; Pollert 1981; Hunt 1980). These studies however, have been predominantly concerned with women as workers, focusing on women, work, and family. Other writers have concentrated on women workers in industrial struggle (cf. Cliff 1984). While this chapter shares some of the concerns of these studies, the point of departure is its focus on women as the 'wives' of industrial workers and the women's role in class struggle.

In conclusion, I return again to the issues confronted in this chapter – the relationship between women's resistance to class oppression and the development of *both* class *and* gender consciousness.

Research methodology

It was my involvement with the Aylesham Women's Support Group which instigated my interest in documenting and analysing the impact of the women's involvement in the strike on their gender and class consciousness and related attitudes and behaviour. In the light of contemporary debate regarding the 'proper' relationship between researcher and researched, the feminist critique of traditional methodological approaches and qualitative versus quantitative research designs, this point is not insignificant. This project grew out of my own involvement in the strike as opposed to being motivated by the desire to collect data from the stance of a non-participant researcher. I began to attend the weekly support group meetings in April 1984. During the strike some sixty to eighty women, mostly miners' wives, attended. After the strike an average of twenty women attended. Thus, for the first time in Aylesham a women's section existed as an expressly political group affiliated to the National Women's Organization which pledges itself to further strengthen the organization of women's groups built up during the1984–5 miners' strike.

I opted for a qualitative research methodology which used open-ended questions. This choice was based on my desire to conduct in-depth interviews which would yield a large amount of information on the women's experiences and attitudes concerning a number of issues before, and after the strike. The interviews were conducted immediately after the end of the strike. Interviews with women in other areas were carried out during the strike by Stead (1987). Follow-up interviews would yield additional information about the long term impact of the strike on the women.

Traditional sociological research methodology associates certain drawbacks with a qualitative approach, arguing that the validity and significance of the results are limited due to 'bias' and an inability to generalize from the particular small sample used. The traditional criteria for interviewing emphasize the one way nature of the interview, in which the interviewer elicits and receives but must never give information, and the interview itself is devoid of personal meaning in terms of social interaction. This is said to eliminate systematic differences in the way interviewers conduct their questioning, and therefore bias, thus ensuring that the data produced are not influenced by the sex, age, or colour of the interviewer. Getting involved with those being researched is said to undermine the validity of the results obtained.

However, the very artificiality of this situation can also be said to detract from the validity of the data obtained (Leonard 1985). In relation to my own project it could be argued that other researchers in the same situation may well have asked different questions, elicited different responses, and come up with different conclusions in their role as a detached researcher. Yet, I believe that my very involvement with the women, the fact that I was no stranger to them, gave me access to information which would have not otherwise been available to me in the one-off interview context. The women were in no doubt as to my political persuasion; I was clearly in support of the strike and a committed socialist. This, I would argue, enabled me to conduct the interviews in an atmosphere of co-operation, mutual trust, and openness. All the women wanted to know what the research was about, why I was doing it, for whom, and constantly enquired about its progress, anxious to see the finished product. The warm hospitality I received was further evidence of their desire to participate in the project – endless cups of tea, coffee, sandwiches, and a meal at the welfare club on the last day the food kitchen was open, followed by a tearful 'booze-up'!

The balance between prejudicing the answers to questions and establishing a relationship which allows the interview to be successful is a precarious one (Oakley 1981). I was aware of this delicate balancing act throughout and endeavoured to take account of it, not only in the questions I asked, but also in making explicit the specific circumstances under which the research was conducted. That a qualitative methodological approach is 'biased' or 'subjective' and therefore invalid is a criticism which I reject as all research accounts are partial realities, overlaid with subjective interpretation by the author. The questions we ask, the information we finally use, and the interpretation of the spoken word ensure this. The problem of recall reliability is also a real one. In asking the women to remember their attitudes and behaviour prior to the strike I accept that their responses may have been coloured by their more recent experiences. None the less, as will be demonstrated, certain patterns emerge with a consistency which highlights definite and significant differences in terms of a before-and-after scenario.

During my study I interviewed approximately 25 per cent of the women activists in Aylesham (and in the course of my research met women from other coal mining communities, whose experiences during and since the strike support the findings and conclusions outlined in the final section). Having randomly selected fifteen miners' wives I conducted my interviews between March and June 1985, each interview lasting from one to one and a half hours. The questionnaire and information about the women included in the sample are given in Leonard (1985). Only one woman I approached expressed a preference not to be interviewed, citing limited time availability due to waged work and domestic commitments. Probes arising from the basic questions varied according to the individual woman's response and were designed to take account of the woman's needs, interests, and experiences. All of the women interviewed were actively involved in the strike.

My questionnaire was designed to shed light on the hypothesis that ideas and practices change as a result of active involvement in industrial struggle, affecting gender and class consciousness. This required examining aspects of the women's behaviour and attitudes before, during, and after the strike. The key areas explored before the strike were previous involvement in political activity and/or workplace disputes, attitudes towards politics, the women's liberation movement and the NUM, the division of labour in the household, work history, and trade union involvement. The key areas explored during the strike were motivating factors for involvement in the struggle, women's changing role in the strike, husbands' attitudes to women's involvement, attitudes towards politics, the women's liberation movement and the NUM, the division of labour in the household, the impact on the woman's relationship with her husband, the overall impact on the woman's attitudes and behaviour, and working with women. The key areas explored after the strike were the future of the women's group, the impact of involvement in the strike on the division of labour in the household, the woman's relationship with her husband, her self-image and attitude towards women's liberation, and the impact on attitudes towards her workplace and trade union activity.

Women in mining communities: a historical overview

The coal industry was nationalized by the Labour Government in 1947 as a result of decades of campaigning by the Miners' Union. This was intended to ensure that changes were to be made with the consent and agreement of all those in the industry, based on a programme of expansion. These principles were consolidated in the 1974 Plan for Coal endorsed by the Labour Government, the National Coal Board (NCB) and the mining unions, in particular the NUM. There was an underlying fear in the early 1970s that the peripheral coalfields of Scotland, Kent, the North-East, and the South might suffer closures. This was further underlined by a 1982 EEC document *The Role for Coal in Community Energy Strategy* (Harwood 1985). In February 1972 a successful miners' strike had led to an increase in wages. In 1974 the threat of pit closures saw renewed strike action culminating in the defeat of Edward Heath's Government.

The return of a Conservative Government in 1979 saw the establishment of strict financial targets for nationalized industries, their piecemeal privatization, and the expansion of nuclear power from 12 per cent to 30 per cent by the end of the 1980s. In October 1979 a leaked Cabinet minute stated: 'a nuclear programme would have the advantage of removing a substantial proportion of electricity from disruption by industrial action of coal miners and transport workers' (as quoted ibid 1985:11).

The early 1980s saw the introduction of anti-trade union laws designed to severely limit the power of workers to strike. The 1980 Employment Act placed limits on picketing and 'secondary action' and sought to penalize the families of strikers by deducting assumed strike pay from the amount of supplementary benefit received, whether or not a striker was in receipt of such payment. The pit closure programme was once again on the cards and rumours to that effect were further confirmed by the announcement in 1983 by the NCB that 65,000 workers would have to lose their jobs to ensure a break even situation in the coal industry by 1988. Ian McGregor, who as Chairman of the British Steel Corporation had made 85,000 steel workers redundant, was appointed Chairman of the NCB with a brief to implement such a programme. The NUM responded by imposing an overtime ban to protest at the Board's demand for an agreement to close 'uneconomic' pits.

On 1 March 1984 the NCB announced the imminent closure of the Cortonwood Colliery and on 6 March made public their decision to cut capacity by 4 million tons and lose 20,000 jobs within a year. This was in breach of the 1974 Plan for Coal, which was pledged to the expansion of the industry and the practice of consultation and agreement regarding any change in the industry. The NUM Executive immediately responded by declaring national strike action which brought the vast majority of its pits to a standstill, involving approximately two-thirds of the 180,000 strong membership. The 1984–5 strike to save jobs, communities, and an entire industry had begun. It was characterized by the great militancy of mining communities, their resilience in the face of controversial police operations and the Tory policy of 'starve them back to work' (Fine and Millar 1985).

While this study focuses on the views of miners' wives, women's relationship to mining has not always been exclusively that of wives and mothers. Angela John (1984) gives an excellent account of women workers in Victorian coal mines and the debate surrounding their exclusion from underground and pit-top work. She focuses on a group of women workers known as the 'pit-brow lasses' who sorted coal and performed a variety of jobs at British coal mines. These women were descendents of generations of women and girls who had worked underground. The 1842 Mines and Collieries Act excluded boys under 10 years old and all females from the coal mines. From then on, female surface workers were stigmatized and depicted as remnants of an undesirable past, heralded as a prime example of degraded womanhood crudely torn from her 'natural environment': the home. Despite the total exclusion campaign waged in the 1880s and its brief revival in 1911, it was not until 1972 that the last two female surface workers were made redundant. At any one time no more than 12,000 pit-brow women were employed, representing 7–8 per cent of all surface workers and only a fraction of the total colliery workforce.

The debate surrounding the pit-brow women demonstrates the ambivalence of late Victorian attitudes towards working class female employment. John concludes: 'In the final analysis, the pit-brow lasses became caught up in the larger debate which confronted fundamental questions about late nineteenth century attitudes towards women, the family, work and class' (John 1984: 222). Although it is true to say that many male miners supported the banning of women from mining work in 1842, Norah Carlin (1984) points out that such a position was far from automatic; in those areas where women did work underground both men and women mine workers had reservations about the Act.

The institutionalization of an ideology and practice of a rigid sexual division of labour, based on the notion of a male breadwinner and female homemaker, took firm root in the late nineteenth century. While women continued in paid employment in large numbers they became increasingly dependent on the male wage, regarding their wage as necessary, given the inadequacy of the family wage, but none the less of secondary importance to their primary role as wife and mother (Gardiner 1974; Rowbotham 1977). A myriad of factors has since served to recreate, in daily life, the views of man as breadwinner, woman as homemaker (e.g. the education system, the mass media and the social security system, to mention a few). Nevertheless, this situation is not without its tensions and contradictions, as became apparent to the women activists during and after the miners' strike.

Women's resistance is not a new phenomenon. What is perhaps relatively new is the recognition and documentation of women's role in class struggle and the impact of that involvement on their consciousness as working class women, doubly oppressed by virtue of their class and gender, and sometimes also by racial oppression. Carole Harwood argues that even 'progressive' historians have used blanket terms like 'labour history' to cover the lives of whole communities, half of whom were female and in some cases were not in paid work.

> Women in coalfield communities become miners' wives, daughters
> and sisters. The calendar of their historical lives is ticked off by
> their men's shifts, their periods of unemployment, their times of
> industrial struggle. The reality of women's own lives, varied,
> colourful and exciting, becomes blurred to the point of invisibility
> and so half the population disappears off the historical map.'
>
> (Harwood 1985:25)

One of the most outstanding features of the 1984–5 miners' strike was the mass mobilization of women in mining communities. For at least 150 years women in miners' families have organized in support of strikes. In 1926 women were active in supporting the miners in their six-month battle after the end of the general strike. In 1972 and 1974 women appeared on some picket lines. There exists a long and continuing history of women in struggle (cf. Cliff 1984; Taylor 1983; Rowbotham 1977). But women's involvement in the 1984–5 strike was on a national scale and at a higher level than ever before. Many women argued and won the right to picket and sit on strike committees in addition to reproducing their 'normal' work – cooking meals and running the canteens. The length of the strike also made a difference in that going back to the old routines becomes more difficult after one year, rather than several months.

Women have had to battle on two fronts: standing up for their communities, their men's jobs, and their children's futures, in addition to claiming their right to be active, defining the conflict as much theirs as that of their menfolk and the NUM (Evans *et al.* 1985). Yet it would be wrong to say that the movement in the miners' strike was a feminist one. Indeed it would be difficult to envisage such a movement emerging without a catalyst such as the strike, given the focus on men and

131

masculinity in pit villages and the fact that the cultural activity of the community is predominantly male-orientated (Loach 1985). The initial impetus to the setting up of the women's support groups was based on class and not sexual politics. However, it would be erroneous to argue that the re-emergence of feminism in the late 1960s was without influence.

The following address by Lorraine Bowler (Barnsley Women's Action Group) to a mass rally in Barnsley Civic Hall in May 1984 serves to illustrate how ideas begin to change in struggle and demonstrates an emerging gender consciousness:

> At the beginning of the strike women from Barnsley group
> wanted to go picketing and we were told that it is a bad enough
> job organizing the men. All I can say to that is women do not
> need anyone to organize them. They can organize themselves. The
> proof of that is shown in this hall today . . . I'm sure that for some
> or most of the women here today it is the same in their homes as it
> has been in mine over the weeks. There are arguments now as to
> whose turn it is to go on a demonstration or picket, and whose turn
> it is to babysit. Talk about job sharing! We've seen it at its best
> over the past eight or nine weeks. In this country we aren't just
> separated as a class. We are separated as men and women. We, as
> women, have not often been encouraged to be actively involved in
> trade unions and organizing. Organization has always been seen as
> an area belonging to men. We are seen to be the domesticated
> element of a family. This for too many years has been the role
> expected of us.
>
> (quoted in Loach 1985: 171)

A change of ideas and behaviour is not an inevitable outcome of women's involvement in struggle. Rather it shows that potential can exist when working class women organize. By taking action for change people begin to perceive a view of the world which conflicts with their old one. But people do not all change in the same way or at the same pace. To what extent did the Aylesham women's political activism change their views of the world about them, their place in it, and their ability to fight for a new social order?

Aylesham

Aylesham is a coal mining village located in the depths of the garden of England, Kent, with a population of approximately 4,000. It is associated with three coal pits, Betteshanger, Tilmanstone, and Snowdown. The latter is situated on the outskirts of Aylesham. As Kent was, and still is a predominantly fruit growing and market gardening centre, skilled workers for the coal industry had to be found from already established mining areas in Wales and northern England (Lilley 1974). Some of the older women to whom I spoke remembered their fathers literally walking from Wales to Kent to seek employment.

Aylesham was planned as a new town for the workers of Snowdown colliery and their families. In 1913 Tilmanstone and Snowdown began producing 15,000 tons of coal each per annum. Chislet colliery was opened in 1918, followed by Betteshanger in 1928. By 1936, 7,300 men were employed in the four pits. From 1936–41 there was a steady decline in workers employed at the pits from 7,300 to 5,000.

It was hoped that the coal industry would stimulate the growth of other industries in the area but it was not until 1951 that the first factory was opened – a shirt factory employing 250 women. Until then mining was the only avenue of employment in the village. Female seasonal employment on fruit farms was, and still is, available. Women also went to neighbouring resorts to work in the distributive trades or seasonal holiday employment (Lilley 1974). In 1967 the Eastry Rural District Council decided to develop an industrial estate which, by 1974, employed some 2,000 workers, most of whom were married women. A relatively high proportion of Aylesham's female population is therefore employed.

The 1972 and 1974 strikes over wages and proposed pit closures in the peripheral coalfields (of which Kent is one) sparked off militant action. Several of the women I spoke to had been involved in organizing food distribution and had occupied the social security offices to secure benefit during the strike. However, their involvement fell short of their activity during the 1984–5 strike. There was no food kitchen and the women did not picket. As one women told me: 'Hardly a dozen of us met. Once the strike had finished that was it. We had food parcels delivered to us which we distributed.'

Prior to the 1984–5 strike there was a women's section in the village which organized activities such as darts, skittles tournaments, outings and holidays, while the NUM organized occasional socials in the local clubs. Although some women used the clubs prior to the recent strike, married women would not go without their husbands, as this was frowned upon. Neither would a women order herself a drink at the bar:

'I can remember women just didn't go out on their own, except for a hen night ... . You do find some women now, two or three of them would go out if their husbands were working, where before they would have stayed at home. Also there was no way before that women would go up to the bar to get a drink, the men would ... . I wouldn't have brought any money out whereas now I take money and sometimes I go and buy a round.'

A picture of separate spheres as described in *Coal is our Life* (Dennis *et al.* 1969) was certainly evident in Aylesham before the strike. The scenario is somewhat different today. Women now use the pit club for their meetings and meet socially with or without men.

The traditional militancy of Kent miners was much in evidence during the strike. Not one miner crossed the picket lines for the first six months and only a handful of those who did lived in Aylesham. The threat of closure to the Kent coalfield was a very real one with two of the three local pits employing some 1,500 miners on the 1984 list of potential closures. Two pits have been closed since the end of the strike and British Coal's decision to close the last remaining colliery, Betteshanger, was announced in 1989. The women to whom I spoke had no illusions regarding the impact of closure on the future of their community. Their foremothers and forefathers had told them of the Welsh 'ghost town' pit communities.

Women's role in the strike

The group of miners' wives initially started to meet in order to organize food collection, distribution and preparation, in addition to fund-raising, organizing outings for the children, and the collection and distribution of clothing. What the women did, in effect, was to set up an alternative welfare system. They attempted to ensure that the strike would not fail through overpowering financial pressures. Although this represented a socialized version of their traditional privatized duties in the home, it is important to note that it was the starting point of the women's involvement in the strike. As time went on the sexual division of labour became less rigid with some women activists emerging as prominent speakers, joining picket lines, and some miners taking up kitchen duties. The degree to which this happened is difficult to assess. Certainly the women's own expectations regarding their role underwent changes as the strike progressed; as Kate told me:

> 'Well I thought we'd look after the children, do the food parcels, you know women's kind of jobs – what men can do but they were too involved in picketing. Then of course we got stronger, going on the picket lines. We were side by side with the men. It was tremendous. I surprised myself.'

That the women gained confidence through the experience of organizing collectively, arguing the case for the strike and identifying the struggle as theirs and not just their husbands', emerged clearly. What began in the minds of many women as a passive supportive role was rapidly translated into a crucial aspect of the struggle. As Kate said:

'Women were the backbone of the strike. We took a lot of the responsibility on our shoulders. It made the men aware that the women were necessary.' The interdependence of the women's group and the NUM was reflected locally by the appointment of one woman whose job it was to liaise between the two groups. Six of the women I spoke to regularly attended the NUM meetings where they had speakers' rights. By their presence these women made it clear that they wanted to be kept informed about all aspects of the strike.

The factors which motivated women to become actively involved in the struggle were many and varied. For some it was the desire to know what was going on, to 'help' and to have the support of other women. Others saw it as a fight to defend their community, against the prospect of life on the dole. Many of the women were anxious to counteract the press coverage of the miners' wives at the beginning of the strike which emphasized women's opposition. This was the initial impetus to Mary's involvement:

'This is what sprung into our wives, seeing them on the telly taking their men to work. I thought well if everybody sees that, they must think all the miners' wives are the bloody same. So our first demonstration in Coalville was to show the other side of the coin, that we weren't all the same. We were supporting the strike. The Yorkshire and Welsh women followed suit.'

The early demonstrations by the men *and* women made the women more determined than ever to demonstrate not only their support for the strike but also their right to take an equal part in it. Helen remembers that day at Coalville well:

'They were spitting at us there – the wives of working miners. A lot of them thought we were pathetic and shouldn't have been there. It should have been the men doing all what we were doing. They thought a woman's place was in the home. Like they'd get our leaflets, rip them up in front of your face and tell you get back and sit in the living room and mind your kids.'

Getting involved initially was an effort for several of the women, such as Pat, who told me: 'I really didn't want to go 'cos I'd never been involved in anything before. I had to force myself to go to the first meeting and I've been to every one since.' All of the women referred positively to the fact that their involvement got them out of the house more often and as time went on they became more aware of the advantage for themselves of that involvement.

Picketing

It is the issue of women picketing which met with most opposition from some men and women. In Aylesham, as elsewhere, women first appeared on picket lines in substantial numbers a few months into the strike. The women's group, on its own initiative, set up a women's picket line at Snowdown when the first miners returned to work. Ten of the women I interviewed picketed locally. Four of their husbands objected, arguing that their wives' presence held the men back as they were worried about the women getting hurt. The remaining six had their husbands' support, though not initially in all cases. Jill's husband tried to prevent her from picketing:

'We had German visitors . . .a miner and his wife, a nurse. They both went picketing and I'd say to him, "Let me go with them" and he'd say no. By the third night I said to Ute I'm going, call me in the morning. I mean how can I talk about a picket line if I haven't been on one? From then on I went regularly with him.'

The local NUM branch officially supported women pickets, but some women had to argue the point with their husbands. Some of the women were themselves against women picketing. As Ann said:

'I don't think the women should put the men in the position of thinking, well, if I do this or that the women are going to get hurt. Plus the men can swear more when the women aren't there 'cos a lot of the older men still won't with women present. I've always thought a picket line is not the place for a woman.'

Although most of the women I interviewed did picket, they may be unrepresentative. A number of support groups did not join any picket lines. Often this was because the men put their foot down saying it was too dangerous and many women themselves were understandably too frightened. Because support was virtually total throughout the strike in the Kent coalfield, confrontations with the police were not as violent as elsewhere.

By virtue of their activity, some of the women became aware of their oppression by men, although they would not name it as such. Whereas, at first, some of the more active women asked their husbands for permission to go to London for rallies, collections, or meetings, the very act of doing so led them to question the practice. What impact did the strike have on family life in relation to the division of labour within the household, i.e. childcare and domestic labour and the marital relationship?

Women, the strike and the family: domestic labour and childcare

Bearing in mind the limitations imposed by recall reliability and the tendency to respond defensively when enquiries are made regarding the quality of our personal relationships, I began by asking women about the extent of their husband's involvement in domestic labour and childcare prior to the strike. Nine women told me that their husbands shared household tasks, particularly when both were in waged work; as in Jean's case: 'It worked quite well. If he was on days he'd get home about 2 p.m., get the dinner and do the housework. When he was on afternoons and didn't get home 'til 8 p.m. I'd do the work.' For the remaining six women the domestic division of labour ranged from nil to 'helping' husbands. However, in most instances the women referred to their husbands cooking the dinner as a regular rather than an aberrant feature of domestic life.

Those women who had always shouldered domestic responsibilities virtually alone, continued to do so. There was however, among some, a change of attitude as to the priority that was given to this. Women can and do make choices regarding the amount of time and effort they put into housework (Oakley 1974). It took the experience of an alternative to domestic confinement to demonstrate this effectively to Pat and Claire:

> 'I'll never be the same again. I've said to my daughter and husband
> I'm not going back to waiting for you to come in from work and
> having dinner ready. I was so bored before the strike. I'm tired 'cos
> I'm out so often now but I'm not so bored and fed up. I've got to
> find an interest in something now like going to night-school.'
>
> (Pat)

> 'Before this strike, apart from the kitchen and seeing to the kids,
> my life ended there. I mean it's just starting now! I was very docile
> and mousified before. He's got to accept me as a person in my own
> right now, he didn't just marry a maid and housekeeper type of
> thing.'
>
> (Claire)

The pattern of men's involvement in domestic labour and child rearing throughout the strike was uneven and is difficult to assess. The shift work pattern in mining facilitates more contact between fathers and children than does a nine to five work regime. But the men clearly had less responsibility in this area than the women. While the woman may have had an occasional night out while her husband babysat, it was assumed that he could go out alone as he pleased. Certainly the extent to which the women were free to become actively involved in the strike was very heavily influenced by the ages of their children. By and large women with younger children were more confined to the home. If they wanted to attend a rally or meeting outside the village it was their responsibility to make arrangements for the children. My evidence does, however, suggest that because *all* of the women were out more often, and were frequently away attending demonstrations or rallies for twenty-four hours or more, their husbands did become more involved with what has been regarded as the 'women's sphere'.

In most households the men went away picketing every other week which, at least in theory, meant that they were available to share house-work and childcare more than when working. This worked out well for Helen who had four children under the age of 12: 'I went on marches and rallies every other weekend. My husband had the kids and I went on my own. We were both equally active.' In contrast Ann was more inclined to take a background role if there was a clash of interests: 'If we both had a meeting on and couldn't get a babysitter I used to stand back and let him go.'

I would conclude on the basis of my interviews that any changes that took place in the allocation of household tasks and childcare tended to be at the instigation of the women rather than the men. This is hardly unexpected given that, at least in the short term, sexual divisions benefit men.

Marital relationships

The strike put whole families in Aylesham, as elsewhere, under tre-mendous emotional and financial strain. There have been both positive and negative side-effects as a result. This was the case not only during but after the strike. Some relationships, where both husband and wife were active in the strike, were more open to negotiation than others. Some of the women finding themselves alone for the first time while their husbands were away picketing had difficulty coping, as was the case with Jean:

'I was on tranquillizers for a couple of months. I still get up and down days which I never used to before. It was him being away all the time at the beginning of the strike and being left on my own with the kids.'

For other women, coping alone was a positive, empowering experience, as with Ann:

'The first week he went away I couldn't stand it being on my own but it made me more independent 'cos I had to be. It made me more aware of what women can do. I know I could handle on my own any situation that cropped up now.'

Some men were at home far more often because of the strike and this sometimes increased tensions between the couple. However, the overriding factor was the unity of striking families in common struggle. All the women felt that the strike had, at one level, brought them closer to their husbands. Yet, at another level, certain tensions emerged where the man was faced with a more self-confident, independent woman. One year of being public wives expanded the women's horizons and expectations. The kitchen sink was no longer the quiet refuge it had been in the past, at least for those women who were active in the group after the strike.

The strike had a considerable effect on women's conception of themselves and their role within the family in approximately half of the cases I looked at. They emerged, after one year in struggle, with a stronger self-identity. Whereas, before the strike, these women identified themselves solely in terms of their position within the family, i.e. as a miner's wife, daughter, or sister, they now have a sense of themselves as people in their own right. This is demonstrated by their continuing political activism (forty women joined the Labour Party), their presence in the pit club which has traditionally been a male enclave, and their redefinition of priorities in relation to themselves and the family. The women have *begun* to challenge that ideology and practice which defines the home as the centre of their universe. The experience of travelling at home and abroad, meeting new people, and coming across new ideas has instigated that challenge.

To what extent has this process of politicization effected a class and gender awareness among the women? For some this appears to have been a temporary phenomenon, while for others there has been a lasting change.

Women and politics

The politicization of thousands of women was one of the most tangible, positive outcomes of the 1984–5 miners' strike (Carlin 1984; Campbell 1984b; Ingham 1984; Rowbotham and McCrindle 1986). The women's resistance to attacks on miners is no departure from the tradition of their foremothers (Campbell 1984a; Harwood 1985), but the 1984–5 miners' strike will be remembered as the one in which women emerged as an unprecedented force in the community. It is a particularly memorable presence given that women were previously absent as a collective political force.

In order to assess the impact of the strike on the women's class consciousness it is necessary to examine the extent of their political activity before the strike. None of the women expressed anything more than a passive interest in politics; as Jill, for example, said: 'All I was interested in was my family, my home and that was it.' This comment is symptomatic of the women's view of themselves as apolitical. Apart from casting a vote occasionally, their concern lay in the private domain with the day-to-day activities of running a home, bringing up children, and often working part-time too. The 'public' world of politics held no attraction or indeed relevance to their situation as they viewed it. It represented an arena over which they were powerless, in contrast to the domestic sphere from whence came their self-definition.

Pauline Hunt's study of working class wives (many of whom are married to miners) reveals similar findings: 'In her cloistered world the houseworker is hard put to see how elections, parliamentary debates, union conferences and strikes have any but a negative bearing on her concerns' (Hunt 1980:99). The maxim that women are a politically conservative force has been challenged by the masses of working class women activated during the strike. Women organizing for the strike far outnumbered those organizing against it. Furthermore, as mentioned earlier, many of the Aylesham women initially reacted against media coverage of the Nottinghamshire wives with their portrayal of miners' wives as opposing the strike. The prior political inactivity of these women is indicative of the lack of a concrete political context of relevance to their lives rather than of conservatism. Being confined to the domestic sphere, both materially and ideologically, restricts women's potential political input. While six of the women were unhappy with the way the country was run they lacked the confidence and a context to translate their opposition into action. As Denise told me:

'The interest's always been there but I've never done anything about it. I could understand what was going on and the sort of class situation we were in, the way we've always had right wing governments, whichever party's been in. But I felt I didn't have the knowledge to get involved in anything. I never discussed politics; I found it boring. I didn't know enough then to form an opinion or say anything I would have considered sensible. I think more women feel more confident now.'

Predictably, the strike catalysed women's politicization. As Kate and Jean told me:

'I never went into this strike political but I've come out as very political. I never used to listen to *World in Action, Panorama* or nothing because I wanted it to be switched off. I had these kids and I couldn't be bothered with all that.'

(Kate)

'Well I aways thought a woman's place was in the house and at the sink doing the cooking and what have you. Now I think the more

you get involved in things the better, because it gives you an
outlook on life and makes you realize what life is about. Now I
make time for other things besides cooking and housework.'

(Jean)

The contradiction between the women's experience of struggle and
media coverage of the strike led to their drawing parallels with other
struggles: national (e.g. Greenham Common (Stead 1987), black
workers, the teachers, cleaners and dockers) and international (e.g.
South Africa, Nicaragua, and Ireland). Their consciousness as working
class women expanded alongside a growth in confidence and strength
drawn from the central role they adopted throughout the strike.

The women's relationship to the NUM also changed during the
strike. Before the strike their relationship to the NUM was negligible.
They knew little about the union and expressed little or no interest in it
beyond its being a 'topic of general conversation' related to pay issues.
However, during the strike good working relationships developed between many local branches of the NUM and the local women's groups.
At the national level the women's objective was to attain associate
membership status in the union. The first ever National Women Against
Pit Closures Conference was held in 1985 and was attended by 500
women activists from the coalfields and 250 visitors. The delegates
expressed their determination to continue the fight against pit closures
in defence of their communities, and their support for the sacked and
gaoled miners. Many referred to the fact that domestic arrangements had
undergone a significant change since the strike – with husbands minding
the children while they were away. Despite the teething problems of the
new organization, its very establishment was an indication of the politicization of the coal mining community women.

Unity of men and women due to the miners' strike is far from
complete. Waxing lyrical about the marvellous role of wives, mothers,
and class fighters washes thin in the light of the 1985 denial of associate
membership to the women. There is still sexism among miners and an
antagonism towards women which needs to be challenged. Many of the
women I spoke to have become more conscious, not only of their class
position, but also of the limitations imposed on their potential for
political activism by their ongoing responsibility for domestic duties.
The continuation of a network of women's groups is a vital means of
ensuring that the challenge to sexism among miners continues to take
place.

In the final part of this chapter I examine the relationship between the
women's movement and working class women. My aim is to shed some
light on the debate regarding the relationship between class struggle and
women's liberation. A central issue in this debate is whether working

class women can fight on two fronts (i.e. class and gender) in tandem or whether the two struggles must be separate.

The strike, working class women and women's liberation

Since the re-emergence of the women's movement in the mid 1960s there has been a heated debate about the relationship between women's liberation and socialism. Socialists want to build a better world based on workers' power with production organized for need not profit. Feminists also want to change the world so that women can be free and equal. A question central to this debate is whether or not feminists can unite with male socialists and trade unionists, or whether their struggle must always be against men. Events during the 1984–5 miners' strike demonstrated how unity can be achieved in struggle. Socialists, who had often argued that women can fight only as workers, were reminded that wives, mothers, and daughters are also part of the working class, whether in paid employment or not. Feminists, who often assume that being a wife only means conflict with the husband, had to face the fact that there can be solidarity in the working class family as well as conflict.

The strike brought many women who thought of themselves as feminists into strike-support work for the first time. Miners' wives who had not thought of themselves as feminists found themselves on picket lines, strike committees, and travelling abroad to raise funds, while their men minded the kids or made the tea, and were at times in conflict with those miners and union officials who sought to restrict women's participation to the soup kitchen. It would, however, be erroneous to deny the continued existence of antagonism. Many men in the labour movement, while happy to see women fighting to support them, are not convinced that women need to fight for themselves. Many feminists are not convinced that men can be allies in the struggle for liberation from class and sexual oppression, pointing to sexist attitudes and male domination of the labour movement as proof that women's fight is still basically against all men.

Women's involvement in the strike and the resultant emergence of a national women's organization provided a structure and context with the potential for commitment to the dual goal of working class and women's liberation. Working class women face the dilemma of reconciling loyalties to class and sex politics (Magas 1971). Whether the potential for unity in struggle is realized or not is dependent on a number of factors, not the least of which are the lessons learned by men and women during the 1984–5 strike. Beatrix Campbell argues:

> For sure, the women have organised as women, they now have a sense
> of their own strength and without a doubt they have created an
> infrastructure of a working class women's movement within the

coal communities. But its very existence is contingent on it being a movement in support of men, and it has the support of men because it is for them.

But the future of this women's movement lies in its commitment to women changing the relationship between women and men. In decades to come, when we come to write and reflect upon the history of this strike as a water-shed in working class politics, the real test of change will be whether this women's movement is allowed to survive – for the women themselves.

(Campbell 1984b)

In the above statement Campbell erroneously assumes that the Women Against Pit Closures movement exists solely for the interests of men. The movement also exists to further the interests of the women them- selves. This is clearly revealed in the Women Against Pit Closures questionnaire (reproduced in Leonard 1985: 63), with its emphasis on mining communities, the organization of women's groups, the promotion of education for working class women and of associate membership of the NUM for women. Middle class feminists ought to exercise caution before arguing otherwise. Sarah told me: 'When a pit shuts it's not just the men that suffers, its the whole village. I think the days where men do all the talking and the women keep their mouths shut is gone.'

The movement of women in mining communities has been based on class and not sex politics (Loach 1985). However, although the miners' wives did not organize because they were feminists or had 'feminist consciousness', the miners' strike has seen the growth of a positive relationship between the women's movement and the class struggle. This can be explained, in part, by the influence of feminist ideology and the presence of feminists in the labour movement who argued that miners' leaders should recognize the importance of the women's organizations and women's right to picket and sit on strike committees. To argue that the women's role in the 1984–5 strike was in essence altruistic, i.e. women supporting the 'men's struggle' would constitute a denial of the strength which the women gained from the powerful role which they played throughout the strike and their claim to fight side by side with the men. The very act of asserting that claim represents a challenge to the view which sees workers' wives as male appendages whose sole task it is to reproduce the labour force.

It was through intense personal struggle that the women I spoke to realized some of their strength and potential. When asked if they had any views on the women's movement prior to the strike, six told me they had never thought about it; four had always thought women should be equal to men in the home and at work. The remaining five held negative views. For example Jill said: 'I suppose I thought they were like – cranks. In my own mind I thought, well, what can women do on their own? Never really bothered about it.'

The hitherto limited appeal of a politics of women's liberation for working class women must be recognized and taken seriously rather than shrugged off as 'false consciousness'. One could argue that such negative views are no surprise given the media ridicule of feminists. Yet it cannot be denied that an ideology which asserts the primacy of sex antagonism over class antagonism is evident in some feminist literature (Delphy 1977; Millett 1981; Firestone 1979; Spender 1980).

The notion that women can only organize and fight separately from men has been justified on the grounds that because men have, for so long, excluded women from most organizations and struggles in the labour movement, it is futile to try to work alongside men who will only dominate women in the same old way. However, a feminism which argues that women must struggle with all women against all men in order to secure liberation makes little sense to working class women. Denise, for example, said:

> 'I was very wary of the women's liberation movement because I could not understand certain points of view. I thought a lot of them were really extreme and I still think that. Women should fight for equality but some of them seem to have got the view that they're better than men and I think they're wrong. If they're going to fight for equality that's what they should be fighting for, not to put down men in the way they condemn women . . . You don't have to be a member of the women's liberation movement to fight for women as women. It's just a general attitude women have to take no matter what organization they're in.
>
> They use it as a separatist movement. They shouldn't. They're fighting the wrong people. I mean you can fight for women as women but then you shouldn't forget there's a lot of people who want to fight for the same things whether they're women or men and that's what they should be fighting for a general consciousness of the way society's run not just that it's against women.'

Separatist feminism denies the material reality of class difference. As Carol told me: 'It wasn't just equality with men, it was equality needed to be gained with other women as well.' While up to a point women do have a common interest in equal rights and can unite to fight for them, as long as we have a class society all women cannot be equally liberated by having equality with men. It is one thing to be equal to a cabinet minister or top management executive and another to be the equal of a bus driver or miner.

During the miners' strike women had their own meetings. Women also sat on the strike committee which gave them access to the sort of discussion and decisions from which they had previously been excluded, and some attended the 'men's meetings'. I would argue that both separate and mixed meetings were necessary. Clearly many of the women found it easier to express their views without men present, and enjoyed the solidarity which emerged among the women. By organizing themselves, controlling their own finances, planning activities, etc. they gained confidence and experience which enabled them to challenge the men. What is wrong, however, is to insist that women can only or must always organize separately.

The 1984–5 strike demonstrated that women's involvement in industrial struggle, as workers themselves and/or as wives of workers, is essential and cannot be relegated to the level of secondary importance or given mere supportive status. The women developed an awareness of their key role in class struggle through first hand experience. A growing confidence in their own ability has precipitated criticism of those male workers and labour movement leaders who wish to deny women their right to an equal position with men in the working class.

Conclusion

After the strike approximately twenty women continued to meet weekly to discuss and plan action on local issues such as the proposal to close the local infant school and the sacked miners, and to plan trips to participate in political action elsewhere. Thus, these women continued to have a high level of political commitment. However, some of the women I interviewed were no longer active members of the women's group. Some, but not all, had young children. For these women the strike represented their introduction to political activity. Once the *immediate* threat was removed they appeared to have retreated from the public to the private sphere. The pressure on the women to revert to their traditional role was very real. As Denise said:

> 'I think a lot of the women that don't come [to the meetings] any more might be fed up or they might find it difficult with their husband's shift. I know it is difficult when their husbands don't want them to go. And quite a few were frightened by the politics involved and would prefer us just to be a social group. Others just wanted to get straight back to the ways things were before the strike.'

However, an accurate assessment of the long term impact of the strike on their attitudes and behaviour in terms of gender (and class) consciousness would necessitate further interviews. Non-attendance at the meetings was not necessarily indicative of a 'return to normal'.

The extent to which the women developed a consciousness of their specific oppression as women was uneven, a point also made by Miller (1986) and Stead (1987). All of the women claimed that the experience of political struggle, which had brought them out of the home, had strengthened their self-image and confidence. They found it easier to air their views in a group context, where previously domesticity had provided no such outlet. An awareness of the constraints which being 'tied to the kitchen sink' placed on their own political horizons and activity was evident. Though they did not see themselves as 'oppressed women', or describe themselves as feminist, none the less the limitations imposed by their expected role in the family became apparent to them. The strike provided a context within which they *began* to question that role. The attempt to break out of the traditional role, even by a minority of women, is a significant outcome of the strike.

In the case of the women who continued to be active members of the group, the evidence to support the thesis that ideas change in struggle is more clear cut. They saw themselves as members of a politically coherent group, established for themselves a legitimate sphere of influence within the pit club and no longer defined themselves solely in relation to the family. For example, Sarah and Denise told me: 'I've changed a hell of a lot to what I was. I'm more aware of what's happening not just within my family but outside as well' (Sarah).

'I think my attitudes changed at home in that I don't think the kids should rely on me like they used to. I feel I've more a life of my own now' (Denise).

One could argue that fifteen to twenty politically active women out of a total of seventy is an insignificant minority upon which to support the thesis. These figures must however be put into a proper perspective. Given that the context for collective action had been removed it was surprising that these women continued to meet at all, and was, I would argue, indicative of their determination to consolidate the personal (though unintended) gains which they had made throughout the year. During the strike the Aylesham Women's Support Group, and no doubt others like it, rivalled the union as the key organizing vehicle within the community (cf. Loach 1985). However, anyone who has been involved in a political campaign (particularly a single issue one) must be aware of the difficulty of maintaining a cohesive group once the immediate struggle is terminated. The emergence of a national women's organization is a concrete indicator of that determination. Whether what began as a fight against pit closures expands to include campaigns on women's rights, discussion of family and personal matters and women's issues remains to be seen. However, the seeds for such discussion and activity have been sown on soil made fertile by the *experience* of being in struggle. Feminists cannot *tell* working class women that they are oppressed. Their own consciousness of their specific oppression is vital.

I have attempted to look at the contradictory and complementary relationships between class and gender by locating my discussion of the politics of class and gender in working class women's experience of active resistance. Exploring these complexities at a concrete rather than an abstract level has proved both difficult and illuminating. For example, a superficial reading of women's role in the strike could lead to the assumption that it merely reproduced the traditional sexual division of labour and reinforced an ideology of the male breadwinner. This approach, however, underestimates the significance of the changes in the attitudes and behaviour of those concerned. The women's activities expanded far beyond the traditional sphere to picketing, organizing, and speaking at meetings and rallies, which in turn raised the question, in many instances for the first time, 'who will mind the children?' Child rearing and housework were no longer the women's only priorities.

Women emerged throughout the strike as a political force to be reckoned with and their collective strength won them, though at times grudgingly, respect and recognition within their own communities. Prior to the strike, women's visibility was largely dependent on their family ties. They defined themselves and were defined in relation to significant others. A sense of their own identity as individuals emerged, drawn from their political activities. Confidence in their ability and right to express political opinions was born out of their own experience of struggle.

Some of the women to whom I spoke were determined to remain politically active and were all too aware that this might produce conflict with their husbands. This represents a challenge to the existing social order in the community where the political and social institutions have been predominantly male-dominated. Forty women had joined the local Labour Party branch for the first time and had started to use the pit club for their own purposes. Certainly there are and will be pressures to return to the established order. Indeed, it would appear that many women have done so. Yet the potential for change in struggle is illustrated clearly by the resistance of those who remain alert to such pressures. That resistance takes place both in public and behind closed doors.

References

Barnsley Women Against Pit Closures (1984) *Barnsley Women*, Todmorden: Arc & Throstle Press.
Beynon, H. (ed.) (1985) *Digging Deeper*, London: Verso.
Bowles, G. and Duelli Klein, R. (eds) (1983) *Theories of Women's Studies*, London: Routledge & Kegan Paul.
Campbell, B. (1984a) *Wigan Pier Revisited: Poverty and Politics in the Eighties*, London: Virago.
——(1984b) 'The other miners' strike', *New Statesman* 27 July.

Carlin, N. (1984) 'Wives, mothers and fighters', *Socialist Review* 66: June.

Cavendish, R. (1982) *On the Line*, London: Routledge & Kegan Paul.

Cliff, T. (1984) *Class Struggle and Women's Liberation*, London: Bookmarks.

Delphy, C. (1977) *The Main Enemy*, London: Women's Research and Resources Centre.

Dennis, N., Henriques, F. and Slaughter, C. (1969) *Coal is Our Life*, London: Eyre and Spottiswoode.

Evans, J., Hudson, C., and Smith, P. (1985) 'Women and the strike: it's a whole way of life', in B. Fine and R. Millar (eds) *Policing the Miners' Strike*, London: Lawrence and Wishart.

Fine, B. and Millar, R. (eds) (1985) *Policing the Miners' Strike*, London: Lawrence and Wishart.

Firestone, S. (1979) *The Dialectic of Sex*, London: The Women's Press.

Gardiner, J. (1974) 'Women's work in the industrial revolution', in S. Allen, L. Sanders, and J. Wallis (eds) *Conditions of Illusion*, Leeds: Feminist Books.

Harwood, C. (1985) 'A woman's place . . . ', in *Striking Back*, WCCPL and NUM (South Wales Area).

Hunt, P. (1980) *Gender and Class Consciousness*, London: Macmillan.

Ingham, J. (1984) 'Women and the pit strike', *Militant* 10 August.

John, A. (1984) *By the Sweat of Their Brows: Women Workers in Victorian Coalmines*, London: Routledge & Kegan Paul.

Leonard, A. (1985) *Women in Struggle: A Case Study in a Kent Mining Community*, MA Dissertation in Women's Studies, University of Kent.

Lilley, M. (1974) *Aylesham: A Study of the Development of an East Kent Mining Community*, MA Dissertation, Eastbourne College of Education.

Loach, L. (1985) 'We'll be here right to the end and after: women in the miners' strike', in H. Beynon (ed) *Digging Deeper*, London: Verso.

Magas, B. (1971) 'Sex politics: class politics', *New Left Review* 66.

Marx, K. (1974) *The German Ideology*, London: Lawrence & Wishart.

Miller, J. (1986) *You Can't Kill the Spirit: Women in a Welsh Mining Valley*, London: The Women's Press.

Millett, K. (1981) *Sexual Politics*, London: Virago.

Oakley, A. (1981) 'Interviewing women: a contradiction in terms', in H. Roberts (ed.) *Doing Feminist Research*, London: Routledge & Kegan Paul.

Pollert, A. (1981) *Girls, Wives, Factory Lives*, London: Macmillan.

Porter, M. (1982) 'Standing on the edge: working class housewives and the world of work', in J. West (ed.) *Work, Women and the Labour Market*, London: Routledge & Kegan Paul.

Rowbotham, S. (1977) *Hidden from History*, London: Pluto Press.

Rowbotham, S. and McCrindle, J. (1986) 'More than just a memory: some political implications of women's involvement in the miners' strike 1984–85', *Feminist Review* 23.

Spender, D. (1980) *Man Made Language*, London: Routledge & Kegan Paul.

Stead, J. (1987) *Never the same again: women and the miners' strike 1984–5*, London: The Women's Press.

Taylor, B. (1983) *Eve and the New Jerusalem*, London: Virago.

Wacjman, J. (1983) *Women in Control*, Milton Keynes: Open University Press.

Westwood, S. (1984) *All Day and Every Day*, London: Pluto Press.

Chapter eight

Women shop stewards in a county branch of NALGO

Jenny Walton

Introduction

Women have been organizing in trade unions for over a century and in 1883 the TUC voted for equal pay for women. Despite this, the slogan 'A woman's place is in her union' has become urgent and significant. It challenges the contrary notion that women's place is at home. But women are not at home; women are in the labour market: by 1987 70 per cent of women were economically active and 64 per cent of women had paid work (OPCS 1989:155). Women make up one-third of trade union membership.

At the beginning of the twentieth century women's collective action was directed to the issues of maternity and childcare through the Women's Co-operative Guild. The Anti-Sweating League won better conditions and the abolition of piece-work. After World War I the number of women in trade unions rose and between 1939 and 1978 the percentage of total members of the TUC who were women increased from 11.4 per cent to 28.7 per cent (Hunt 1982:157). Latterly, measures have been adopted to further encourage women's involvement in trade unions and to look after their interests, such as the TUC Women's Conference and the TUC Charter for Women.

Another assumption that is challenged by the slogan 'A woman's place is in her union' is that men's trade union activities are based on the need to maintain their dependants. The labour movement has been founded on men believing that unity is strength, and with this comes the right to make demands for working people. Working people though, has always meant working men and the demand for the family or living wage has implied a dependent wife and children. This has impeded the development of a coherent policy on women's pay and diluted union concern with issues which affect women, such as equal pay, low pay, and the problems of combining work with family responsibilities.

Enormous social changes have forced attention on these issues. Official statistics show that 42 per cent of lone mothers are in full- or part-time work (OPCS 1989:157) and that the so-called 'typical' family unit of a married couple and dependent children represents only 28 per cent of total households (OPCS 1989:103). If wage labour is no longer purely a male activity then we should not expect trade unionism to be just a male activity either.

So women join unions, but then what happens to them? The expectation is that women trade union officials will follow the path set by men and get down to wage negotiations and collective bargaining. This has not happened to any significant degree and women in trade unions are criticized for their apparent lack of activism and unwillingness to take industrial action. Any explanation requires close examination, but would seem partly to do with women's unease with existing trade union structure. Traditionally, men's commitment was easy to measure because they would stand up and be counted and have vocal representatives. Women have never been public in this way. Working outside the home has, until recently, been considered a secondary role for women; their 'real' job was domestic labour and mothering, whereby no matter how hard they worked they were subservient to the male. So, to establish a communal bond outside this authority and to go on to make demands on an even more powerful male management system has not been an easy task for women workers.

Women's experience in the labour market is very different from the experience of men. As the TUC has pointed out, women form the vast majority of part-time workers:

> Between 1961 and 1980, while total employment fell by about 400,000 the number of people working part-time doubled. In 1980 out of an employed workforce of 24 million there were 4.4 million part-time workers, 84% of whom were women, the vast majority being women with family responsibilities.
>
> (TUC 1983:5)

By March 1988 the corresponding figures were 5.3 million part-time workers out of an employed workforce of 25 million, 83 per cent of the part-time workers being women (DOE 1988: Table 1.1).

It has been argued that women make up a secondary labour force to which Barron and Norris (1976:53) have applied five main attributes: 'dispensability, clearly visible social differences, little interest in acquiring training, low economism and lack of solidarity.' Although, as Maura Luck shows in Chapter 2, not all of these characteristics are applicable to women, the lack of solidarity which Barron and Norris describe does place women workers in a pattern which is self-reinforcing. When faced with the possibility of industrial action, women in service jobs which involve caring are well aware that if they withdraw their labour it will often be replaced by that of other women who will have little option but to provide the service for free. The cost of the action is not in lost production or threats to overseas markets, but in human suffering. It is also a very powerful weapon with which to criticize women's action and weaken public sympathy. Women are not just seen as turning their backs on their employers, but on their 'natural' role and women have not been willing to do that. Women need employment and union structures which allow them to find their own effective strategies.

In *Getting It Together* Jenny Beale says that women need unions for the same reasons as men – to protect and improve conditions at work and as a force for social and political change (Beale 1982:4). She also says that women are not taking up a democratic position within the trade union movement (1982: 7–8). Women are almost entirely absent from local negotiations, few women hold high office in unions, women lose out over sectional interests, and women's interests are not given priority. To bring about change in all these areas is a formidable task, especially under a government which promotes an ideology which supports women's traditional role in the family.

This leads to a very important question: what continues to prevent women from participating equally in the trade union movement at a time when the TUC appears to have taken positive steps to encourage the participation of women at all levels? Some interesting work has already been done, for example by Stageman (1980), Harrison (1979), and Fryer *et al.* (1978). I set out to give this matter some attention in my own union, the Kent County Branch of the National Association of Local Government Officers (NALGO), which has 6,000 members. I was not able to find out how many members are women, but I would expect that more than half are, since the County Council staff is divided in the proportions shown in Table 8:1 (Higgins 1981).

Table 8.1

	Women %	Men %
Full-time staff	26.9	23.1
Part-time staff	42.3	7.7
Total	69.2	30.8

Other studies, Stageman's most specifically, have asked women to list, in order of priority, factors which they thought would increase their participation. I thought it would be interesting to expand this topic by talking to all the women stewards in my branch and that this would be of particular relevance given the general absence of studies of women

151

who have positions of responsibility within trade unions. A women who is a steward may be assumed to have some degree of commitment, and by using these women in my research I expected to discover more information about women who are already participating in the union at a higher than average level. Once something is known about their attitudes, work profile, and personal situation we are in a better position to understand the women who are not active. My misgivings about asking women to select factors which they think would make them more active are that however willing and honest the women set out to be, it is in some ways an imaginary exercise and on a personal level it is very difficult to predict how things would be different if other variables were altered. The more popular choices will, of course, have the greatest significance, but this still fails to account for people's ability to change and to explain the complex reasons behind their choices. For instance, two of Stageman's most popular factors were 'fewer home responsibilities', and 'having a greater interest in union affairs' (1980:69). I am not sure that these actually tell us very much, especially after my interviews with women who were rarely satisfied with their own degree of participation; those who were satisfied appeared to be some of those who were least involved in the work of the branch.

There is, of course, a difference between being a member and a steward, but from my own experience of being a member and then a steward I was dissatisfied with both and although being a steward made me a more involved member, it revealed many more opportunities for feeling inadequate. I wanted to find out if other women had had the same experience and how they dealt with it. More than that I sought to go beyond personal shortcomings to see if a number of women's experiences would point to institutional and cultural factors which would provide some explanation.

NALGO

NALGO nationally has published a survey of members entitled *Equality?* (Rees and Read 1981), which provides information about the activity of women members within the labour market. The study concludes that women still operate predominantly as a secondary labour force. Whereas men accommodate working and being the parents of pre-school children, women have a break in service. This must affect the seriousness with which they regard themselves as workers. The study revealed enormous differences in salaries: 57.6 per cent of women earned under £5,000 per annum, whereas only 11.5 per cent of men earned under the same figure. In 1980, 99.5 per cent of male workers were full-time paid workers, while 81.9 per cent of women were full-time. Of the part-time women workers, 80 per cent worked between seventeen and thirty hours a week, and 91 per cent were married, compared with 54 per cent of full-time workers. Continuity of service was interrupted for 40 per cent of cases, 75 per cent to stay at home and look after children. Of course, a number of women also delay starting work in order to care for their children, forgoing training and career prospects into the bargain. Women in NALGO had fewer educational qualifications than men: 'Twice as many men as women had A levels and four times as many had ONCs, HNCs, degrees and postgraduate degrees or diplomas' (Rees and Read 1981:19). In-service training with employer sponsorship and day release showed large discrepancies, although the researchers also looked at who requested sponsorship and found that 79 per cent of the women had never asked.

NALGO as a whole had 50 per cent female membership, although the length of union membership was greater for men. Among the sample of the *Equality* survey of 5,000 members, 351 shop stewards were interviewed, 70 per cent of whom were men. The stewards

> appeared to differ from the sample as a whole in contrasted
> ways for the two genders. The men were more likely to be married,
> for example, while the women were less likely: indeed, 16.5% of the
> female shop stewards were separated, widowed, or divorced.
> Fewer had children, while for men the proportion was about the same.
>
> (1981:22)

These levels of union activity display both differences from and similarities to the case of the Turkish factory workers studied by Yildiz Ecevit in Chapter 4, young Turkish women without children being the most active group, whereas divorced and widowed women were the least involved in union activities, all of the shop stewards being men.

So it seems that British women who lead traditional lives are less likely to become shop stewards, whereas the traditional male is not stepping out of role if he becomes a steward. The power of conformity appears to be well in operation here and for traditional women who may aspire to be stewards there are few acceptable role models. The imbalance is heightened by the ease with which the traditional dominant male takes on the role of shop steward. If inside unions, there is seen to be an equation between being a good shop steward and dominant male behaviour, then the task for women is vast. They must either learn to behave like dominant men or develop another way of presenting themselves and their issues which is comfortable for them, effective, and acceptable to the union bureaucracy and the employers.

Kent NALGO

The Kent County Branch of NALGO has been operating a Joint

Consultative Committee (JCC) since 1979. There is a JCC for each department, seventeen in all, and each JCC consists of representatives of staff and employers. The JCCs meet several times a year. During 1982–3 when I took my sample, seven departments had no women stewards, but a combined total of twenty-four men stewards. It is usual to have a steward for each twenty-five members. The remaining ten departments had a total of 167 stewards, 67 of whom were women. I interviewed 60 of these women in the first two months of 1983 and one questionnaire was returned by post from a woman who had recently retired (see Table 8.2).

Table 8.2

Department	Number of women stewards interviewed	Number of women stewards in department	Number of men stewards in department
Architects	3	3	6
Education	20	20	22
Fire	1	1	2
Highways and Transport	2	2	15
Libraries	14	15	2
Probation	2	2	1
Social Services	15	20	30
Supplies	1	1	7
Treasurers	2	2	9
Trading Standards	1	1	2
Total	61	67	94

Background information provided by the survey

The members who were represented

The women stewards worked with and represented mainly women in most cases. In all but seven instances over 80 per cent of their colleagues and members were women. The vast majority of these women were working full-time on clerical grades. Of the seven stewards who did not represent mainly women, two represented 50 per cent men and 50 per cent women, four represented about 40 per cent women and 60 per cent men, and one woman represented all men.

The influence of other shop stewards
How stewards work together and what influences they have on each other is important, especially in a branch the size of Kent County,

covering such a large geographical area. I wanted to find out if the gender of the steward the women were in closest proximity with made any difference, so I asked how many other stewards from their shop were women and how many were men. Thirty-nine of the sixty-one women stewards worked on their own. The remainder had the contacts shown in Table 8.3.

Table 8.3

Women stewards	Number of other stewards in same shop
4	1 woman
4	2 women and 1 man
2	1 woman and 1 man
2	1 woman and 6 men
7	1 man
1	2 men
1	3 men
1	7 men
Total 22	26

It might be expected that the women who worked on their own would attempt to reduce their isolation, as well as increasing the involvement of the membership, by encouraging discussion at a local level. This did not happen; of the thirty-nine stewards who worked in offices without frequent contact with another steward, twenty never held workplace meetings, and fifteen only held meetings when they felt that there was an issue which was worthy of discussion or, very occasionally, when the members asked for a meeting. Compared with the whole sample in which twenty-four stewards never held meetings and twenty-seven only held them when there was an issue to discuss, the shops with one woman steward had the least number of meetings.

The response from stewards who held meetings when there was something to discuss was fairly positive, especially when interest had been generated by informal discussion prior to the meetings. However, two stewards said that the most lively discussions had resulted in generating feeling against traditional trade union behaviour, one about not wanting to strike and the other about voting 'no' in the ballot to affiliate NALGO to the Labour Party. Holding meetings at a local level seemed to be for these stewards, a dispiriting experience, so perhaps they failed to hold regular meetings because this was such a discouraging experience for them.

Stewards who did not hold meetings did talk informally to members about business and it may be that this was a more useful way of passing on information. I also asked if women's working conditions allowed them to talk to one another and the majority indicated that there were few barriers to informal communication. One reason which was given for not having meetings was that women could not attend at lunchtimes because they were married women with duties such as shopping to carry out. Informal discussion was also seen as a way of generating interest prior to meetings in the cases where stewards held meetings irregularly.

The four women stewards who worked with one other steward consisted of two groups of two women. In both cases the women appeared to have a positive effect on each other although there was a stronger partner in each case. I felt that the importance of contact with another woman steward was verified when, later in the survey, I asked about women's attitudes to women-only courses and all four of these women felt such courses to be useful and said they would consider attending.

The two women who said they worked with one other woman and one man were separate cases. In each case the man was considered to be the senior steward. One woman became a steward because she thought clerical and administrative staff lacked representation. The other woman was interested in women's issues, but felt she was operating under the shadow of the male stewards.

It seems that those whom the stewards see as constituting their reference group is important. No group means that the steward is unlikely to remain involved, but small groups containing other women means that apathy from the membership is not so influential. The presence of male stewards did inhibit women.

Women stewards as managers

The view that women stewards are atypical and more likely to take on dominant male type behaviour is an interesting one to examine because of the number of women stewards in Kent County Branch who hold supervisory jobs and staff responsibilities. This may be seen as an advantage when it comes to negotiating with senior management, but it may also hinder their perception of the members' problems – it is a commonly held view that being both a steward and a manager is contradictory.

Twenty of the fifty-four stewards with full-time jobs had respon-sibility for other staff. Out of the twenty, only six women were, strictly speaking, managers on management grades, but the other fourteen were administrators and office supervisors. Twelve of the twenty had taken routes to becoming a steward which were slightly more planned than the average for the sample, whereas just under half of the sample told me they were stewards because there was no one else to do the job. There was some feeling that a managerial element in union representation was desirable. One women said the steward 'Needed to be someone with clout, not a junior assistant' while another said 'There was no one else to represent me who had the guts to do so'. Only one woman specifically mentioned seeking nomination because she wanted to work for women in the union but she did not continue for a second year. She told me her main reason for not standing again was because of her health. However, her experience as a steward, although diplomatically described, had not helped her to pursue her original aim. She shared her shop with an active male steward who selected issues for her members' attention, did most of the talking, and all of the negotiating. The new steward was also a manager, but a man.

A significant proportion of the women stewards who were also managers had held office at branch level and within their departmental JCCs. Out of the twenty, seven had held office, including that of chairperson of the executive committee and the two sub-committees. Four of these women had also been to NALGO's annual conference, some several times, whereas only two other women stewards from the rest of the sample had attended. How effectively the women who were also managers represented other women is difficult to say. They did stress the desirability of the absence of conflict in their dealings with higher management when they negotiated on JCCs. For example, in the libraries department, a professional review, together with the introduction of new technology has meant a reduction in women's jobs and in hours. This was achieved amicably according to the stewards who worked in libraries.

As part of my interview I asked women if they considered themselves sympathetic to the women's movement. The women who were managers indicated on the whole that the women's movement was quite separate from their own experience and work. This was the case even when women told me about the discrimination in favour of men they had suffered themselves. Among the women there was a recurring attitude of complacency with their own position; 'Women's problems are of their own making', 'Women have only themselves to blame', 'I can't understand why women get themselves into such a state in the first place'. One woman who had been very active in the union and recognized sexist behaviour, went to some lengths to explain that gender was not important and that if you behaved like a skilled professional, recognition and approval would be forthcoming.

These results indicate that the process of becoming a manager has the effect of desensitizing women to the problems they themselves have faced. They did not, on the whole, find the roles of manager and union steward contradictory, but perhaps they would not have remained stewards if they had. One did, at a later date, give up her stewardship. There was no one who sought to use her status to encourage women to oppose management over the erosion of their pay and jobs. As far as I could tell, agreements were reached amicably through natural wastage and reduction of hours. I was told that most women whose jobs became part-time preferred it that way and those who were not happy decided not to protest formally about the change in their working hours.

Trade union participation and domestic experience

Attendance at meetings

I asked the women stewards how often they went to branch meetings, of which there were three a month. They were always held in Maidstone, began at 5.30 p.m., and were open to all stewards. The two sub-committees met in a large room with stewards sitting at large tables at right angles to a top table for the chairperson, branch secretary, branch organizer and minute taker. The Executive Committee meetings were held in County Hall in the very imposing Kent County Council Chamber, with the chairperson, branch secretary and chairpersons of the sub-committees at benches on a raised dais. Stewards sat in large leather chairs in semi-circles round about, each with their own microphone which the branch organizer switched on when each person began to speak. The ceiling is very high and on the walls hang much larger than life, portraits of past council leaders – all men. Their names are inscribed on oak panels on the end wall. The men's toilet is just across the corridor; I have still failed to locate the women's toilet.

Table 8.4

Attendance at meetings	Number of women
Once a month or more often	19
Once every 2 months	2
Once every 3 months	3
Less than every 3 months	37
Total	61

The women's frequency of attending meetings is shown in Table 8.4. These figures are discouraging if participation is measured in terms of attendance at meetings. By no means did the majority of male stewards attend every meeting, but there were always a lot more men there than women.

I then tried to find out how the women who attended least would categorize the practical circumstances which made it difficult for them to attend and asked them if their lack of attendance was due to any of the following factors:

(a) time;

(b) distance and travelling;

(c) children or other dependants;

(d) disapproval from members of their household.

Twenty-four women attributed their low attendance to categories (a) and (b) combined, five attributed it to (c), three to (d), and five had other reasons.

The three women who cited disapproval from household members all had interesting things to say. One said that her husband was not keen on anything but her being domesticated, then went on to talk about her domestic role being the reason why she was not more involved in the union. She obviously regretted this very much, but thought that, at the age of 50, she was past the time when she could have any meaningful involvement. Our interview took up the whole of her lunchbreak rather than the half she had planned for and as I was going out of the door she settled to her typewriter and said with a grin, 'Well, we haven't got anything for tea tonight!'

Another woman told me that when she first became a steward her husband was furious about the political overtones and she had never been to a branch meeting. Another married woman who had children, but of an age when they were able to look after themselves, did go to meetings from time to time although her family hated it. When I asked if domestic work was more evenly shared because of union work she made the heartfelt comment, 'You must be joking. The preliminary of any union meeting is me getting up at dawn to prepare a casserole and a big pudding!'

None of the five women who said children or other dependants were the main reason for keeping them away from meetings had very young children. What was becoming evident was that although family responsibilities were a significant cause of women's limited involvement in union activities, this was to do with how women and their families saw their role within the family. There were few women with young children in this sample, so it would be interesting to compare this group with other women stewards. It may be that few mothers of young children are ever stewards, because they do not see the two roles as compatible. This would mean that providing crèches would not suddenly produce an upsurge in women's union activity. This is not to say that crèches should not be provided as women need to learn to expect this resource, but the conditions and ideology which accompany women's dual roles must change in a far more profound way in order to permit their greater involvement in trade unions.

It is probably the case that more men than women stewards had children under 10 years old. If this is correct it would confirm that being a father is not incompatible with being a steward. One man said at a meeting that he likes to be away from union meetings by 8 p.m. so he can be home in time to say goodnight to his children. If only being a parent were always so easy!

The women who attributed their poor attendance at branch meetings to the time and travelling distance involved, related these factors as much to their jobs as to their families. Women who would have needed to leave work by mid afternoon talked about the extra weight this would put on their colleagues and said they could not keep asking people to cover for them. No one mentioned the benefits of having an active shop steward. They were all very concerned about their responsibilities at work.

What was perhaps more significant, and something I will take up later, is that once women had made an investment of time to travel to and attend the meetings they wanted something in return, and when the meetings became a neutral and even a negative experience, their attendance dropped. Thus, it does not seem that changing the times of branch meetings would mean that many more women would attend. Attendance would probably increase if being a shop steward became a more respected job and more staff were available to cover for the time it took.

Table 8.5

Option	Number of times chosen
Job	28
Training courses	8
Other education	14
Current family	5
Original family	15
Being a steward	21
Other	21

The domestic experiences of women were not always in contradiction with their union participation. The attitudes they developed from their experiences at home had often been influential in their wanting to be a steward in the first place. I asked women what had been the main determinants in their becoming stewards. I gave them a number of options shown in Table 8.5, and they chose the option or options which seemed to apply to them. Five women chose current family life; four were referring to their husbands, one to her father. Twenty-one said their original families had been influential; eighteen referred to their fathers and three to their mothers.

Alienation from trade unions

The theme of alienation ran through all my discussions with women stewards. Their experience at meetings was often disappointing, both in terms of their own participation and the observations they made of other people's behaviour. They were rarely using up spare time, especially if they had to leave work by mid afternoon or earlier to be in Maidstone by 5.30 p.m., and they wanted the time spent in meetings to be worthwhile.

I asked women why they went to meetings and, apart from eight who said they went to oppose industrial action, most women gave me rather bland answers about the need to represent members. What was significant was that they told me more about why they did *not* go to meetings. They spoke of being interested in the beginning, but of losing interest after listening to what they regarded as time wasting exercises by people who had different ideas from their own.

Table 8.6

A –	You are shy and find it difficult to speak out in a large group.	
	frequently	15
	sometimes	21
	never	24
B –	You feel that other people can say what you want to better.	
	frequently	12
	sometimes	32
	never	16
C –	You don't understand fully what is being discussed.	
	frequently	3
	sometimes	30
	never	27

The experiences of women who said they went to meetings infrequently because they felt alienated were reflected in the whole sample, although women dealt with this in different ways. It did not always stop them from going to meetings, but it did affect their participation when they got there. In one question I asked women to choose how often a statement best described their own experience in an attempt to find out what difficulties women have in common. A summary of their replies is shown in Table 8.6.

The fact that so many women were prepared to put themselves into the 'frequently' and 'sometimes' categories indicates that speaking at meetings is a considerable problem for women. Interestingly, the women's low level of participation in meeting discussions is not correlated with their degree of understanding of the issues. Their degree of understanding was relatively high, so this was not the reason why they found it difficult to speak.

I asked women if they felt they contributed more when they felt passionately about something. Fifty women answered an unequivocal 'yes', and many gave the impression that they could not understand why I had asked the question, because the answer went without saying. Six women said 'no' because they thought that emotion and intellectual effort could not be combined. Five of these women were on supervisory grades with responsibility for staff and had to chair meetings in the course of their jobs. It was not just how they felt themselves that concerned them, but how they expected to be viewed from the outside and emotion was seen as detracting from their credibility. One woman said you must feel passionately, but not be passionate.

The theme of alienation came out strongly when I asked women to describe what it was like when they had difficulty in speaking at meetings. I also asked them if they thought this was something to do with the other people who were present. They did not always believe they were put off by other people, but often attributed their failure to speak of their own shortcomings. Those who were aware of the dynamics of the group felt that there was an inner group which had its own hierarchy to which, as new stewards, they were unable to gain admittance and which only listened to its own people. Women talked about not wanting to make fools of themselves, but noticed that other people did so, without it apparently affecting their self-confidence. They saw a big difference between being a newcomer and being a member of the 'closed club'. When they were new, women felt they were not always welcome to speak and when they did speak they felt there was a danger that what they said might place them in a group with which they did not want to be aligned. Women spoke of being on the receiving end of hostile, unfriendly reactions at a time when they had not been around long enough to make their positions clear and could not possibly have been a threat. One woman said that she had to force her way into discussions, which she found difficult because she was not domineering and aggressive, and this was required behaviour. There was a difference between the way women behaved in the course of their jobs and at union meetings, where they found they could not say a word; 'It was crazy'.

In order to find out more about women's observations of meeting behaviour I asked women about the extent to which they thought argument about procedure and union rules took precedence over the content of the debate. The replies are shown in Table 8.7.

Table 8.7

Arguments about procedure and rules take precedence over content of debate	No. of women
Frequently	19
Sometimes	24
Rarely	3
Never	10
No answer	5
Total	61

Bearing in mind that to say this happens frequently is a far stronger statement than to say it happens sometimes, nineteen in this first category is a considerable number, especially as women did not see themselves as taking part in these arguments. It was another form of interaction between members that they were excluded from. The general view was that arguments about procedure and rules were unnecessary and there was nothing to be gained by joining in. The women were aware, though, of the importance of such arguments to the people who were involved. I asked a supplementary question about who participated most on those occasions and seventeen of the nineteen women who said this happened frequently said the participants were mainly men.

Women from the group of twenty-four who said these arguments happened 'sometimes', were less critical because of what they saw as the need for the debate to be controlled. It was during these sorts of arguments that they noticed the emergence of dominant personalities who became more important than the chairperson, and they were men. From the group of twenty-four, twenty-two women said that it was mainly men who were the participants.

The ten women who said arguments about rules and procedure 'never' took place were not as far removed as it might seem from the women in the other two groups, because their interpretation of proceedings was that a more business like approach to meetings would actually serve to control the dominant personalities.

I moved on to ask the women this question: 'Do you find that men will on occasion dominate a woman who isn't as lucid in debate as other people present?' This question was designed to assess the degree of sexist behaviour which took place at meetings. I did not use the term sexist as I thought women might find it offputting or not understand. In many ways this was the central question of the survey, but I felt that dwelling on the issue directly any more than I did would have been expecting too much of women. This is because one of the most important features of male oppression is that to a great many people it is invisible and to ask women to catalogue their own experiences of being dominated sets up contradictions which would make their answers doubtful. I hoped to avoid this in the question by asking women what they had observed in relation to other women. The answers were that thirty-one women said they had noticed this sort of behaviour and twenty-three said they had not. Two of the latter women qualified their answers by saying that although men do not dominate, they do most of the talking. Seven women felt they could not answer because of their lack of experience at meetings.

I would like to divide the group of thirty-one into ten and twenty-one. Ten women said it had happened and the question clearly had meaning for them, but they were not able to give me any examples. The group of twenty-one filled out their answers with descriptions of how they recalled this happening. They had seen women who were having difficulty speaking, being treated by men with derision to the point where they would be unlikely to speak again. Men had dismissed women's contributions as if they were a waste of time and had been unnecessarily complicated in the way they debated issues they knew more about. It was not always personally directed, but took the form of men not listening when women were speaking or raising eyebrows when women's rights were mentioned. Four women spoke about men's attitude to a clerical regrading claim which was based in part on the need to recognize how women's work has always been undervalued. Seven women in the course of their answers, although not always to this question, talked about the use of voice and language. Men were more likely to be heard because they had big voices which carried further. They were also seen as being more adept at presenting what they wanted to say so as to bring notice to it, whereas women tried to be as simple and straightforward as possible.

Women's roles as trade unionists

In the course of this study I became aware of the nature of the limitations which are placed on women as trade unionists. We have already seen that women stewards as managers appear to be less tolerant of women who have not achieved as much as they have and as such are seen as responsible for their own fate. There was also the feeling that it was more 'natural' for men to enter into the heart of the debate and women allowed this to happen even if they did not respect the arguments they were listening to. There was a tendency for women to see their role as stewards as a kind of unofficial personnel officer. Twenty-six of the women I interviewed saw this as a meaningful part of the job. They spoke of the links they formed between management and workers, of resolving work-related problems, and also giving attention to people who had personal problems. They were clearly more comfortable with this aspect of the work than they were speaking at meetings or formulating pay claims. As they had become more aware of people's needs they became critical of the County Council's provisions in this area. One woman who had been involved in negotiating service and conditions believed that the County Personnel Department value the union because it takes so much work off their hands. Women obviously felt a heavy degree of responsibility both as employees and as stewards. Being a steward for whom personnel work was significant was an attempt to reconcile this contradiction. It was evident that once in this position, their ability to bring about change was limited.

The women who did not view personnel work as the role of a shop steward experienced clear disapproval from management. One woman had received the comment that her sympathies were likely to affect her social work practice adversely. Another had encountered resistance about having time off for meetings, but she had overcome this because she said she was not as easily dominated as the last steward, also a woman.

From the group of twenty-six who believed they did personnel work, fifteen had not experienced disapproval from management while eleven had. It does not seem that this view women had of the role of steward protected them from management disapproval, possibly because management's view of what they were doing was quite different. The types of censure which the women experienced ranged from jokes or snide comments to being taken aside and told to keep their duties at work and at NALGO apart and warned that it might not be good for their careers if they did not. One woman had been given a special room in which to confine her union activities and her responsibility for staff training had been taken away on the grounds that she would not have enough time. The woman was well aware of the remonstration that this was meant to imply and was amused when, because of other staff changes, she was asked to take back the staff training – which she did. Another woman who worked in an office in which there were three other stewards, all men, noticed that the officer manager seemed to do his best to avoid talking to her about union issues which were likely to affect the working of the office and would seek out one of the men to talk to, if at all possible.

Industrial action

Of course, the way to incur the highest degree of disapproval from management is to take industrial action and I tried to assess how far women would press their demands, and what, if anything, they would strike for. I tried to assess the women shop stewards' attitudes to industrial action by asking them if they had ever taken part in any form of industrial action and what sort of issues they might be likely to take action over. Twenty-three of the sixty-one women said they had taken action and would do so in the future if the issue warranted it. At the time I did not think that this was a true test of their militancy. Most of these women had never been in the strategic position of making demands and achieving them through industrial action. For most, their action had been limited to a demonstration of discontent, such as a lobby on County Hall to protest against cuts in public expenditure or a day's action in support of health workers where they had nothing to lose except a day's pay. They spoke about how important an instruction and not merely an authorization from the union would be in any future action, and said that if they did not agree they would resign from the union. However, the high level of participation by women that occurred during a dispute which took place while I was writing up this study showed that, contrary to popular belief, women are prepared to strike over issues which are particularly contentious. I also asked women about their political beliefs, expecting left-wing sympathizers to be more in favour of industrial action. Eleven of the twenty-three women were supporters of the Labour Party, but eight said they did not have strong political beliefs.

Nineteen women had never taken industrial action, but said they were willing to do so over issues like unfair dismissal or redundancies. Some of these stewards clearly would already have taken industrial action if support had been forthcoming from their members. One library assistant felt that posts which had been lost could have been saved if there had been widespread support for industrial action which would have limited the libraries' service, but not stopped it altogether. Another librarian saw the explanation of this not happening as the high degree of job satisfaction that library workers get and their willingness to serve the public, which overrides their willingness to work to their job description. Ballots among members in all departments of Kent County Council have rarely been successful in gaining grassroots support for industrial action. Only one woman from this group of nineteen was specific about her politics. She described herself as a Tory and said that this was not a contradictory position with her trade union work.

The women who said they had never taken industrial action and were not likely to do so also numbered nineteen. They were particularly opposed to strike action. Those who spoke about the positive values of negotiation over industrial action had never been on the appeals and negotiating panel; neither were they active in their JCCs. Most said there was no connection between their political beliefs and being a steward.

Potential for change via trade union participation

There is an equal opportunities working party in Kent, but this had not developed to the stage where women could see that it could help them to articulate their difficulties and provide a forum for airing and remedying the injustices that some recognize in private. Some women had not reached the point where they could perceive that these injustices were legitimate. They described their lack of participation in the working party in a variety of ways, but what was clear was the need for education.

It is perhaps to be expected that women who have lacked the benefits of many formal educational qualifications would not immediately see the importance of trade union education. In Stageman's (1980) survey, five groups of public workers were asked which factors they believed would make it easier for them to participate in the union. Participation in education courses was one of the options, but this was rarely chosen by the women, even though they did not have to choose one factor in preference to any other. A possible explanation is that the priority given to domestic commitments would preclude them from regarding education courses as a viable option.

I an unaware how many men stewards in Kent NALGO had been on courses, but a considerable number of women (twenty-seven out of sixty-one) had not had any trade union education. The most basic course is a three-day induction course for new stewards with a standing agreement with the employer that stewards can be allowed time off to attend. In the case of recently appointed stewards it might be expected that it would take a few months before they participated in a course. However, only three of the stewards who had not attended a course had been appointed for less than a year. Three others had been appointed for one year and the rest for between two and six years.

One woman spoke about how much she would have appreciated a course early on, but she was not offered the opportunity until she had been a steward for two or three years and by that time she felt she had gained a lot of knowledge on her own. Another woman said she was keen to go on a course and even though she worked part-time, did not have the kind of home commitments which would have prevented her from attending. Five others had enrolled for courses, but in the event were unable to go, one because her child was ill and three others because of the difficulties of taking time off work. They did not seem to resent the work-related reasons and talked about their reluctance to let their colleagues down.

Thirty-four women had been on training courses. Eighteen had only been on the introductory course, and fifteen of them still felt they lacked knowledge, not because of shortcomings in the courses, but because of the amount of information they wanted to acquire and the complexity of the issues. Sixteen women had been on longer courses or more than one course. Seven of them felt they had sufficient knowledge, but talked about the importance of continued use and application of what they had learned. This group contained the women who were most active within the union.

Trade unions are now beginning to recognize the importance of education for women stewards and the TUC's Women's Charter says that special encouragement should be given to women to attend training courses. The positive value of women-only courses is slowly becoming more acceptable as women experience the benefits. I asked the women stewards if they would be interested in attending a course just for women, then listed some of the benefits, asked if they agreed and, if they were interested, what other advantages they saw. The question often surprised women and they reacted as if it was a completely new idea. Only one woman brought it up before I did. Thirty said they would go on a women-only course, twenty-five would not and six said they might.

Twelve of the women who said they would go on such a course had not been on any courses at all. The advantages these women saw was the work experiences which women have in common and the opportunity to talk about women's issues without men asking if it was a relevant topic. They said they would feel more comfortable and that women are better company. A further eight women who said they would attend a women-only course had already been on one mixed course. They thought that women on their own would be more open about their opinions and participate more, as well as sharing the same problems.

The positive reaction to women-only courses was not displayed by most of the women who had been on several courses. Sixteen women had been on several courses and only four of the sixteen said they would like to go on a women-only course. The only conclusion I can draw from this is that we have returned to the limitations revealed earlier: that women who excel either as employees or as trade unionists are less likely to be sympathetic to the forms of oppression which less successful women experience.

Conclusion

It is well established that women have an inferior position in the labour force. This survey provided evidence that this position is reflected in the trade union movement. There is little likelihood of women at the beginning of their careers, with young children, becoming active shop stewards. There are almost no role models, back-up facilities, or even any appreciation of the need for resources. Women managers who are stewards seem to show some of the least understanding of these problems, probably because of their satisfaction with their own efforts.

For too long women's low level of involvement in trade unions has been criticized by male trade unionists, although such criticisms have been somewhat muted in the light of women's active participation in industrial disputes such as the miners' strike, as discussed by Avril Leonard in Chapter 7. Criticisms have been based on the assumption that women have not been involved in unions because they did not want to be. This implies that women have had a free choice, but we know that in reality women's lives usually follow a very predictable pattern, bound by forces which give them very little choice. Women's domestic responsibilities and exclusion from certain areas of paid work discourage their development as trade unionists. Those women who do become involved in union activity are forced to do battle not only with employers who are determined to cut hours and conditions of work, but with the patriarchal beliefs and practices of the union itself. Within the county of Kent these conditions are equally, if not more, prevalent than elsewhere. Cuts in public expenditure and the introduction of new technology both mean that jobs are threatened and the union's ability to protect women's jobs has not been encouraging. Against such a background it is little wonder that so few women are prepared to sit for hours in oppressive rooms listening to men argue about the suspension of standing orders and which amendment they are voting on.

Like the library workers interviewed by Maura Luck in Chapter 2, the women I spoke to were a stable workforce and frequently talked about their commitment to their jobs – an understandable emphasis, given the strong hold of the myth that women only work for pin money. They felt that there was little appreciation by others of the time involved in effective union work, even in just travelling to meetings. The women did not want to let their colleagues down, and this reference group was probably very important to them as they did not have a corresponding reference group among union stewards. The women who felt most isolated and went to the fewest meetings did not share their union responsibilities with any other women stewards and did not seek support from ordinary union members by holding regular meetings. The women who worked closely with at least one other woman steward were more active in the union. Their contact with other stewards also helped to protect them from management disapproval.

It is only recently that positive action measures have been considered with the objective of overcoming the constraints on women's involvement in unions. Of the women whom I interviewed in Kent, 44 per cent had never been on an introductory union training course and 83 per cent of those who had been on a course still felt the need for further training. Most of the women were receptive to the idea of women-only training courses, so if they were available, both the women and the union as a whole would benefit. Such courses would also decrease the degree of isolation which the women experience when they become stewards.

There are few opportunities for rewards from union work; the women I interviewed became stewards, in the main, out of a sense of duty and went to meetings to find out what was going on. Enjoyment did not come into it. A fair proportion of women did tell me about individual disputes they were involved in – regrading claims, disciplinary action, and health and safety matters. Their successes had been exhilarating, but were few in comparison with the dispiriting times when individual disputes dragged on without solution. The women usually received some help from the branch office, but the disputes with which they were involved were not regarded as collective issues worthy of debate or wider action.

At the time when I carried out the survey the women's experience of industrial action on anything other than a token basis was nil. Two-thirds of the women imagined that they might take action in the future. At the time this seemed an unrealistically high proportion. However, after I had completed the survey, in August 1983, a male shop steward was sacked for refusing to carry out a job which would have been contrary to a NALGO instruction regarding a dispute about gradings in family support centres. Four hundred members of the social services department came out on strike immediately. Of the fifteen women shop stewards from social services whom I interviewed, eleven were on strike for over four months; only four never went on strike. The women who went on strike displayed a high degree of resolve against a background of approximately 1,000 male and female employees who received instructions to strike, slightly over 400 who followed the instruction at the highest point in the strike and 200 who were on strike for over four months. The experience in Kent blows wide open the notion that women who have high levels of jobs satisfaction do not take industrial action – social workers do get satisfaction from providing a public service and have shown that women as well as men are prepared to fight for them.

References

Barron, R.D. and Norris, G.M. (1976) 'Sexual divisions and the dual labour market', in D.L. Barker and S. Allen (eds) *Dependence and Exploitation in Work and Marriage*, London: Longman.

Batsone, E., Boraston, I., and Frenkel, S. (1979) *Shop Stewards in Action*, Oxford: Basil Blackwell.

Beale, J. (1982) *Getting it Together*, London: Pluto Press.

Beechey, V. (1979) 'On patriarchy', *Feminist Review* 3: 66–82.

Brown, R. (1976) 'Women as employees: some comments and research in industrial sociology', in D.L. Barker and S. Allen (eds) *Dependence and Exploitation in Work and Marriage*, London: Longman.

Brown, W., Ebsworth, R., and Terry, M. (1978) 'Factors shaping shop steward organisation in Britain', *British Journal of Industrial Relations* 16(2).

Coote, A. and Kellner, P. (1980) 'Hear this brother: women workers and union power', *New Statesman Report* No.1, London.

Department of Employment (1988) *Employment Gazette* 96(10), London: HMSO.

Ellis, V. (1981) *The Role of Trade Unions in the Promotion of Equal Opportunities*, Manchester: Equal Opportunities Commission.

Equal Opportunities Commission (1982) *The Fact About Women Is . . .*, Manchester: Equal Opportunities Commission.

Fryer, R.H., Fairclough, A.J. and Manson, T.B. (1978) 'Facilities for female shop stewards', *British Journal of Industrial Relations* 16(2).

Glucklich, P. and Snell, M. (1981) *Women – Work and Wages*, London: Low Pay Unit.

Harrison, M. (1979) 'Participation of women in trade union activities', *Industrial Relations Journal* 10(2).

Hartmann, H.I. (1979) 'The unhappy marriage of Marxism and feminism, towards a more progressive union', *Capital and Class* 8: 1–33.

Higgins, J. (1981) *Equal Opportunities: A Survey of Women in the Secretary's Department*, Unpublished Paper, June.

Hunt, J. (1976) *Organising Women Workers*, London: Workers' Education Association.

——(1982) 'A woman's place is in her union', in J. West (ed.) *Women, Work and the Labour Market*, London: Routledge & Kegan Paul.

Lewenhak, S. (1977) *Women and Trade Unions*, London: Ernest Benn.

NALGO (1979) *NALGO Equal Rights Survey*, London: NALGO.

—— (1975) *Equal Rights Working Party Report*, London: NALGO.

Office of Population Censuses and Surveys (1989) *General Household Survey 1987*, London: HMSO.

Rees, T. and Read, M. (1981) *Equality? Report of a Survey of NALGO Members*, London: NALGO.

Rights for Women Unit (1983) *Newsletter*, March, London: National Council for Civil Liberties.

Robarts, S. with Coote, A. and Ball, E. (1981) *Positive Action for Women*, London: National Council for Civil Liberties.

Stageman, J. (1980) *Women in Trade Unions, A Study of Trade Union Branches in the Hull Area*, Industrial Studies Unit: University of Hull.

Technical, Administrative and Supervisory Staff (TASS) (1975) *Women's Rights And What We are Doing to Get Them*, London: Amalgamated Union of Engineering Workers/Technical, Administrative and Supervisory Staff.

Trades Union Congress (1971) *Facilities for Shop Stewards*, London: TUC.

——(1982) *Women Workers Bulletin*, London: TUC.

——(1983) *Women in the Labour Market*, London: TUC.

Chapter nine

Money and power

Evaluating income generating projects for women

Joy Lyon

Introduction

This chapter investigates income generating projects in the context of linked struggles to overcome underdevelopment and the subordination of women. Policies and projects emphasizing income generation for women in the 'South' and particularly in rural areas, can be seen as a part of the approach to 'integrate women into development', a concept which became a focus of international and national development agencies during the mid 1970s.

In 1970 the United Nations Research Institute for Social Development (UNRISD) stated:

> There is a profound contradiction between women's condition as
> the chief agricultural producer and the rudimentary nature,
> sometimes the non-existence, of technical and co-operative means
> designed more specifically for them. The agricultural extension
> service is almost totally directed to export crops and thus to men.
> Rural activities programmes for women are oriented more towards
> their functions as mothers and wives than as agricultural producers.
> In these conditions it is perfectly obvious why there are growing
> frustrations on the part of women about their status and
> participation.
> (African Training and Research Centre for Women, UNECA 1975)

A gradual process of recognition of the lack of attention paid to women's interests in development planning and policy-making was brought to a head in International Women's Year in 1970, when, at the United Nations Conference on Women in Mexico, a call was made for 'intensified action to ensure the full integration of women into the development process' (Elliott 1977). This stimulated an abundance of research into women's condition and the implementation of various rural development programmes involving women's participation.

Two major perspectives can be seen to have provided the impetus behind this resolution. First, it was consistent with other national and international human rights agreements pointing to the need for more equitable treatment of women in their productive roles and action against discrimination on the basis of sex. Second, it was consistent with current views in development thinking which recognized the failure of present schemes to reach the needs of the poorest. Earlier GNP-raising strategies of Economic Growth and Growth with Distribution which aimed to increase production and consumption through the diffusion of western capital, advanced technology, and entrepreneurial spirit had been seen to result in rising unemployment, and growing social and spatial differentiation: benefits had manifestly failed to 'trickle down' to the majority of people. The inherent threat of major social and political upheavals had made it imperative for some strategy to be devised for economic growth to reach the poor and raise their standard of living. Emanating from this was a reorientation of development strategy towards reducing poverty through the satisfaction of basic needs, with particular emphasis on rural areas and consequently on women, who represent the majority of many rural populations. The goal was to ensure the supply of food, clean water, shelter, and clothing, and to generate supplementary income through employment to meet these needs.

The International Labour Office World Employment Conference in 1976, focusing on the basic needs approach and the need for special attention to women, pointed to their preponderance among the poorest of the world's poor. The conference argued that in order to promote economic growth, the present underutilization of female human resources, a consequence of allocation of work of low productivity to women, must be amended. For development to proceed towards material improvement and greater equity the conditions of women's work, their access to productive resources and participation in decision-making at all levels were targeted for improvement.

The approach brought with it an impulse to 'integrate women' as agents in the strategy if it were to be successful: for it was increasingly evident that much of the responsibility for the provision of essential goods and services falls to women, not men. There was also the general assumption that men have benefited from development planning, but have not passed these benefits on to women. However, rather than challenging the underlying issue of the sexual division of labour within the household, the strategy takes this sphere as immutable, as if the problem of women being left out was not part of that development and therefore required special planning. Rather, it is a problem of the processes by which women have been disadvantaged, and the deeper structural constraints on fair distribution.

Whatever the good intentions of the 'integrationists', there are false and patronizing connotations in their views, as Papanek suggested:

> a curious ambiguity in the concept of *integrating* women in the development process hampers the achievement of this goal from the start. For women *are* full participants in all processes of social change, in spite of the fact that they may be affected differently than men. However, these differences often seem to confirm the false notion that women are less central to major social processes than men. In turn this misperception leads many to assume that women are a backward sector of society that needs to be 'integrated' in order to be 'modernized'.
>
> (Papanek 1977)

As a development strategy this approach is suspect given the context of dependency and the continuing imperatives of capital accumulation. Inequalities between men and women are in part an aspect of uneven development; likewise a widening gap between them can be detected. Just as economic growth in underdeveloped countries primarily benefits the developed metropoles, it increases inequalities within those countries, benefiting the few at the expense of the majority. In this sense, class inequalities cut across sex inequalities; a minority of women may share the benefits too, and hold significant political positions. In the absence of thoroughgoing structural change, the advocation of self-reliance (directed to the poor) can be conceived of as social reformism, a means of alleviating or even justifying the effects of a concentration of resources and wealth in the higher echelons of the economy and society.

These roots and characteristics of the 'integration' approach are relevant to any evaluation of policies and programmes 'for women' that have emerged over the last decade, providing the framework for a critique in terms of the limited potential they have for a radical transformation in the lives of women and relations between the sexes. A more positive thread to emerge from some of the case studies is the potential of women themselves to identify the sources of their subordination and oppression and to fight effectively against them.

Women's hidden role in production

Even after a decade of discussion of the inadequacy of conventional indicators, women's economic contribution is still ignored, or at least grossly underestimated, in censuses and other statistical data. Official statistics can be very misleading. For instance, in 1973 the US Department of Labor stated that 5 per cent of African women were economically active, while the UN Economic Commission for Africa reported that in 1974 women did 60–80 per cent of agricultural work, which amounted to up to sixteen hours a day during the planting season (Tinker 1976). The indication is that agricultural work done by family members is not counted as work; nor is exchange labour, household work, childcare, or 'informal sector' work. Often women's work is fragmented so that it is hard to measure or evaluate (Beneria 1981; Recchini de Lattes and Wainerman 1986). Since statistics fail to show women working, planners have not planned for women to work. Yet development projects do involve women, often invisibly, while it is men who receive training, new seeds, loans, and so on. In effect, women's independence decreases; even if they do benefit in some ways, the gap between them and men widens. If planners were to investigate women's productive contributions, projects would be more likely to support women's work and open new opportunities for them. Since their important roles in subsistence production have been ignored, 'development' has widened the gap between women's and men's earning power.

Being invisible on the economic front has meant that when obliged to incorporate 'women's issues' into the planning process, there is a tendency for agencies and institutions to slide this obligation into a social welfare or special considerations category (Rogers 1980). In this way women's issues are kept marginal, relegated to special sections in development institutions and to women's departments of welfare-oriented ministries within national governments. The result, as Rogers argued, is that international agencies' allocation of funds to women's affairs tends to be restricted to social welfare programmes, which pay little attention to women's agricultural-related work and are segregated from major development programmes. Relatively few and scantily funded projects reflect the tendency towards reinforcing gender segregation and continuing disregard for women's agricultural activities and special needs in major development institutions' policy-making (Rogers 1980).

In addition, agricultural extension programmes tend to focus attention on male farmers, overlooking the importance of women as major contributors to farm labour and as family breadwinners in their own right. This tendency is a reflection of the perceptions of project planners and authorities, who see women in western terms, as essentially domestic workers whose primary responsibility should be in the home and not in the fields. Lele (1975) argued that as a result, extension services have not attempted to increase the productivity of the work women do, but instead have tried to reduce women's participation in agriculture by promoting more homebound activities. Extension programmes for women have often been exclusively oriented towards domestic concerns, such as nutrition and hygiene. Despite their intrinsic value, the problem lies in their being regarded as subsidiary, as the exclusive province of women rather than men. Restricting programmes for women to these functions, in which they are already skilled given available resources, leaves little room for improving on women's economically productive activities, for instance by developing food crop technology rather than cash crop technology.

The debate was initiated by Esther Boserup (1970). She argued that 'female' farming systems precede 'mixed' or 'male' farming systems which emerged with the introduction of the plough, pushing female labour out of agriculture. Under colonialism and with economic development this trend was accelerated. Boserup's early examination of the differential impact of economic change on women and men saw the primary motive for providing work for rural women, either in agricultural or non-agricultural occupations, as drawing on their capacities for increasing production in the rural areas and ensuring that an improvement in men's earning power in agriculture is not significantly offset by a decline in women's work participation and hence in women's earning power. Further, it is seen as a preventative measure against female migration to towns in reaction to a lack of opportunities in the village for them when their earning power has been taken over by men using modern methods and machinery.

While Boserup's analysis offers some useful insights, it is clearly inadequate. The data on rural-urban migration alone demonstrate that capitalist development has different effects for both sexes in different places; there is no simple push-pull motivation. The actual situation is evidently more complicated than her analysis would suggest, since capitalist relations themselves are introduced in different ways. In some places there may be commercialization of former subsistence crops, or new crops grown with no change in the technology used. For instance, as Huntington (1975) points out, in Brazil large-scale commercial farming of coffee, sugar, and cotton developed using the traditional ('female') hoe and slash and burn agriculture. Elsewhere, for instance in India and Indonesia, new technology, the introduction of high yielding varieties of seeds or new types of land tenure (with, perhaps, a shift from sharecropping to wage labour) may be the significant elements.

Women may have been excluded or marginalized from certain aspects of production, but in many cases their subsistence work or unpaid agricultural labour increased, so their overall contribution was not 'squeezed' so much as the *returns* to and the specific nature of their contribution. Moreover, farming innovations, although directed to men, frequently increase women's work burdens, and if males are encouraged in cash cropping this can lead to the diversion of female labour from food crop production; it is this, coupled with male monopoly of the income from crops, rather than an actual decline in women's work participation, which has a detrimental effect on women's earnings and hence the welfare of the family. When men are drawn into increased agricultural activity they tend to withdraw from off-farm activities, leaving more to women who already undertake the more critical bulk of household responsibility, with the result that women's leisure time is sacrificed. In the case of Ghana, as described by Bukh (1980), integration into the market economy was characterized by the migration of male labour or their absorption into commercial crop production. Women were relegated to food crop production and other small scale subsistence activities, and were often solely responsible for the upkeep of the household. Men controlled the most important sources of cash – cocoa production and wage labour – yet failed to allocate their income to household expenses. Women's workload increased; constraints on their time and labour availability meant that the more accessible land became over-worked, with resultant lowering of productivity and nutritional levels. The amount of cash that could be raised from small surpluses was minimal.

Capital penetration is in no way a uniform process; it interacts with subsistence production in various ways. Its effects must also be identified; women's subsistence work may become less productive, women may lose access to new technology, or women's work may stagnate while men's opportunities increase. Beneria (1979) describes three cases of the impact of capital penetration on women's economic participation. In the South African case, migration to mines and urban centres removed males from agricultural activities, leaving women responsible for tasks related to reproduction: household work and subsistence food production. The Jamaican case illustrates a situation of a higher proportion of women than men engaged in waged labour in the plantation economy. In a situation of very low and insecure earnings, men declined to work on the plantations, opting rather for petty trade or migration to urban centres. Women, in this case, had a primary role as breadwinners in the waged sector, as well as bearing responsibility for child rearing and family maintenance. In West Africa women traditionally took responsibility for the upkeep of themselves and their children through subsistence farming and trade in farm products and processed foods. Capitalist penetration and commercialization of the economy offered disproportionately greater opportunities for men to earn cash for themselves in a range of occupations. With greater mobility, access to transport, and trading contracts, men also made inroads into women's trading functions, dominating the modern trading sector. Women's former relative economic independence, and hence ability to support dependants, was progressively undermined.

Joy Lyon

Income generation for women in Zimbabwe

A case study of income generating schemes for women in Zimbabwe, based on fieldwork which I carried out in 1983–4 and also using information from studies by the Zimbabwe Women's Bureau (1981), UNICEF, and the Ministry of Women's Affairs and Community Development (1982), demonstrates the necessity for women to define their own needs for self-reliance and illustrates some of the difficulties which are involved in implementing this. During the early twentieth century, following the colonial conquest of Zimbabwe, a capitalist economy was developed, based on farming, mining, and manufacture, drawing on the resources and labour of the pre-capitalist economic system. The 'traditional' economy underwent great changes, but was not destroyed; elements of it were deliberately kept intact by colonial policy. Prior to colonial intervention, there were between men and women (and juniors and elders) clearly established relationships of subordination and domination, inequalities in access to and control over resources, in exchange, distribution and consumption, which were exacerbated by the introduction of a cash economy. Mechanisms existed whereby husbands (and elders) could systematically appropriate the surplus production of wives (and juniors), a system of production which could be manipulated to meet the needs and interests of colonial capitalism.

Provisions were made for men only to labour in urban areas and mines, since women's labour was seen as essential to the agricultural sector, to sustain the family and provide insurance against sickness, unemployment, and old age for the male migrant, which his wage did not cover. Women became *de facto* heads of households, responsible for the day-to-day management of fields, livestock, ploughing, and child-care. These increased burdens for women went unrecognized. Their status fell further relative to men's, whose contribution was in the more highly valued cash sphere. The overall control over women's labour remained, with migrants visiting and resident male elders keeping watch meantime. Husbands continued to make major decisions as to when to sow and harvest, which seed to use, and when to sell the produce or cattle.

Male migrants' cash wages became essential to the household's viability, as the agricultural system declined and needs expanded. Women became increasingly dependent on men's remittances to buy food and new commodities, while men preferred to spend on individual consumption goods and beer. Since independence, land has not been significantly redistributed, despite schemes for resettlement and other agricultural programmes; good quality land remains the preserve of white farming. The communal lands population is estimated to be

178

double the land's carrying capacity and the demographic imbalance remains; over 80 per cent of the population are women and children under the age of 15.

The Zimbabwe Women's Bureau was formed in 1977 as a direct response by representatives of various women's organizations to the 1974 UN Plan of Action for the Integration of Women in Development. Its objectives are to conscientize women about the necessity of involving themselves in income generating projects and to increase women's self-reliance. In a survey carried out by the Zimbabwe Women's Bureau (1981) following independence in 1980, 3,000 rural women expressed their problems and needs. From this study, as well as from one carried out by the Ministry of Women's Affairs and Community Development in conjunction with UNICEF (1982), the most pressing need to emerge was economic, for women to find an independent source of adequate cash income to meet their responsibilities for providing for family welfare. Many women recognized the legal discrimination they suffered, as regards their minority status, inheritance of property, divorce, child custody, and their position under traditional marriage.

Women cited difficulties in gaining access to sufficient land and equipment to grow enough food for the family, and in controlling its use and product: 'I have much difficulty as a woman. I work hard on the farm and yet I get nothing at all. We wives are taken only as labourers', '. . . all the money I get from growing things is taken by my husband.' They also expressed difficulties in gaining access to extension services and in obtaining loans. Women resented being unable to qualify for resettlement schemes in their own right, or to own land as *de facto* heads of households (which applies to as many as 70 per cent of households in one district).

Overwork was seen as contributing to poor health, high blood pressure, and back troubles: 'As a woman I think I am the person who does most of the work at home. I look after the family as well as the fields, the vegetable garden, and the chickens and cattle.' This was compounded by a lack of labour-saving devices, such as wheelbarrows and scotch carts to help carry maize to grinding mills, crops from fields, and water and wood. Inadequate access to health services, educational, and communication facilities were all areas in which women wanted to see changes.

Women lack representation at all political levels. After local government elections in 1981, in forty-eight districts only 22 out of 1,204 local government councillors were women. Many recognized the problems this caused: 'Most women are not represented in the councils. Yet women are the ones who know what must be done in the rural areas for them to be developed. After all it is the women who live there'; 'It is

179

very hard for us because we are not given a chance to speak at meetings'; 'We want to participate in local decisions and to be chosen as leaders of organizations that are not only for women.'

The vast majority of women said that they needed to earn money, to meet the rising cost of living; the high prices of food and clothing in rural stores. It is women who are responsible for providing the household essentials, school uniforms and fees, and farming inputs: 'Women need to earn money because they are the ones who face the shortages at home because husbands do not earn enough to support the family'; 'Women need to earn money because most of the expenses at home have to be met by her. When a man gets money, he spends it on beer and girlfriends.' Women expressed a need to earn so as not to be financially dependent on husbands: 'We don't want to quarrel with our husbands day and night because of money. We need to earn our own money and bank it through our own hands.'

Small-scale income generating activities were found to be common, undertaken individually or in groups, covering vegetable gardening, poultry raising, handicraft production, and crochet. Transportation and marketing of produce were cited as particular problems. Women resented their husband's control over the small amount of cash they earned (though some concealed it). This prevented women in most areas from using banks or savings clubs. Most used any cash earned immediately for family purchases.

Since independence, with a socialist party orientation, the number of registered producer and collective co-operatives has grown rapidly; yet women's role in them is minor compared with their predominance in 'pre-co-operatives' formed into income generating projects. These deal mainly with non-agricultural activities (baking, soap-making, crafts, school uniform making, poultry keeping, market gardening). The implications are that women are mainly expected to generate supplementary incomes in rural areas, from non-agricultural petty marketing and industrial activities, as well as to spearhead community projects for literacy and health care in the communal lands.

Investigations into income generating projects that are sponsored by local and foreign non-governmental organizations and the Ministry of Community Development and Women's Affairs show that the groups face problems which raise doubts about their long-term viability and effectiveness in combating the manifestations of women's subordination illustrated in the Zimbabwe Women's Bureau survey. Despite the active encouragement of income generating projects by community development workers and representatives of other agencies, in many cases no sound criteria appear to be applied in the selection of projects undertaken by groups, either by the women themselves or by the supporting agencies. Groups are united in defining their prime need as cash income: '. . . without income, women have to ask men for everything.' However, many provide members with only low levels of returns and income, owing to undercapitalization and inadequate sources of finance, poor marketing skills, the absence of storage and transport facilities, and lack of technical and managerial expertise.

Although project decision making is entirely in the hands of women, there is a tendency for groups to rely heavily on external agencies for their overall organizational coherence. The social composition of groups tends to be skewed, with better-off families more likely to be beneficiaries of projects, while the poorest and most oppressed groups are not reached. Where women of polygamous marriages are present, they are more likely to be the first wives, who are able to delegate other tasks to junior wives. Sometimes membership fees payable on joining are prohibitive to many women, or participation is dependent on completion of a course, for instance in dress making, which is too expensive for many women and without provision for childcare for its duration.

Many of the groups are involved in producing marginal products (such as crafts) or products facing competition from large industries (such as bread and soap) which rely on sophisticated wholesale marketing and aggressive advertising techniques. Groups making school uniforms have run into financial difficulties owing to the fact that they are forced to sell at very low prices in order to compete with commercially produced uniforms. Others have had to cope with the whims of local school heads, who change their uniform requirements at short notice, leaving the women with unsaleable stocks they have built up over time. There is evidence that some heads have been persuaded, by payment of commission, to reject uniforms made by local women's groups in favour of those produced by a large commercial concern.

The majority of income generating activities are labour intensive and therefore super self-exploitative, or compete heavily with domestic work and normal agricultural activities for the labour time of women. This tendency is in part a reflection of the projects having largely been promoted by middle class urban women and foreign donor agencies. Women frequently walk very long distances to collect water and wood and loads must be carried by head porterage. Some tasks have to be left undone on days when the women undertake project work and this can lead to conflict with their menfolk, especially when little tangible benefit results from the women's participation. The women's enthusiasm for their project work enables them to resist this opposition, and to attempt to show themselves to be working harder on the family fields on other days to avoid further criticism.

Projects thus tend to reinforce women's traditional roles and the patriarchal value system that places the burden of social and health welfare provision on women. Hence, groups of women undertaking income generating projects are also ideal targets for Blue Band margarine cookery demonstrations and similar sales promotions. Few attempts have been made to get men and women to perform the same roles both inside and outside the home, and to arrange domestic work co-operatively, even though this was the practice in the camps in Mozambique and Zambia during the liberation struggle: 'Our men here in Zimbabwe, they don't help their wives doing the jobs. They just say everything that is supposed to be done by the wife must be done by her. We have no help here. It's their custom, men in Zimbabwe.'

After independence income generating projects became the fashion, and often diverted women from the vital struggle to gain more control over the economy. Women have been restricted to a narrow sphere of women's issues, and this has prevented them from participating in decision-making at local, district, and national level. As the groups tend not to debate wider socio-economic and political issues they are very vulnerable to the manipulations of unscrupulous politicians.

Zimbabwean women's subordinate status was confirmed by the granting, until recently, of Grain Marketing Board cards to men only, even though they may be absent for much of the year, depriving women of direct access to cash generated from agricultural surplus production. The structural impoverishment of the communal lands, which severely diminishes the potential for surplus production, and the sexual division of labour which has allocated subsistence food production to women and alternative employment to men, have yet to be decisively confronted. These, coupled with the 'customary' male right to wives' earnings, jeopardize women's struggle to provide adequately for the welfare needs of themselves and their children. Husbands' tendency to spend a disproportionate amount of the 'household's' income on personal consumption compounds the problems. In the light of these observations it is clear that the introduction of income generating projects is not in itself tackling the roots of rural poverty and the subordination of women.

Yet, at the micro-level, for women to begin organizing together to attack their problems and to raise incomes can be a start. Women in Zimbabwe have been determined to maintain control over the cash raised and to allocate it according to what they perceive as priorities. There are indications that women have been under pressure from their menfolk to spend all the group's earnings immediately, as pressing needs dictate. Yet many women are resolute in their defiance of this, prudently choosing to save for reinvestment and expansion of activities. If women are able to save reasonable amounts of cash, usually through bank accounts, opportunities for credit provision open up, facilitating the purchase of labour-saving devices such as wheelbarrows and scotch carts for group or individual use and the further expansion of income generating activities. Consideration of the Zimbabwe case has thus shed light on the extent to which income generating projects can lay the basis for more concerted challenges to traditional gender stereotypes. It provides a useful context for a more general examination of the potential and limitations of the income generating schemes which have been introduced in other areas during the 1970s and 1980s.

Engineering fertility rates

One argument for increasing the productivity of the work that women do and promoting income generating opportunities for women has been that this will reduce population growth rates. Raising the productivity of household and subsistence tasks would reduce the demand for child labour. The creation of new sources of employment and income for women would provide sources of status and security presently found in high birth rates. So long as women value children for their labour contribution and for social security, motherhood will remain their primary role and birth rates will remain high. Projects which only emphasize welfare provision for women serve to reinforce this mothering role, as has been the case even where a reduction in population growth has been sought.

Dixon's (1978) research into non-agricultural small industries in rural India, Nepal, and Bangladesh set out to test such hypotheses. She argued that if women are in productive work this will reduce, or delay fertility. If women combine together in groups it becomes more possible for them to obtain credit, and the groups form a basis for solidarity from which consciousness can be raised. The provision of rural employment opportunities is also seen as instrumental in curbing migration to cities. Dixon argued that for employment provision to have maximum effect on population growth, young unmarried women should be the prime target group. They should be working away from the traditional home and agricultural environment in central village or small town workplaces. The women should participate in the organization and functioning of the enterprise, and support services such as training, literacy, health, family planning, and childcare facilities should ideally be provided.

Although such plans can be seen to contain many elements that should, in theory, enable women to gain greater control over their lives, to advocate them explicitly as a means of engineering fertility rates is suggestive of an attack on women's freedom and self-determination. Besides, Dixon's case studies of the milk co-operative scheme in Gujarat, the jute works in Bangladesh, and the carpet weaving project in Nepal do not bear out her optimism concerning the benefits of rural industries to women. Lack of control over money supposedly results in women's low status and increased motivation for frequent childbearing, so that income generating is important. But Dixon takes the case studies out of their own context. There is a lack of detail concerning the relation of the schemes to local social and family structures. She sees them as revolutionary alternatives to home economics based projects in that concentrating on income generation has potential for redistributing power. Projects supported in these cases are part of community development so that their power to change either overall economic structures or women's position is very limited. It is essential that women control production, the retail of the products, and the distribution of the income generated. One of the problems Dixon overlooks is that the incorporation of women in social production has many limitations in 'liberating' women. It can mean that women simply move from the domination of male kin to the domination of male supervisors and management. Financing organizations support these schemes, yet do not want to support research into structures of households and the distribution of resources that would provide appropriate guides to policy-making. They simply want to get money to people as quickly and easily as possible.

Traditional handicrafts: an inappropriate base for expansion?

In many cases, where income generation has become a focus, projects have originated from welfare rather than development concerns. As a result they have not been based on sound economic planning. New handicraft projects, which could be seen as an attempt to resuscitate lost employment, have to depend not on the local market, but on a narrow and fluctuating foreign and tourist demand, for what, in that context, are non-essential and purely decorative objects. Often raw materials are expensive and difficult to obtain, products are not of high quality, and women themselves are not active in the overall organization. The steady production required for efficient marketing can be hard to keep up given seasonal peaks in agricultural work and other demands on women's time. Such welfare oriented projects tend to end up actually promoting the dependency that they meant to alleviate. They tend to get little funding, but occupy women's time in laborious processes, effectively excluding them from broader programmes and policies that would help raise productivity.

The Mhadubani painters (India), described by Jain (1980) are a case in point. The commercialization of a traditional form of artwork, used in ritual and ceremony, was promoted as a relief project at a time of dire need following drought conditions in the area in 1967, and continued thereafter. Transferred from floor and wall painting on to paper and cloth, the art products gained international recognition and generated significant income for some individuals. Being dependent on external markets, fortunes fluctuated, marketing being beyond the control of the producers, and decline in demand followed a relatively short lived boom. The advances made by women painters in terms of status as income earners in households have not been reinforced by more enduring improvements in their education, health, and nutrition, and general village improvements have no basis for continuation. Males of the well-off artist households have siphoned profits off into expenditure on luxuries at the expense of necessities such as expenditure on food, medical care, and children's education. Overall, as a welfare project based on unsound craft production, it provided wealth for some, for a time, but with no accompanying, on-going development or structural change, only ultimately increased dependence.

Co-operation or exploitation?

Some of the case studies described by Jain (1980) highlight further problems stemming from women's lack of control over the activities they undertake to generate income. Even where a project has not originated from an explicitly export-oriented or factory-tied activity, its growth into this sphere can cause loss of initial control by women, and the project's potential to improve the lot of women can be eroded. The Lijjat pappad industry in India started with a group of seven women and then, supported by official institutions, expanded into an organization of 6,000 over twenty years. The rolling of dough into various types of breads and snacks, utilizing the existing skills of women, working from home, developed into an economically successful enterprise. Yet, effectively, it merely exploits cheap labour as these breads go to the world market; the women's involvement in the organization represents their proletarianization rather than the creation of new roles and a fair income for them. Women do have a greater degree of participation in the day-to-day management and operation of the local co-ordinating centres than in the dairying co-operatives; women are members of the organization, act as intermediaries, have the right to participate in decisions relating to the centre, and to elect members to the managing committee. Communication and consultation channels are strong. Yet the uppermost levels of the organization, the overall management and liaison with the wider commercial world, are the preserves of men. Decisions as to what to produce, how much, and quality specifications are beyond the control of the producers. Raw materials are distributed with a stipulated minimum production rate, in return for piece-rate payments. Moreover, there are strict rules and regulations to which the women must adhere, particularly in relation to the separation of work and social contact. In this way women are prevented from raising issues pertinent to their condition as women within households and neighbourhoods. This makes a mockery of the emphasis laid on the organization as for women, by women, epitomized by the reference to all workers as 'sisters', the so called Sisters Saving Scheme (a fund generated by a compulsory levy on each payment made to a pappad roller and distributed as loans in times of need). Policy in this case is divorced from theory; it is formulated outside an analysis of the evolution of the economy as a whole, and within the organization there is an explicit strategy which prevents women from using it as a base for organizing in pursuit of their own interests.

Women the silenced producers

Women may gain access to co-operatives and organizations, constitute majority membership even, but fail to participate in or have representation at the administrative levels and in management. The AMUL co-operative in Gujarat, a sub-section of a major dairying scheme in India, is a case in point. It was started as a means of raising income from a sole activity, in which women were already widely involved, and thus appeared to be an appropriate base for a project catering for women's needs. It operates on a very large scale, aiming to reach 7.5 million women of dairying households. However, the way in which women milk producers are incorporated, and the structure and goals of the co-operative scheme itself, are problematic. Women perform the bulk of the labour in dairying and its management, although they do not own the stock. However, they are not registered members of the co-operative societies, except in a minority of cases; hence they are denied access to the decision-making bodies. Women are entirely absent from the management and staff structure.

The overall scheme is primarily profit oriented, commercially geared to supplying city demand, and male-dominated. While expediently overriding traditional money lenders' and private traders' exploitation, the interests of the individual female small producers are ignored. Preferences for higher daily prices for their milk are overlooked in favour of periodic rewards for profits made, which are paid to the registered male household head. Furthermore, these rewards, as well as decision-making roles, are distributed according to size of shareholdings, thus reinforcing the economic advantage of better-off farmers. As producers, the women ultimately receive technical inputs and other supporting services to improve the efficiency of dairying, but it was the men who were mobilized, addressed at village meetings, and targeted for co-operative organization, not the women. The scheme has resulted in increased output, but for women it means more time and energy input for little more income (the women are reported as saying they have no access to money in times of need), and no more independence or control over their production than in any putting-out system, the category to which the scheme effectively belongs.

'Success' cases

An investigation by ESCAP/FAO (1979) into rural women's income raising activities in nine South-East Asian countries set out to reveal 'successful' projects with a view to replication in other villages. The international agencies viewed the income generation schemes as important means of increasing overall income in rural areas, rather than of addressing women's particular needs in relation to the allocation of household resources. The schemes are said to be oriented towards increasing women's income and independence; yet the studies, although cited as 'success' cases, do not address the dynamics of household structures and thus fail to demonstrate that women have achieved real independence in a structural sense.

Women's organizations laid the basis for the income generating activities described in many of these cases, and were an important aspect of their 'success'. The projects were often initiated under the leadership of one 'outstanding' woman, a club being formed to undertake a variety of fund-raising activities in addition to 'home improvement' efforts. In Dusan, Korea, proceeds from the women's rice saving scheme, field labour, nursery produce and compost sales, and co-operative shop, enabled the women to open a bank savings account. In the case of a co-operative store venture in the Philippines, the initial motivation came from an official food-for-work project. This proposed reward in food rations for the implementation of a useful project. It fell to women to pursue this goal at a time when men were busy planting crops. Women undertook the planting and sale of vegetables and from this initial project went on to further income generating activities, establishing the store from the proceeds.

The organizations formed by women provided the solidarity that proved essential to overcome obstruction and intimidation, or the non-co-operation, of those in control of support services such as credit, technical training, and marketing. Many groups started without outside assistance, but income was raised most successfully when, organized and motivated, the women gained support in the form of access to government extension services. In Dusan, women gained support for a livestock project in the form of advice on the selection and raising of cattle and training in modern livestock management techniques. In Malaysia the newly formed Women's Farmers' Club obtained grants for starting rice noodle manufacture along with agricultural extension services and inputs, subsidized or on credit. This organization was formed as an offshoot of the Farmers' Club in which women had little opportunity to participate, as its activities clashed with household labour demands as well as with their vegetable growing and poultry raising activities. Rice noodle project work (time consuming and laborious) had to be fitted in with seasonal demands for women's labour in paddy transplanting and harvesting, when noodle production had to cease.

What comes across from the studies as the essence of this kind of 'success' is organization. In most of the examples this is hierarchical, stressing 'outstanding' leaders, and there is evidence of tensions. Yet with a defined organization, more interest is generated and channelled (door-to-door canvassing was common), bargaining strength *vis-à-vis* commercial and political interests is gained, and it facilitates the pooling of small amounts of savings from which, over time, credit can be provided to individuals.

Organizing women or women organizing?

Women have frequently worked communally and existing women's groups can and have acted as a base for development, often more effectively than projects designed for women from above. Okonjo describes one such group in Nigeria, whose workings indicate some of the features of credit provision which are important to women (cited in Buvinic *et al.* 1979). Small sums are deposited by members at frequent intervals, to avoid the tendency for the money to get spent on other things. The whole sum saved by the women is loaned to members in turn, or allocated to a particular member in an emergency or at a time of special need. Members act as guarantors for each other, taking responsibility for the repayment of the loan if the loan taker is unable to repay it. The loans are spent on children's education, investment in retail trade businesses, improvement or rebuilding of housing, clothing, and food. The women see their credit group as preferable to formal institutions, such as the local post office, as these require larger deposits, do not provide for emergency withdrawals, and do not permit loans or frequent transactions.

Women face obstacles in obtaining credit for the upgrading of their economic activities over and above those faced by the poor in general. The problems involved, and the advantages to be gained through tackling them, are highlighted by Bruce (1980) in an account of market women's co-operatives formed to assist in the provision of credit in Nicaragua. Formal banking and credit institutions require forms of collateral, such as land and other property, which is not owned by women, so access is denied to them. Often these institutions do not have credit programmes that suit the types of work women do, so the size and terms of loans and the repayment schedules tend to be inappropriate. The formal settings and procedures, fixed opening times, and the literacy necessary for comprehending and undertaking the paperwork involved in credit institutions are further barriers to women's participation.

Benefits for some: others lose out

In many cases the initial inspiration or encouragement for income generation schemes came from the better-off and better educated women and their contacts, enhancing their ability to approach community development officers and other officials. Their emphasis, as in the example of the Mung Ho women's group in Thailand, tended to be on 'constructive use of leisure time' to add to family income. There is a tendency for this to result in further accentuation of economic differences between households, if certain more advantaged groups of women gain at the expense of others. In one case, in Tamil Nadu, tailoring and plastic bag making efforts were confined to better-off women. Harijans, the untouchable castes, who constituted 4 per cent of the village's population were hesitant to participate in the Mahila Mandal's 'ladies' circles' project and so failed to gain from the economic benefits the project brought to the village. The harijans had less opportunity to join the group since the majority, both men and women, were employed throughout the year by non-harijans in agricultural labour. Clearly these women need their own organization to pursue their particular differing interests, to counteract the tendency for the success of the Mahila Mandal's project to widen economic gaps between the castes within the village. In Dusan, too, the club members became better-off than other villagers, priding themselves in their ability to make charitable efforts to 'help the needy' and to 'cheer up the military'. In the Philippines co-operative store project there was opposition from poorer villagers who could not afford to buy shares and hence could not purchase goods on credit.

Women lose control: men step in – and out

Women's control over the activities they undertake is essential if they are to benefit fully. Case studies illustrate that women may control the day-to-day running of the project, but lose control at the level of overall production and marketing. This is particularly liable to happen where the income raising activity is geared towards the export market, typically producing goods on a putting-out system. Such were the vagaries of the toy animal assembly project in Korea. There the women were dependent on the amount and kind of work the factory decided to allot them, and faced problems of low, irregular wages from the factory, as well as health hazards from the dust from the animal stuffing, and boredom from monotony.

In Nepal, women undertaking vegetable production to raise income lost control at the level of marketing. Since the vegetables had to be transported to town for sale in the early morning when the women's time was taken up with domestic chores, men took over the marketing. As there was no fixed market place, and street selling was illegal, the men were forced to sell quickly to shops and individuals, usually below the price they had estimated, the produce then being resold to consumers at a much higher price. In this way the rewards to women's labour fell to men, leaving the women in a position of having to plead for cash. The project reporter recognized the advantages to be gained through organizing permanent marketing and storage facilities (along with cooperative distribution of seed and fertilizer among women) so as to enable the women to sell the vegetables later in the day when they had more time available. However, the suggestion that the men could undertake domestic chores in the morning, allowing women to be free to market their produce, was not put forward.

In undertaking new activities, the reallocation of women's time implies some shift in the sexual division of labour in the household, which, through the contradictions it highlights, can raise consciousness and potentially reduce rigidities. The ESCAP studies showed that although men's support for income raising activities was appreciated by the women, there was little evidence that their support had extended to more specifically facilitating women's efforts, through participation in 'women's' household tasks; the men instead continued to 'relax at home', to protect their leisure time and to let the women get on with their efforts. In Dusan the women took a typical conciliatory attitude towards their menfolk, following initial ridicule at their handling cattle. Their leader emphasized her diligence in serving her husband and family as a priority as instrumental in gaining male support for the project, and interest and assistance both in project tasks and in related objectives such as renovating old kitchens and improving wells. In the rice noodle project in Malaysia, husbands were the ultimate arbiters in major problems in the women's ventures.

Organization and consciousness: contrasting cases

Organization and activities undertaken with the aim of raising income are no guarantee of an increase in women's status within the household and community, but can be a first step towards self-reliance and consciousness of wider and more fundamental problems, as Mary Castelberg-Koulma also shows in her study of women's co-operatives in Greece in Chapter 10. The Self-Employed Women's Association (SEWA) of Ahmedabad, India (Jain 1980), a trade union of 10,000 low income members, provides an example of how women can organize successfully to raise income from their present occupations, gain confidence to confront obstacles and to pursue other goals on a basis of self-reliance. The membership of SEWA covers twenty trade groups including handcart pullers, used garment dealers, vegetable vendors, junksmiths, and petty traders.

SEWA was formed in 1972 as an offshoot of the Textile Labour Association (TLA). This was previously a welfare oriented women's wing, assisting women in mill workers' households by organizing sewing and other classes. Investigations by the leadership revealed the exploitative nature of the work these women subsequently undertook, and the absence of unionization and protective labour legislation. Action was stimulated when a group of women headloaders from the cloth market, although not members of mill families, approached the women's wing demanding that attention be paid to their appalling wages. Assistance was given to them in negotiating price-fixing agreements with the Merchants' Association. Women of other trades followed suit in approaching the TLA with their grievances. Common problems were severe debts to money lenders who charged extortionate interest rates, harassment from the municipal authorities and police, high rentals on equipment, poor housing, overwork, and ill health.

A public meeting was called by the TLA women's wing, at which women spoke about their problems and the need for protection, and suggested forming their own organization to deal with them. The organization attracted large numbers of women, primarily interested in the possibly of increasing their income through improved conditions of work. Fieldworkers were deployed to investigate problems, resolve individual grievances, and represent collectively members' interests to the authorities. A co-operative bank was established and managed by women, providing credit and saving facilities, assisting the supply of raw materials and equipment, technical assistance, and help with marketing and financial management. The SEWA Trust set up childcare centres, maternity and medical insurance schemes, occupational training, and functional literacy programmes.

The SEWA organization has been a means through which women have gained self-confidence, the strength and skills to objectify and deal with their own problems, avoiding dependence on the delivery of development services from outside sources. Women associating with others and drawn into public participation in dealing with banks, insurance companies, and municipal and police authorities have developed a new self-perception and consciousness and have gained the respect of men and their families.

Having built up a successful organization, the women of SEWA have since suffered set-backs and obstruction from the non-worker, higher caste male-dominated parent union. The TLA no longer recognizes SEWA as part of its organization, expelling it from the premises provided and demanding withdrawal of its union funds from the SEWA bank. It is postulated that:

> TLA leaders felt increasingly threatened by the women's advance towards self-independence, and methods of struggle which were not only opposed to TLA policy of compromise and collaboration, but also provided a dangerous role model to the male workers. They also resented the press publicity and widespread recognition given to Ela Bhatt's work.
>
> (Karl 1981)

Despite this rejection, the SEWA leadership has expressed its determination to carry on, and its confidence in the strength of the membership and wide support for its efforts.

Income generation for women: a universal 'solution'?

Just as the effects of capital penetration are not uniform, strategies such as income generation cannot be assumed to be appropriate to all situations. Whether or not generating income can have a positive effect depends very much on the total context of 'development' in any particular location, from relationships within the household to relationships with national and international capital. The potential varies: where population density is relatively low and responsibility for crops is allocated on the basis of sex, such as the case of African women's responsibility for food crops, women could be helped to raise productivity and men could also be drawn into food crop production to reduce child and female labour. In other situations though, for instance in Indonesia where there is a surplus of female labour in agriculture and possibly a less sharp division of tasks, the creation of alternative income generating opportunities is needed, rather than efforts to increase the productivity of current agricultural activities. There can be no blanket prescription indicating which policies will be positive and which negative, for this can hinder rather than help to improve women's position.

Among women, class and strata differences can be identified. For example, in richer households women tend to be less burdened; poorer women are more likely to be in agricultural labour, producing food for their own household or, if landless, undertaking labour for others. Some may work for wages in rural industries (such as tobacco processing), some produce commodities at home for the market (such as woven carpets, beedis, beer, lacework). Many spend long hours in fuel and water collection for household use. Some migrate from deteriorating rural conditions to cities to work as domestic servants, prostitutes, and so on. In many cases women's lack of income is not a reflection of lack of work, but a lack of returns to their labour. To take on a form of income generating activity outside their normal workload may be absurd given the existing time constraints. In such cases it may be far more appropriate to replace some of the tasks rather than add more work, in the absence of more far-reaching strategies to tackle the root causes. As Palmer observes:

> statisticians may be able to prove that real family income has risen as a result of economic change, but it requires more than a statistician to explain why, for instance, nutritional levels fall while wristwatches, transistor radios and bicycles (all largely utilized by men) find their way into the household.
>
> (Palmer 1977)

There is obviously a logic in paying attention to increasing women's cash earnings, but there is a problem with introducing new activities where women are already working up to sixteen hours a day. For opportunities to be beneficial to women there must be a reduction in their traditional burdens, or there is a danger that men may take advantage of the new opportunities resulting in a wider income gap between men and women. Whatever 'independent' activities may be introduced for or by women, they are still subject to the constraint of being part of a household organization, as regards labour allocation and the distribution of rewards. Without radical transformation of this institutional structure there can be little real progress for women. Access to the labour market is hardly a route to autonomy when women's pay and conditions of work are so much worse than men's. Sanday (1974) argues that contribution to subsistence appears to be a necessary, but not sufficient factor in determining women's status. If women are excluded from valued social production they lose their power base and control over resources. If women do not have control over resources to begin with, increasing their income may simply provide a further source of dominance for men. Owing to the imbalances in the allocation of income within households, the income generated will not necessarily increase income for women themselves, since it may well get directed to men and to children, rather than giving women independence. In this case the income generated will have fulfilled only a role of decreasing overall poverty, without necessarily having improved women's welfare. The aim of any income generating activity should be to reduce dependence, not just to exploit cheap labour.

Clearly, the 'household' is not synonymous with the family, nor is it a constant homogeneous category. Household income is not an adequate indicator of relative welfare. The idea of a constant household-family with a male head, whose internal relations and exchanges are irrelevant, is a myth that goes some way to explaining the ineffectiveness of some policies, and the detrimental effects of others. People live in different households at different stages in the life cycle, in different relationships, which affect their activities and status. The fact that women are allocated the bulk of reproductive tasks within the household sexual division of labour helps maintain their subordination by limiting the extent of participation possible in outside production. Any income that can be generated by women does not automatically enhance women's position, so long as they remain subordinated within the household and in the wider society. If the activities taken up are seen as (or are in fact) marginal or supplementary and their reproductive roles continue to be perceived as primary and not reduced, then women are not structurally any better off. So long as the economic content of women's subordination in marriage – domestic labour – remains unchallenged, 'economic independence' has little meaning.

Conclusion

A critical analysis of the 'integration' approach points to its shortcomings as a far-reaching 'solution' to the underlying imbalance of power between the sexes. Women have been viewed in terms of their potential contribution to overall development, the emphasis being on raising productivity rather than on the equitable sharing of both overall labour input and the fruits of that labour between men and women. It has been seen that in emphasizing 'women' as a category apart, development planning geared towards women can result in their ghettoization. The approach still suffers from the legacy of undervaluing the contribution women make to the economy in different societies, which is, in part, a reflection of the view of all women, by many statisticians and development planners, in a western stereotyped image.

Rather than attempting to impose on women additional tasks based on western values of domesticity (which tend to reach only the better-off minority anyway), assistance could be directed towards reducing the time and energy spent on domestic tasks to a minimum. Inefficient tasks could be identified and women could be assisted by the application of appropriate technologies, for instance to cooking, water collection, and post-harvest food processing, though such technological improvements should not be directed exclusively to women, thereby confirming their position in the domestic sphere. If women's burdens were relieved in this way they would be freer for training, decision making, and participation in new remunerative activities. There is clearly a problem in purchasing improved technologies for tasks that do not produce exchange values. This is one reason why women need to raise cash and obtain credit which they can control and allocate appropriately, in areas where men are reluctant to invest.

The assumption that the benefits of development are redistributed towards women through their participating in income generation schemes is often invalid. When women's labour is already largely committed to unpaid household labour it seems, on the surface, to be appropriate to develop new extra-household activities to raise income. But relations of production within households are structured in such a way as to maintain women's subordination and dependency. Domestic relations of production are not autonomous of changes in the wider economy; as conditions there change, relations within the household also adapt and change; the sexual division of labour undergoes shifts which, given inequality over time and unequal access to valued resources, has detrimental effects on women, which are rarely resolved solely by innovations such as schemes for raising cash incomes. If women genuinely gain control over their labour and its rewards improvements are possible, but men must be integrated into the process; by relinquishing their control over women's labour, time and rewards, there can be a balance and reciprocity. Women have to get together, to organize to make the challenge. To raise income, and to purchase household oriented technologies, can be a step. It is not a solution, but there is possibly more potential for change via structures larger than the individual household where resistance is strong and men have no incentive to change the status quo.

References

African Training and Research Centre for Women, UNECA (1975) 'Women and national development in African countries; some profound contradictions', *African Studies Review* 18(1): 47–70.

Beneria, L. (1979) 'Reproduction, production and the sexual division of labour', *Cambridge Journal of Economics* 3(3): 203–225.

—— (1981) 'Conceptualising the labour force: the underestimation of women's economic activities', *Journal of Development Studies* 17(3): 10–28.

Boserup, E. (1970) *Woman's Role in Economic Development*, London: George Allen & Unwin.

Bruce, J. (1980) *Market Women's Co-operatives: Giving Women Credit*, New York: Seeds.

Bukh, J. (1980) 'Women in subsistence production in Ghana', in *Women in Rural Development: Critical Issues*, Geneva: International Labour Organisation.

Buvinic, M., Sebstad, J. and Zeidenstein, S. (1979) *Credit for Rural Women: Some Facts and Lessons*, Washington: International Centre for Research on Women.

Dixon, R. (1978) *Rural Women at Work*, Baltimore: Johns Hopkins University Press.

Elliott, C.M. (1977) 'Theories of development: an assessment', in The

Wellesley Editorial Committee (eds) *Women and National Development*, Chicago and London: University of Chicago Press.

ESCAP/FAO (1979) *Learning from Rural Women*, Bangkok.

Huntington, S. (1975) 'Issues in women's role in economic development: critique and alternatives', *Journal of Marriage and the Family* 37(4): 1001–1012.

Jain, D. (1980) *Women's Quest for Power*, Ghaziabad: Vikas.

Karl, M. (1981) 'Income generation for women', in *Women and Development: A Resource Guide for Organization and Action*, Geneva: ISIS.

Lele, U. (1975) *The Design of Rural Development: Lessons from Africa*, Baltimore: Johns Hopkins University Press.

Palmer, I. (1977) 'Rural women and the basic needs approach to development', *International Labour Review* 115(1): 97–107.

Papanek, H. (1977) 'Development planning for women', in The Wellesley Editorial Committee (eds) *Women and National Development*, Chicago and London: University of Chicago Press.

Recchini de Lattes, Z. and Wainerman, C.H. (1986) 'Unreliable account of women's work: evidence from Latin American census statistics', *Signs* 11(4): 740–750.

Rogers, B. (1980) *The Domestication of Women*, London: Kogan Page.

Sanday, P. (1974) 'Female status in the public domain', in M. Z. Rosaldo and L. Lamphere (eds) *Woman, Culture and Society*, Stanford: Stanford University Press.

Tinker, I. (1976) 'The adverse impact of development on women', in I. Tinker and M. Bramsen (eds) *Women and World Development*, Washington: Overseas Development Council.

UNICEF/Ministry of Community Development and Women's Affairs (1982) *Report on the Situation of Women in Zimbabwe*, Harare: Ministry of Community Development and Women's Affairs.

Zimbabwe Women's Bureau (1981) *We Carry a Heavy Load*, Harare: Zimbabwe Women's Bureau.

Chapter ten

Greek women and tourism

Women's co-operatives as an alternative form of organization

Mary Castelberg-Koulma

Introduction

Women's labour provides an essential prop to the tourism industry, making heavy demands on the domestic skills traditionally assigned to women. Women occupy jobs ranging from receptionists and chambermaids to being the mainstay of small family enterprises and their related activities. Yet few studies address themselves to the effects that tourism has on the local female population. This chapter will therefore examine the effects of mass tourism on Greek women and some attempts which women have made to establish alternative forms of tourism organization.

Interviews with women employed in the mass tourism industry in Greece reveal that tourism, via the provision of wage-earning opportunities, has enabled them to gain more independence than their counterparts of previous generations. However, the material gains of the last two decades have been tinged with losses of other kinds. Among these are the insecurities resulting from the seasonality of the industry and the disruption of traditional lifestyles – the winter ghost towns, the summer importation of urban non-indigenous culture and the dependence upon guests for economic survival. The unease felt by most women is particularly related to the social effects of tourism on gender relationships, clearly displayed in the tourist scenario.

An examination of the cultural construction of gender, which concerns ideas about appropriate male and female sexuality and behaviour patterns, reveals the impact which tourism has had on Greek women. The principal interaction is dominated by a relationship of male host/female guest while the indigenous women remain peripheral. The *Kamaki* phenomenon, in which Greek males attempt to pick up foreign women, has become something of a cult in touristic settings. Most of the Greek women interviewed felt that this adversely affected their lives and relationships and clouded the acquisition of any material gains. Greek women's peripherality can also be seen by the contrasting represent-

Mary Castelberg-Koulma

ations of Greek and foreign women on postcards sold in resorts throughout Greece. The Greek woman is usually portrayed as an old crone, dressed in black, in an 'underdeveloped' rural setting. The barely clad foreign woman, in contrast, is a sexualized object, depicted in semi-pornographic poses. These male-gazing images attempt to reflect the dominant scene, to the detriment of both Greek and foreign women. The holiday ethic of 'getting away from it all', fostered and sanctioned by western consumer ideology, offers most tourists little chance of drawing conclusions other than the marketed stereotype. An understanding of the implications for Greek women's perception of their own identity is not part of the tourist package.

Given the present situation and its particular implications for women, the introduction of Greek women's agro-tourist co-operatives is a welcome form of alternative organization. Owned and controlled by Greek women, their creation over the last few years has offered both a potential contradiction to the dominant form of host/guest interaction and a positive initiative for Greek women. Evaluation of their achievements and limitations is therefore important. This can best be achieved within the context of an examination of prevailing gender constructs; in particular, of traditional Greek male and female role expectations and behaviour patterns.

The males

Male children in Greece and much of the Latin speaking world are greatly welcomed at birth. The mother's prestige is enhanced as her offspring promises more 'hands to the family'. On the other hand a daughter and her consequent dowry provision is a burden to the family. Mothers tend to pay more attention to their sons and their behaviour plays an important role in the cultural construction of masculinity (Herzfeld 1985). In many ways the origin of 'machismo' can be found here. The overpowering role of the mother who rules and nurtures a young boy's life and who consequently deserves a lifelong respect and trust that is assigned to no other woman is a contradiction to women's lack of public power. Thus, a boy tends to see his mother as a contradiction of power and powerlessness. The consequence of this for a male child is to assert his masculinity and to identify with his father as a reaction to maternal power. The mother's attention and favouritism towards her son tends to reflect his narcissism and confirm his self-importance. In turn, the son's respect for his mother can be seen as an expression of his own ego by his connection to her.

In terms of man's sexuality and nature, various attributes and acts of infidelity or pre-marital and extra-marital affairs can be explained away. Reactions to this behaviour can vary from resentment and resignation to concealed admiration. Women tend not to act until family resources could be squandered. Expression of male sexuality is necessary and vitally important. Hirschon (1978: 67) writes: 'A man's sexual needs are incontestable; enforced or prolonged absence from sexual intercourse is believed to have serious physical and mental consequences, possibly even leading to insanity.' These models of male upbringing and masculinity patterns are related to traditional concepts. They vary in intensity according to location and are subject to conflicts and change. In the touristic setting the male hosts play out the roles bequeathed to them. Unsanctioned expression of their sexuality consolidates their masculinity. This is played out on the female guests (*touristries*) serving as a focal point of male-female interaction. In places where mass tourism exists for seven months of the year the ratio of tourist females to local males is as high as 10 to 1 (Koussis 1984:147). Greek men gain easy access to foreign women who often fall victims, willing or unwilling, directly or indirectly, to the *Kamaki* sub-culture that has become a household name in Greek society. This applies to men of all classes who are to be found on beaches, in bars and discos, or anywhere tourists congregate in order to 'catch' a tourist woman. *Kamaki* means harpoon and 'to make *Kamaki*' means to take the necessary steps to pick up a tourist, the analogy being that the female is the fish. *Kamaki* men have a variety of motives in this pursuit, ranging from opportunities to go abroad to just spending a nice summer, sometimes allowing themselves to be treated by the *touristires*. Their pick up tactics can consist of lying or subtly simulating situations where the tourists can be unwittingly duped (Bowman 1988). The anonymity and transience of the holiday can explain their success in many ways. The access to *touristries* also means that the men have the opportunity to discard the aspects of their culture that fail to suit their needs while they 'modernize' themselves outside their cultural bounds.

The Females

In contrast, indigenous women in most rural situations are still bound by the traditional cultural constraints assigned to their role, of which mothering and maintaining the well-being of the family are essential components. This function implicitly emphasizes the home power-base, upholding a strict division of labour and a lack of participation in public life and the outside world. At birth girls in Greece do not receive the same status as a boy child, the dowry provision being seen as a liability (although this has been abolished by the Family Law Act 1983). Girls are brought up to uphold a sense of shame, defined by Friedl (1962:80) as 'a sense of inner embarrassment at the thought of revealing oneself either the physical self (modesty) or the inner emotional self.' While a girl is growing up she has a constant vigil to keep within the ideals of shame. These are guarded by her family, the menfolk, and even younger brothers. In turn the men's control of the women enhances their own honour and masculinity. Any loss of shame by the women reflects on the men. Women's sexuality is thus controlled physically and psychologically; virginity is of prime importance. These values belong to traditional assumptions and practices, but they remain on an unconscious if not conscious level. Older generations of women bringing up young women and girls have been exposed to them. Women's sexuality is determined by the cultural messages they receive, not only from their kinsmen, but also from other women (see Chapter 4 of this book and also Wikan, 1984, for a comparative view).

To Greek women of this tradition the ideal man is the *pallikari*, 'a youth who is handsome, manly, narrow-hipped and nimble' (Campbell 1964: 279), a person who is strong enough to maintain the support and honour of his family in the home and in the community. He complements her in her capacity as mother and guardian of the home. Her sexuality is expressed in these terms and solely within marriage.

Close to the ideal of 'the good woman' is one who is subservient to males, is known to suffer as a martyr for her family and uphold sexual purity throughout marriage. Espin's work on Hispanic women equally applies to the tradition of 'shame' culture of women in Greece:

> Sexual pleasure in marriage may be seen as lack of virtue. To regard sexual behaviour exclusively as an unwelcome obligation toward husband and a necessary evil in order to have children may be seen as a manifestation of virtue. Some women express pride in lack of sexual pleasure and desire.
>
> (Espin 1984:156)

In many rural areas of Greece where tourism is rampant many of these attitudes have been internalized by generations of women. 'Many Greek women see sex as a bad thing. They don't know their bodies. They're ashamed of them. They have complexes. The men don't give her a chance of a sexual life in order to control her and this goes against him' (Marina, an architect on the island of Kos). Yet many of these public attitudes conform to the extreme cultural expectations of women's sexual role and protect the woman in preserving her honour and that of her family. To base a judgement on women's sexuality on public statements in a culture and tradition that requires silence on such matters and to assume that most women have denied their sexuality is misrepresentational. Further studies are needed to shed light on how women react and negotiate their role within this system.

It is important to see how the indigenous women within this value system perceive female tourists and how they view their interactions with their kinsmen in the latter's role as host. Women tourists represent an antithesis to the values Greek women were brought up with – especially those of the older generation. Therefore, maintaining their roles could be seen as upholding 'the last bastion of tradition' (Espin 1984:160). In this sense Greek women in touristic rural settings are representative of oppressive cultural norms. They are often ignored, remaining peripheral in their own countries. For rural women a lack of access to western culture is thought to reflect in them a lack of world-liness and inexperience. Phenomena such as nude bathing (part and parcel of the holiday package of many tourists) remain incom-prehensible as well as threatening, particularly to women of older generations:

'Nude bathing: I don't like it. I lived in Athens for nineteen years. I never saw that anywhere. Only here. You see them going around naked. I don't like it. I've lived in another environment in other years. I would like them (tourists) to be a humbler (*pyo tapino*). We can't do anything. We simply go past them and we see. Before you went to the sea to have your swim and you didn't see that. In this village women live in another world ... .No, we lived quietly. I told you what I thought about nudism and the drinks they drink; that they touch one another in the roads; that they make love; all that. I'm against that. I don't accuse them. It's only that I've lived in another environment. The only thing I want to know is whether they would do that in their countries. I don't think they'd do it . . . someone would say I'm backward but to change now . . . I can't.'
(Anthoula, 49 years old, on the island of Kos)

Yet the recent decades of tourism seem to have brought out the implications of encouraging full expression of male sexuality. As it now stands it can be seen as an impediment to the well-being of the family, even threatening male honour. Maria Koussis writes from interviews in Crete:

Kseftilistikame (we lost our dignity) that is exactly how one would describe us. Married men don't pay attention to their children but go grab tourist women. They are disinterested in their own children and families. We lost our dignity without really wanting to.
(Koussis 1984:132)

This has an effect on the way women relate to their men in the sense that men can no longer guarantee the honour necessary to maintain a family. In this sense they negate women's role and the values women learn to respect and admire in men. An oppressive dignity is usually maintained, somewhat reminiscent of the stolid faces representing Greek women on the postcards sold throughout Greece. The Greek woman is nearly always displayed as the crone clad in black and positioned in rural surroundings, usually in connection with domestic chores. She is desexualized. However, as in the case of South-East Asian women discussed by Wendy Lee in Chapter 5, representations of foreign women conform to racist sexual stereotypes. The usually blonde, sun-tanned foreign woman is displayed in semi-pornographic poses – a sexualized object.

It is worth questioning whether tourism will in any way create a dynamic for change in Greek women and a questioning of traditions and practices and self-awareness which could pave the way to a different division of labour and expectations from the males they relate to and nurture. Whether tourism contains a dynamic for transformation of current gender relationships depends on what other forms of alternative organization there are. If these can grow, develop, and mature, gaining the support of women and the realization that a better deal is offered to them, then a strong material base may lay the foundations for a change in consciousness.

The women's agro-tourist co-operatives

I would argue that an important prop to laying the foundations for change are the women's agro-tourist co-operatives which offer women participants in rural areas a chance to earn money for themselves through tourism. This national project is an experiment, principally organized from Athens and initiated under the socialist government in 1985. It is important to stress that the co-operative conceptions never originated from the aim of improving women's condition in tourism, but as an employment opportunity for rural women. Nevertheless, the co-operatives offer a welcome contradiction to the prevalent position of women in tourism in Greece. Not only are the co-operatives important as a material base that may act as an impetus to change, but they can also enhance 'creative encounters' (Gregor 1985: 192) and a quality tourism of a more equal nature between hostesses and guests. Besides this they are an indigenous model of development and whatever evolves from this experiment will stem from within Greek culture.

This on-going experiment is directed towards women who live in small villages where mass tourism is not operative. This means that there are no rival enterprises or non-co-operative schemes to draw them away. Most of the women involved in the venture have no cash income of their own so joining a co-operative is a unique opportunity for them to become wage-earners. Additionally, management and decision-making and the work they perform is under their control. So far this situation is unparalleled in the autonomy it offers to women. Most rural women have never directly earned money for themselves, let alone been responsible for an enterprise. The women also have little formal education to apply their skills other than in farming and domestic chores. The co-operatives give them the chance to be paid for what they have always done.

From the guest's point of view, this type of tourism lends itself to encounters where the guests have made conscious efforts to visit a country whose infrastructures have not mimicked their comforts and lifestyle. Implicit in this is an avoidance and absence of the imported features usually associated with mass tourism, including food and entertainment. The venture caters for guests unconcerned with importing their cultural accoutrements and avoids the implicit escape-route type holiday which western consumer ideology disseminates.

For female guests the co-operatives are beneficial in the following ways. First there is an element of safety from the usual problems of harassment women experience. Second the female guest, more than the male guest, has a chance to be drawn into aspects of women's culture, in contrast to the case of sex tourism in South-East Asia. It is a way of understanding the culture from the hostess's point of view and of gaining access to her meaning system. This can contribute to dispelling racist stereotypes of women's position in either society. It is a way, perhaps, for 'the losers' to unite and turn the tables on the present situation for their own benefit.

The co-operative project originated from Chrisanthi Laiou Antoniou, Prime Minister Papandreou's adviser on women's affairs, and who was leader of the Secretariat of Equality – part of the Ministry to the Prime Minister. The Secretariat was set up as part of a conscious Government policy to improve women's affairs by the PASOK party (Pan-Hellenic Socialist Movement). The first agro-tourist co-operatives for women were set up in 1985, with the objective of generating income for rural women (*agrotissa*), who were seen to be the most oppressed women in Greek society. Within this national context it is also important to stress that other women's co-operatives were set up in non-touristic enterprises. These include cake, sweet, and Greek pastry making (*zaharoplastiki*), handicrafts (*hiroteknia*), and interior decorating (*eleochromatiston*). The agro-tourist co-operatives are to be found in Ambelakia in Northern Greece, Petra on the Island of Lesvos, on the Island of Chios, in the village of Arachova near Delphi, in Agios Germanou near the Yugoslav-Albanian border, and in Maronias in North-Eastern Greece.

Structure and organization

Women who wish to become co-op members undergo a training period where they are taught to use their skills for touristic purposes. The courses are held in accordance with the availability of the women from their seasonal tasks and the women are paid to attend them. They are also taught the ideology of a co-operative enterprise and how it should work and function. In practical terms the women are taught how to receive guests and how to run the co-operative restaurant. An elected president is appointed to the co-op and decisions are made by the administrative council, presided over by her. The council consists of the members, the treasurer, the vice president, and president. Meetings are held once a month and elections every three years.

There is also a secretary who allocates the rooms to the guests, collects money from them, and is responsible for ensuring that the Government retains 10 per cent of the income. In Ambelakia the secretary was a civil servant especially appointed to the task. The setting up of a co-op can depend on the *Nomarchial* (district) Committees of Equality which are voluntary bodies led by an Equality Officer. These committees help the work of the *Nomarche* (district leaders). Whether a co-op is set up or not can depend on how strong the Nomarchial Committees of Equality are.

In terms of finding members, the initiative is attractive to many women. Rural areas suffer from general unemployment and low incomes. Many women who wish to return to production at around the age of 35–40 have little opportunity for doing so: 'The co-operatives offer this [work] to them because an employer wouldn't take them so old and unskilled not even in the public sector so they see the co-operatives as a solution to problems' (Spokeswoman (co-ops) Secretariat of Equality). The co-ops work with support from national governmental organizations such as EOT (the National Tourist Organization) for publicity and marketing, the Agricultural Bank of Greece for loans, OAED (the National Employment Bureau), EL. KE. PA. (the Greek Centre of Planning and Development), and E.O.M.M.E.X., which is responsible for teaching traditional handicrafts. Additionally, much of their patronage is derived from indigenous tourism and Government incentives to promote social tourism (*kinonikos tourismos*). This tourism is for Greeks of all ages and old age pensioners who are on low incomes and are entitled to Government subsidies if they choose to go on holiday anywhere in Greece.

Incentive schemes were organized so that the women wanting to participate were able to alter their houses while preserving the traditional style. They were all lent 200,000 drachmas for improvements and had the right to borrow more for extra expenses if necessary. The idea was that women would let rooms in their houses with access to a bathroom with hot water and would offer their guests locally produced food for breakfast. Some co-operatives such as the one in Ambelakia offered local food in the co-op restaurant, which was run by different women on a rota basis. The information about co-ops is distributed by National Tourism Organization offices in Greece and abroad. Prospective foreign visitors are asked to fill in a form with a few personal details, with the aim of matching guests and hostesses; for example guests with children are sent to households with children of compatible ages.

On arrival in Ambelakia, for example, guests go to the co-op office in the village square to notify the secretary. There they meet their hostess and are taken to her house and shown their rooms. When the guests leave they pay the hostess and the payment is taken to the secretary in the co-op office. Later the hostess is reimbursed, the co-op keeping 15 per cent. The breakfast fee charged to the guests is paid to the hostess directly.

The co-operatives as an alternative form of organization promoted by the State

The co-operatives provide an opportunity for work for rural women who find little or no work in the labour market. The women's main concern is, justifiably, to earn money in whatever way they can. The ideological component, vitally important for a co-op to run successfully, is seen as less important than material needs. Few of the women who join see their work as a contradiction to capitalist profit-making practices. In addition, problems can occur as women leave their own individual working partners or associates who consist of close relatives or affines who are accustomed to working together. Yet, co-operatives in Greece are alternative forms of working which are also part of tradition. For example, the village of Ambelakia can boast of setting up the world's first co-operative which, in the seventeenth century, was famous for selling natural dyes and threads to Vienna. In the 1950s Greece had a total of 7,127 agro-co-operatives with a membership of 718,000 (Sanders 1962: 201). Due to the small size of agricultural holdings it was more feasible for farmers to organize in co-operative groups to sell their produce. Women were members too, but were registered in their husband's name. However, women members were excluded entry to the male domain of the village coffee shop (*kafenion*) where most of the buying and selling of produce took place.

The co-operatives stem from historical traditions, but the 1980s experiment is designed to favour women exclusively. The initiator of the project, the leader of the Secretariat of Equality, said:

> The organisation of women's co-ops would be a step in giving economic independence for women. Inside the co-ops women would be politicised, they would learn democratic principles by

exercising their vote, by working on committees, by controlling the funding. They could learn the language of economics.

(Livas 1986: 2)

What are the growing pains of an experiment where the State has made a conscious effort to empower rural women? It seems that one of the issues is the difficulty emerging when a nationally and centrally conceived idea is implanted on a traditional rural economy focusing on women who have been oppressed for centuries. (Before the PASOK Government came to power rural women were not even entitled to a pension.) What does this effort at empowering rural women involve? First, it is the State which defined the course aimed at bettering the lives of rural women. The work is carried out by the women's organization, EGE (the union of Greek women), whose members also work as civil servants at the Secretariat of Equality, which is an organization with women's interests in mind. This is not a ministry, but like most Government bodies, satisfactory results have to be produced justifying the amount of investment and usage of tax payers' money. The women civil servants working on the co-op experiment at the Secretariat are all under pressure for the co-operative project to succeed and are sincere and hardworking in their continuous support. However, a conflict emerges as the women civil servants, in their roles as agents of the State, attempt to disseminate co-operative ideology to rural women who just desperately need paid work.

Conflict also emerged from partisan politics and from rival political parties and their women's organizations, whether from the left or right. Resentments, criticisms, and bitterness ensued from what other nationally-based women's groups and organizations saw as a monopoly of power for the women's organization of the PASOK party. Supporting or not supporting an experiment such as the co-operatives could be seen as a way of undermining PASOK's power, both nationally and regionally. In contrast, women in rural areas traditionally vote in line with their husband's wishes. Political or public life and the opportunity for participation and control is a very new experience for them. Dependency on the State and the ruling party leaves the co-operatives' future open to insecurity. Yet, without State support in the form of loans and training programmes the project cannot grow.

> 'I don't know what would happen if the state didn't support them (the co-ops). That's the big problem for all the co-ops. It's been the biggest problem that we had to set them up this way up to the time they would stand up to a free economy competitively. To work with the ideology of self-determination but with the economic result as private enterprise.'

(Spokeswoman Secretariat of Equality)

Not only are there set-backs due to working alongside a capitalist system, but difficulties are rooted in the particularities of Greek rural culture. Every village has its own pre-established sets of relationships and initiatives from outsiders (including the State) are usually resisted:

'Working together (*synergasia*) is difficult generally in the co-ops. The women have always learnt to say 'I'. That's a tremendous thing to face. They compare themselves to others. They keep things back and don't give what they should.'

(Spokeswoman Secretariat of Equality)

This tendency is not exclusive to women and poses problems for change in rural areas. As far back as 1962 Sanders wrote of the problems co-ops faced if the members did not see immediate results and if the credit and repayment systems failed to present the members with future long term goals. The keeping of records, membership lists, preparation of reports, and the understanding of parliamentary procedure are activities that are beyond the skills of rural people. Due to this lack of understanding there is often a 'tendency to be chronically critical of management, the Government and perhaps the whole idea of co-ops in general.' (Sanders 1962: 197).

Kinship and family organization and ideology can divide rural women, as the experience of the Ambelakia co-operative reveals. Some of the women co-op members I interviewed felt negative about the idea and only stayed in the co-op because they had committed themselves to five years. Besides this, women of different ages had differing interests. For example, married women with young or adolescent children had more interest in the co-op than young, single women or widows. One woman, a widow in her sixties, had accumulated many debts through credit allowances. She had overspent her initial loan, but repairs and changes to her house to preserve its original style had meant that she had to borrow more. She resented the repayments and the debt. Her lack of literacy skills had made her vulnerable and she was unaware of the concept of long term investment. She had gained additional comforts and improvements to her home, but a life of poverty and insecurity had made her justifiably overcautious and simple about her needs. She felt the changes to her house were a show of great extravagance and she had been victim to this. Her criticisms of the co-op were vented by traditional gossip techniques. It was difficult for her to air her grievances at co-op meetings and to resort to a different method of criticism besides gossip. A younger woman member said: 'We started off well and then there were personal interests and they wanted to cheat (*kombiness*).' Another said: 'Some women – they think some women are stealing. It's all written down – everyone can check the books. They are suspicious (*kachipopsia*). They do things behind your back.'

Yet, given the heritage of local institutions, rural culture and women's oppression it seems inevitable that the initiative for the co-ops, mobilised by feminists within the State, should be beset by a number of problems. The question raised is whether this material base can in any way pave the way for a change in consciousness among women, challenging the definitions of sexuality brought about by the *Kamaki* phenomenon. It is also necessary to question whether the material base is strong enough to survive in the context of a conservative Government. Will the co-ops evolve as a viable alternative so that women will organize themselves despite withdrawal of State funding and perhaps the removal of the Secretariat of Equality? As in the case of the women's bookshop discussed by Jane Cholmeley in Chapter 11, one of the prime factors determining the duration of the co-ops will be financial success. If women see that financial success is bound up with working together for the good of all, then the co-ops stand strong as an organization that can rival capitalistic enterprise. If the experiment also shows that a slow form of empowerment can be derived from collective work, then there is a chance of survival and a way for them to move forward.

Rumblings of change?

At the moment there are some rumblings of change despite the conflicts. In Ambelakia the financial returns were strongly and enthusiastically greeted: 'Yes, we're satisfied. It's extra for me 50,000–60,000 drachmas. Isn't that a profit (*kerdos*). It's rare to find women who work like they do in the towns.' In Ambelakia the co-op's financial viability has also ensured that the women have little interference from the men. The men were suspicious at first but: 'Somewhere they understand it's in their interests. It's not anything bad. It brings money to the village.' Besides, the work of the co-op is principally domestic so men would not be involved anyway. The course of time will see whether any change has been made in the division of labour. The president said: 'We don't want men in the co-op. If we have men they'll order us around for everything (*tha mas kani koummanto*) – for the money. We don't want men. The men help us as much as they can but outside the co-op they don't bother us.'

The co-operatives, it could be argued, reinforce rather than challenge the traditional division of labour by confining women's work to domestic tasks and perhaps doubling their workload. The course of time will tell whether any change is made in the domestic division of labour. However, it is significant that women in Ambelakia have begun to take over space originally designated to men and play a role in public life:

'It's very easy for the women in the co-op to go for a coffee to the *kafenion*, something they wouldn't do before. In Ambelakia it's happened. In the islands it's even easier. In Ambelakia they didn't go previously. The co-op office is next door to the *kafenion*. When they finish they go next door and drink. They have more of a presence there. When we go to the village we stop at the *kafenion* after five hours journey and they [the women] are with us. After one or two times this breaks slowly the fact that it's forbidden for women. Those things have happened.'

(Spokeswoman Secretariat of Equality)

The women who go to the *kafenion* (the main coffee shop/restaurant in the village) enter a male domain, but this is in the context of their work. They are not seen as overtly challenging a norm as they are going about their business, i.e. entertaining guests, receiving women co-op officials from Athens. When they are visible in these public places they are not performing leisure functions exclusive to males. (It's also questionable if they would have time to.)

Yet the women *have* entered a male domain and they perform functions relating to the outside world. This, I would argue, is an initial step in giving them access to power outside the home. This has also been achieved without upsetting any balance which can displace them from power in the home. This situation can therefore be compared positively with earlier co-operatives in rural areas. In addition the co-operative activities have expanded opportunities for women which can include travel and meetings with outsiders. They relate to the outside world on their own terms by virtue of the fact that they are involved in an important public venture. They also manage and control their own enterprise which, as Joy Lyon has argued, is a prerequisite for more fundamental change. The president said:

'The woman has come out more. She has more knowledge. Personally I met many people now with the co-op. I meet *Nomarches*, people in other services, with banks. I go and they know me now. They all know us . . . with the Secretariat of Equality in Athens, with Greeks we didn't see before.'

She also mentioned that she had attended seminars and met people from all over the country. She said: 'You speak of your difficulties there and how to face them – with the Secretariat of Equality, the Ministry of Culture.' Similarly: 'Look something has changed – your knowledge. You get to know people. You know hundreds of people' (co-op member).

Mary Castelberg-Koulma

The noticeable feature about the village of Ambelakia the night I first arrived was the presence of a number of women in the *kafenion* in the village square. Some of them led the dancing and others were eating and drinking at a large group of tables reserved for a party of German guests who were staying at the co-op. The local men, on the other hand, maintained a low profile, sitting among themselves, playing cards and backgammon, and sipping their drinks. The whole scene seemed to reiterate what the secretary had told me: that the co-op had 'opened the women's spirits'.

The women were all unanimous in finding the training programme a positive experience. Many had attended, despite having a heavy farm and domestic workload. They found their training was advantageous as it had transformed their knowledge and skills in the domestic sphere into work that would assure them an income. 'How to serve visitors in the restaurant, how to serve customers, collect plates, everything, especially for me as we have a shop; where to put forks and knives and how to cater for a big party; how to receive the guests in the rooms' (co-op member). Despite the various divisions and disagreements, the women wryly mentioned the poetic metaphor that they had heard on their training course which had affected them. The instructor had said: 'The co-op is like a pomegranite. Don't let the pomegranite open and let the seeds scatter about.' They had called the co-op restaurant 'The Pomegranite' (*to rothi*).

I had observed the pleasure and gratitude of the large party of German guests who had occupied most of the rooms. The co-op president had said: 'The service we give them, the hospitality, it's not like a hotel. The quietness (of the village) and the love the women show towards every visitor.'

Conclusion

The co-operative experiment not only contains within it the dynamic for a quality tourism and a new form of encounter between hostesses and guests, but it also constitutes a direct challenge to the present position of Greek women in relation to tourism. Whether that challenge is effectively taken up depends on maintaining the financial success of the co-ops so that the important ideological component can develop and grow. This would allow further consolidation of the experiment and provide impetus for expansion, releasing the women from dependence on tenuous and possibly impermanent State support. It would also enable women to internalize their initial empowerment and to continue to connect this with other areas of their lives.

The experiment also requires that its present successes are more widely disseminated and that policy makers themselves see it as an alternative which can benefit the majority of Greek women involved in tourism. Women in rural areas of mass tourism need to be more aware of autonomous alternatives open to them and, perhaps more importantly, women's peripherality needs to be taken more seriously. This would give women the opportunity of voicing their discontents concerning the social effects of tourism on them.

The overall success of this experiment needs to be assessed over time. At the time of writing it is in its very early stages. It cannot boast of competing with mass tourism and multinational tour operators – it was never meant to anyway. It does, however, demonstrate one way in which the racist stereotypes typical of tourism in Greece, South-East Asia and other parts of the globe can be challenged. The experience of the Ambelakia co-operative shows how women have become successful wage-earners and have improved their public position in the village and elsewhere. Any further judgement is premature. For future reference it will be of immense importance to track the changes in members' lifestyles and behaviour patterns in order to assess the impact the co-op has on their lives and relationships. The on-going financial success of the agro-tourist co-operatives is the key not only to the survival of this alternative form of organization, but to the development of changes and challenges on other levels. In this respect they are an important way of improving women's lives not only in tourism, but also in the wider public sphere.

References

Bowman, G. (1988) Fucking tourists: Sexual relations and tourism in Jerusalem's Old City. Unpublished manuscript.

Campbell, J.K. (1964) *Honour Family and Patronage. A Study of Institutions and Moral Values in a Greek Mountain Community*, Oxford: Oxford University Press.

Espin, O.M. (1984) 'Cultural and historical influences on sexuality in Hispanic/Latin women: implications for psychotherapy', in C. Vance (ed.) *Pleasure and Danger. Exploring Female Sexuality*, London: Routledge & Kegan Paul.

Friedl, E. (1962) *Vassilika. A Village in Modern Greece*, New York: Holt, Rinehart & Winston.

Gregor, S. (1985) *Village on the Plateau: Cretan Women in a Changing Economy*, PhD Thesis, University of Manchester.

Herzfeld, M. (1985) *The Poetics of Manhood*, Princeton, New Jersey: Princeton University Press.

Hirschon, R. (1978) 'Open body/closed space: the transformation of female sexuality', in S. Ardener (ed.) *Defining Females*, London: Croom Helm.

Koussis, M. (1984) *Tourism as an Agent of Social Change in a Rural Cretan Community*, PhD Thesis, University of Michigan, Ann Arbor.

Livas, H. (1986) 'Women's Co-operatives', Feature Stories, Athens News Agency, Academias 20, 4 March, Athens.

Sanders, I. (1962) *Rainbow in the Rock. The People of Rural Greece*, Cambridge: Harvard University Press.

Wikan, U. (1984) 'Shame and honour: a contestable pair', *Man* (NS) 19: 635–652.

Chapter eleven

A feminist business in a capitalist world

Silver Moon Women's Bookshop

Jane Cholmeley

Introduction

On 31 May 1984 at 9.30 a.m. a group of women gathered outside 68 Charing Cross Road for the opening of Silver Moon Women's Bookshop. Dale Spender said a few words, cut a ribbon, and we all stood on the pavement feeling exhilarated, self-conscious, determined, and terrified – each emotion assisted by an intake of champagne and orange juice. At the end of our first day's trading we had £250 in the till, spent by supportive friends who had been saving up their book purchases for us and by the passing purchasers who did not know and were not interested in the difference between Silver Moon and Mills & Boon. That £250 was the first return and outward sign of two years of planning and hard work that had brought a women's bookshop to the high street in Central London.

Why had we set ourselves this objective? How had we got there? First, I would like to consider the question – 'why?'. What motivated the two, then three, women who founded Silver Moon? Looking at the forces that defined and set up this particular challenge involves identifying a context of difficulties that we felt as individuals working in conventional structures. These had led to clashes and frustrations, out of which we were motivated to try and develop something new. 'The personal is political' has been a major political concept of recent feminism. It certainly applied to all three of us. Therefore it is appropriate, first, to examine our individual working experiences, because this was the context of our frustrations, providing the motivation for change.

In late 1980 I was in my sixth year of working for the British Printing Corporation. I was the foreign rights manager, running a department with a turnover of £1.2 million per annum and earning a good salary. I loved my job; my prospects were excellent. Then the sky fell in. Between December 1980 and April 1981 there was a four month industrial dispute when the management locked out the National Union of Journalists staff. Foreign business trips were transformed into picket line duty. The good salary became 'strike' pay of £35 per week. From my point of view, the management totally lost the good-will of their staff in their drive to maximize profits and, by their own capitalist standards, were massively incompetent, allowing the share price of the company to plummet to 13p so that the company was vulnerable to a hostile takeover bid. The takeover happened in the middle of the dispute; work was resumed; some staff left. I returned to work under specific personal guarantees – which were cynically broken within two weeks. Life at work became intolerable. Just over three months later I left with minimal severance pay. The point here is not to rehearse a drama, but to illustrate in microcosm that apparently secure conventional structures – even faithfully served – can, in fact, be precarious and frequently become intolerable. It was a totally radicalizing experience. The world would never look the same again.

Sue Butterworth, who was involved with Silver Moon from the beginning, and Jane Anger who joined a year later, both had similar experiences. The former was a conscientious and loyal editor for a leading UK bookclub. Due to what might be regarded as management ineptitude, the department she worked in became redundant and she was dispensed with. The latter, who joined Silver Moon planning in April 1983, was the only one of us to have left work voluntarily. She worked for the British Council and eventually found the structures stifling and the hierarchy oppressive. She also increasingly came to question her allegiance to the Council's political objectives. Jane resigned, stepping into the risk of Silver Moon. We were pushed; she jumped, which was a measure of both dissatisfaction and courage.

So, for various reasons each of us felt an urgent need to earn a living in a different way. Normal forms of business and government organization had been personally destructive and had formed in our minds the feminist thinking whereby we discarded them. Now, being outside, where should or could we go? It was a time for realistic assessment: what could we do? What talents and assets did we have? What changes could we envisage and, of these, which could we effect? For all of us our skills and intentions added up to books plus feminism. Without the capital to start a publishing company we targeted a feminist bookshop.

The answer to the question why we set ourselves such an objective, has so far been biographical and largely a reaction to negative circumstances. Our objective was also fundamentally focused by positive political analysis. Our intention was to provide a permanent outlet for women's writing. From Harriet Martineau via Virginia Woolf, Dale Spender, Tillie Olsen and Andrea Dworkin today, there has been a continual and valid complaint that women's voices are not heard and that women do not have access to distribution. The situation has gradually improved. *The Mill on the Floss* could now be published by Marian Evans without the necessity of a male pseudonym. Women's publishing houses do exist; women's magazines now cover more than the domestic sphere. But problems still remain. Many women/feminists are writing and many women/feminists are reading, but between the supply and the demand there is not an easy free flow. There are restrictions, problems, and prejudices that constrain the availability of women's writing. For example, The Women's Press could not get regular shelf space in many shops. Their answer to being excluded in this fashion was to create a mail order book club, but this only services the subscriber and not the occasional or new purchaser. A visit to almost any high street bookselling chain can be a sobering experience. Women's interest is defined as romance. 'Real' fiction is dominated by male writers. Women writers get nowhere near an equal or fair share of shelf space.

The Greater London Council Arts Committee had also identified this problem. In their *Bookshops Review of Policy* report (Greater London Council 1983) they stated:

> That market forces and the interest of a popular informed cultural democracy are not synonymous is, in our present society, fairly obvious. Nowhere can this be seen more clearly than in the provision and accessibility of bookshops. For some decades the number of comprehensively stocked bookshops . . . has been in decline, whilst censorious and limited range chain stores such as WH Smith and Menzies have taken over the market in bookselling.

The Greater London Council (Garnham 1983) identified that for disadvantaged groups: 'It is access to distribution which is the key to cultural plurality.'

The Greater London Council was abolished in March 1986 by the Thatcher Government. Under the leadership of Ken Livingstone the GLC had developed a radical and socialist approach to the arts. Their policy was developed by co-opted specialist advisers who examined arts resources, processes, and art forms, prioritizing the interests of groups who had never before (and have not since) had access to institutional power and money, e.g. black people, women, gays and lesbians, and disabled people.

Our priorities were similar. We felt that at critical points all along the distribution process, women's writing was and is being curtailed and restricted. Even these days, most publishers' sales forces are male, with many being uncomfortable at best and hostile at worst to women's writing. Many bookshops will not stock feminist titles, or will stock only the most obvious and unthreatening ones. In library supply, buying decisions are frequently taken at a level where job segregation has taken hold and the buyers are male. Occasionally implied hostility to women's writing bursts forth into outright prejudice; for example, Councillor Robert Davis of the City of Westminster demanded that 'the recent City Council booklet on "Books About Women" should not be permitted, especially where emphasis was given to books on "feminism" ' (*Women in Libraries Newsletter* 1983). In 1988 the passing of Clause 28 as part of the Local Government Bill prevented local government money from being spent on the 'promotion of homosexuality'. This amendment could be interpreted so that no local library or publicly funded school library would be allowed to use public funds to buy books with gay and lesbian content (unless that content is hostile). This gives legislative validity to what has previously been contained as individual bigotry.

Our tender to the Greater London Council stated: 'Many of the existing channels of book ordering, review and distribution are un-sympathetic to feminist writing, seeing it as hostile or as an exploitable passing fad. We feel it is vitally important to have a women's outlet for women's writing to ensure its promotion and continuance.' The idea of setting up a women's bookshop was an obvious challenge. A women's bookshop would be a pivotal point in the distribution system. Given the experience and resources available from each of us, it would also be a project of achievable size. Our personal needs plus our political objective together formed the motivation.

The identification of a project that is vital and achievable is a point at which idealism and realism come together into action. But founding a women's bookshop was an ambitious objective. What did we mean by it and how did we achieve it? Between April 1982 and April 1983 we began to define our concept of a women's bookshop. Through that year we developed our intentions for the bookshop. We wanted:

(i) a living wage – we could not afford to think otherwise and we believed that women should be paid for their work;
(ii) to create a bookshop to aid the spread of feminist ideas and to generate income for women writers;
(iii) as central a site as possible – we felt that it was extremely important, both politically and economically, for our women's bookshop to be out of the margins and into the centre;
(iv) above all else we wanted autonomous control of our own en-deavours.

It is worth adding here that as all three of us are lesbians, autonomy and control were especially important. To be fair to our previous employers, none of us had personally suffered direct discrimination because of our sexuality and publishing is, generally speaking, a liberal area of employment. But whenever or wherever a lesbian is employed there is always the underlying fear of discrimination. Lesbians and gay men have too often been unjustifiably sacked because of their sexuality and there is little or no legal protection. Autonomy was essential for all of us. During this year, we added the objective of setting up a women-only café within the bookshop. We intended to provide a safe and secure place for women; a prime site example of women-only space. We defined these principles as a framework for our feminist business.

After a year of theoretical dreams, there followed thirteen months of frantic activity. How did we achieve our objectives? What tasks and problems did we face? In what respect were they complicated or made easier by our feminist/political intent? From the outset we assumed a contradiction between the purposes and practices of a feminist business and the present capitalist status quo. Given our past work experience and our resistance to it, this was an understandable assumption. Was it borne out in fact? From April 1983 to May 1984 we spent every spare minute working towards the establishment of the bookshop. It was a tangled skein of events and I have therefore rationalized events into four main themes: finding premises; raising finance; forming a company; and working as feminists.

Finding premises

'The type of shop you have and the sort of people who use it, will largely be determined by where it is and what it looks like. Your choice of premises will say more than any other single factor about what you want to do with your shop' (Federation of Radical Booksellers 1984:6). As an estate agency lecturer once remarked: 'There are three things to remember about property: (i) position, (ii) position, (iii) position.' Agreement from both radical and commercial ends of the spectrum. Why? Once again, to quote from the Federation of Radical Booksellers (1984:6):

> Bear in mind that even local activists can't always be expected to make special journeys to visit you . . . . There is a danger in being located too much off the beaten track. Passing trade can be very important, and a more central and more expensive shop unit may ultimately make better sense than back street premises away from traditional shopping areas. Your stock levels and many of your overheads – wages, phone, etc. – may be the same, wherever you are located; your sales certainly won't be the same.

Practical considerations dovetailed with our political intentions. We wanted to make women's writing centrally available and highly visible as a political statement. We intended this as both a declaration of validity to all feminists and as a major technique of outreach into the general market-place.

217

Intentions are all very well, but how realizable are they? The Federation of Radical Booksellers say 'your *choice* of premises', but is there in fact a choice? We began with a map – the first capital investment of Silver Moon – on which we marked all the other feminist and radical bookshops and their assumed catchment areas. It would be impolitic and economically stupid to gatecrash someone else's local territory. We originally targeted West London. Every Saturday and Sunday Sue and I went walking the streets with our new puppy in tow. It was a miserable and rainy spring. Our notebooks got soggy and illegible. We got wetter and more distressed as the weekends went by. We learned to watch for the 'sunny side of the street', which way the pedestrian traffic turned from the tube stations or bus stop – 10 yards the wrong way can kill you – where was the hub and where the periphery? We tried guessing where an area would be in five to ten years' time – going up or declining? We watched and scribbled and got tired feet.

Once we began to get the feel of an area, we then had to gather practical details of square footage and costs. West London – ranging very approximately around Portobello Road, Queensway, and Marylebone High Street – we discovered to be sky-high unobtainable. Most of the property was owned by institutions and pension funds. A rare freehold of very small size could command a price of £300,000 (1983 prices) and, leasehold, could be rented for approximately £20,000 p.a., plus rates, plus premium. We also discovered a prime catch-22: many agents would not even send property details to someone who was not already an established trader.

We moved areas towards Covent Garden, Holborn, and the British Museum. The available units were more mixed, therefore more possible; prices were still high and premiums higher still. The centrality of our aim looked beyond our grasp. We began to think that we had been utterly unrealistic. The economics of specialist bookselling and the supply and demand conditions of the London property market seemed to be in two different worlds. No wonder that under this framework, high street bookselling is becoming more and more concentrated in the hands of the powerful chain stores.

Then on 16 April 1983 we had one of those pieces of luck that you can scarcely believe. The Greater London Council advertised two shop units on the Charing Cross Road with the proviso that 'consideration will be confined solely to bookshop use' (*The Bookseller* 1983:1453). All the footslogging and depressing calculations that we had been doing in the preceding twelve months made us recognize what a once in a lifetime opportunity this was. We were in the right place at the right time. Our thoughts, planning, and motivation had prepared us to move fast. The GLC wanted to preserve the traditional character of the

Charing Cross Road. In addition, our project was in line with the policy priorities of the GLC. However it would be untrue to say that the GLC let us have the lease on 68 Charing Cross Road purely because we proposed to set up a feminist bookshop. It might have been my hope, but there is certainly no evidence to suggest it. Indeed, the Council's Valuation Department was obliged 'to act in a reasonably business like manner having regard to the Council's fiduciary duty to its ratepayers' (Greater London Council 1982:1). The GLC wanted a bookshop on our site, not a video shop or yet another T-shirt and jeans shop. That they got a feminist bookshop in one of the outlets (the other became an art bookshop) was, I hope, a bonus for them. It certainly was for us. 'Working for London' and caring for the quality of life in London, the GLC's particular brand of cultural intervention broke the property impasse. Not only did we get a central site, we got a site on *the* bookselling road of the UK.

The process from seeing the advertisement for 68 Charing Cross Road on 16 April 1983 to eventually signing the lease on 31 October 1984 was complicated and fraught. Legal technicalities and planning permissions had to be sorted out. At one time we faced demands for open-ended personal guarantees of around £100,000 plus. We even got caught in the so-called Paving Act – Local Government (Interim Provision) Act 1984 – which, during the Government's dismemberment of the GLC, gave the Minister of State power to oversee the disposition of all GLC leases, including ours. Five months after we had started trading, our lease was finally approved. The whole process from beginning to look for premises to a signed lease had taken two and a half long and difficult years, but the prize of a women's bookshop, proudly and centrally on the Charing Cross Road, was an achievement beyond even our wildest dreams.

Raising finance

On 22 June 1983 we had an offer of a prime site bookshop in the most famous bookselling street in the UK. We had provisionally accepted a rent of £7,000 p.a. exclusive. The first thing we had to establish was how much capital we needed and how we could raise it. The building was utterly dilapidated and we had to calculate the capital costs of renovation, fixtures, fittings, stock, fees and insurances, etc. We then had to prepare business plans of income and expenditure to prove to sources of finance (and ourselves) that the scheme would be viable. An architect friend gave us an estimate for the cost of rebuilding. We estimated the rest of our capital costs by rudimentary but effective methods, e.g. number of feet of shelving x average number of books per foot x average cost of a Women's Press paperback = £16,000 for the cost of stock. To estimate the cost of the café, we sat with catalogues and costed every item we could think of. After sixty-three hours we arrived at the overall capital figure of £64,156.56. This figure was later revised, by cost savings, to £47,214.

This £47,214 seemed an enormous amount of money to raise, but I never doubted that we could do so. Four types of sources were obvious ones to approach: (i) the GLC; (ii) family, friends and ourselves; (iii) banks; and (iv) other grant giving bodies. We approached fifteen different grant giving bodies without success. In trying to get grants and donations we adopted the tactic of separating out a small item of the costs and trying to tailor it to the interests of the prospective donor; e.g. we approached the Greater London Arts Association for assistance to set up the art gallery component; we approached disability charities for contributions towards the very high costs of the access building works. However, we failed to meet the necessary criteria: for the Greater London Enterprise Board, we were not creating enough jobs – only four and they required a minimum of twenty at that time; for the Arts Council, their definition of community bookshops was 'bookshops in positions where none other is available: and this can hardly be said of the Charing Cross Road' (Arts Council 1983). Obviously the Arts Council define community by geography only. The GLC thinking that defined a community bookshop as 'any bookshop (that) operates in a geographical area of social or cultural need, *or that caters for a specific group with particular social or cultural needs* (my italics)' (Greater London Council 1983:5) was obviously too liberal an interpretation for the Arts Council to swallow. As our shop was in the City of Westminster and we would be paying our rates to Westminster City Council, we also asked it for financial support. The City of Westminster, the second richest borough in the UK, was totally unhelpful: no loans schemes; no job creation schemes; they did not even reply to our requests for information about disablement provision.

Our unsuccessful (and indeed our successful) attempts to obtain finance were an object lesson in the criteria and definitions which are used to control access to finance. We discovered some very interesting control mechanisms. Most donating charities give to trusts and charities. A commercial enterprise that needs assistance for a non-commercial purpose, e.g. access for the disabled, does not qualify. Furthermore, charitable aims must not be political. Building water troughs for thirsty horses is charitable, but trying to change the second class citizen status of 52 per cent of the population – women – is political, and therefore not allowable. But the GLC was a grant giving body where the criteria did fit. The GLC priorities were, *inter alia*, that: funds should be sought from other sources, not just the GLC; and

> Highest priority will be given to those projects which are trying to
> establish permanent facilities, participation in a communication
> and distribution network, such as a community bookshop . . . to
> encourage a greater involvement of women . . . gay groups . . .
> where possible groups should show a democratic and collective
> working process, e.g. equal wages, group policy management.
>
> (GLC 1984:5)

They could have been written for us. All of the previous criteria had
been reversed by the GLC; still the piper calls the tune, of course, but a
totally different tune, with funds to back it up. Our application for
£32,614 was submitted on 30 June 1983 (the revised figure of £47,214
having been reduced by raising nearly £15,000 from other sources), and
after seven months of being put under the microscope financially and
politically, the grant was given on 17 February with the words: 'Given
the crucial importance of feminism, there is an undoubted need for a
new community bookshop and women's club . . . Silver Moon is a
project of strategic importance' (Arts and Recreation Committee
1983:4).

In addition to the generous GLC grant, we had also approached our
bank for a loan of £15,000 under the Government's Business Guarantee
Scheme. We fully expected the loan to be given; the amount was
modest, our business plan was sound. My only anxiety was that interest
rates, running then at 14 per cent, would be a heavy burden to bear.
Extraordinarily, we did not get our loan. Five months after the
application had been submitted, the bank manager wrote us a virtually
incoherent letter saying that he had forgotten to process the application. I do not believe that there was anything sinister in this; just a
case of inefficiency. The manager was transferred shortly afterwards
and we withdrew the application, no longer needing the loan. The new
bank manager who, unlike his predecessor, does not make jokes about
the GLC giving 'all that money to the ladies', is supportive but not
intrusive.

Finally, we raised approximately £15,000 from friends and relations.
Two well-known authors between them lent us £1,500 at 6 per cent
interest (matched to deposit account rates). Our families lent us £7,000
interest free. This was generous and humbling because none of them
would describe themselves as feminists. They supported us personally,
but did not subscribe to the aims of the shop. (I am glad to say that all
these loans were paid back in full within three years.) Sue and I provided
the balance of the money.

The amount of capital finally available to us was £47,214, of which
£32,614 came from the GLC and £14,600 from personal sources. Such
a situation raises two important questions: (i) could we have created

Silver Moon without the GLC grant? and (ii) how did the sources of money affect the distribution of control within Silver Moon?

First, could we have created Silver Moon without the GLC grant? Without the GLC we could have raised the £14,600 personally and a bank loan of £15,000 or maybe a little more. So would approximately £30,000 have been enough compared with the £47,214 we did have? The GLC were extremely clever and frugal in their grant giving, contrary to the accusations of profligacy that central government has levelled at them. They insisted that we spend half of their money on the building (the other half being spent on stock which could have been redeemed). Their dilapidated building was refurbished and made good by their capital and our labour; an ideal partnership.

Without the GLC we would have had to set our sights lower, starting with the bookshop only and not the café (ironically, as it turned out), skimping on the building work and doing more ourselves, leaving the basement floor as it was – an utter mess and closed to the public – taking more extended credit from publishers on stock, etc., but it would have been possible. Since opening the shop we have spent substantial amounts (approximately £6,000 per annum) on improvements, as well as paying back £12,000 worth of loans. Had we started at a lower threshold of say £35,000, the money would have been allocated differently and we would have reached our opening level of stock, building alterations, etc. about eighteen months later. But of course the GLC grant gave us more than hard cash, it gave us confidence, impetus, and the financial cushion to make a few mistakes without their being fatal. We owe the GLC an enormous debt of gratitude, but without them all is not lost. Without GLC money it would have been slower and harder, but I am convinced that it would have been possible.

Second, questions of control were a constant theme through our fund-raising efforts. One of our primary objectives in setting up Silver Moon was to have control of our own endeavour. In addition to the requirements given above, the GLC laid down two further conditions: (i) that 'the group give an undertaking that should they cease operation within five years they will refund to the Council the value of the equipment to date'; and (ii) that we 'agree that in the event of any profit being achieved at any time within the next five years these profits should be spent on bookshop activities' (Arts and Recreation Committee 1983:1, Appendix IV). Hopefully, the first condition would not arise and we would be complying with the second condition anyway, as sound business sense. The £14,600 personally raised came without any external strings attached. Questions of control did, however, arise internally in that two of us had provided £14,600 of personal finance and the third person had not been able to contribute. This imbalance led to repercussions to which I refer later.

Forming a company

Three hardworking feminists do not a corporate entity make. We knew the bank would insist on some recognisable legal entity, and the addition of a third and later fourth person to the team obviously had structural implications. What choices were available and what were the implications of each? This was all new research to us and during the course of it we discovered some fascinating implications. At the beginning we identified five options: partnership; collective; co-operative; charity; and company limited by share capital. Some of these were easily dispensed with.

Partnership? The bank disapproved. There is no limited liability (though we quickly learned that the notion of limited liability is much hedged around by personal guarantees). Moreover, a partnership is usually deemed more suitable for the professions, e.g. solicitors and architects, than for a commercial organization. Collective? A collective has no legal entity. A co-operative? Our information was that a co-operative must have seven members. We were only three and we felt that to have a majority of 'sleeping' non-involved members would be neither sensible nor desirable. Charity? Unfortunately, improving the status of women is deemed a political and not a charitable aim. The Charity Commissioners and the Women's Liberation Movement, from their different perspectives, would probably agree on this.

That left us with the absolutely standard, off-the-peg, capitalist path of a company limited by share capital. Silver Moon Limited was legally formed in July 1983 with the all-encompassing Memorandum of Association that stated: 'The objects for which the company is established are (A) (I) To carry on business as greengrocers, grocers, fruiterers, suppliers, growers, distributors, exporters, importers, retailers and dealers generally in all articles of food and consumable items and *to carry on business as a women's bookshop and café*' (this last added in a different typeface). We immediately fell foul of the GLC's company's criteria which quite reasonably would not give public money to a company structure that could make and keep private profits. The GLC insisted that we re-form as a company limited by guarantee. As this type of legal entity we can take normal business decisions; this second Memorandum of Association defines the aims and objects of the company and states: 'The income and property of the Association shall be applied solely towards the promotion of its objects . . . .' We moved from greengrocery to more sympathetic aims: 'to promote and provide an outlet for writing by and for women; facilitate the extension of women's networks, promote women's training and education, provide a safe meeting place for women.'

The significance of this change of legal status is that a company limited by guarantee is grounded in co-ownership philosophy. During the company's life (and also if the company is discontinued for any reason), its objectives cannot be changed nor its assets personally pocketed. Thus, a company limited by guarantee is not designed as a capitalist vehicle for private profit. Similar to the labour movement co-operatives in ideals, it also meets the need of very small numbers, i.e. under seven members. A company limited by guarantee is a rather clever hybrid. In a small and somewhat unpublished way, this legal form is in itself a challenge and vehicle for change. In terms of 'start-up' we were on our way. Obviously, there were scores of other questions to settle and work to be done, but the three essentials of finding premises, raising finance, and forming a company had been achieved.

Working as feminists

By 1988 Silver Moon was nearly four years old in trading terms (six from conception). In those four years we learned, developed, and made changes. We made mistakes and we made improvements. We tested out theories (ours and other people's) and found some wanting and some entirely appropriate. The whole process was exciting and exacting. The most noticeable change at Silver Moon over this time was the closure of the café in August 1985 and the subsequent expansion of books into the basement in May 1986. Even today women come in and ask for the café. The café was such an optimistic and integral part of our dream. 'The café will provide a safe, comfortable, confident and secure meeting space for women' we had declared in our financial proposal to the bank. We had expanded this rationale in our grant application to the GLC: 'We believe that women have traditionally suffered in mixed space, men invariably taking up more room while making more noise. Women are too often harassed in wine bars and cafés or are made to feel uncomfortable in the 'male space' of pubs. We deserve and need our own space.' Many women loved the café; felt the bookshop/café combination to be an ideal. Others, including Sisterwrite, warned us of a financial drain and massive labour commitment; they were right. On a good day, with gales of women's laughter resounding up the stairs, we were reminded of Emma Goldman: 'The sound of women's laughter is the sound of revolution!' But unfortunately, the good days were too few and too far between. We got certain essentials wrong. The café, with 24 seats, was too small to be viable. Our planning permission did not allow us to cook and we did not have room to do so. We could only serve cold food and hot soup – not ideal for the British climate. None of us had worked in the catering industry; that we felt we could run half of our new business from a foundation of ignorance showed a terrifying optimism/arrogance. The café was not visible from the street which was detrimental. Sandwich bars and other eating places all around us were packed with office workers at lunch time, but we never learned how to reach that market. I think there was a not entirely unfounded suspicion that the Silver Moon café was a lesbian meeting place! This deterred the daily office trade we needed.

In May 1985 we applied for a beer, wine, and cider licence in an attempt to upgrade the café. After all, there is more profit on a bottle of wine than a cup of coffee, and it raised possibilities of evening opening and giving the shop a more social/community function. The application was a long and exceedingly expensive operation and in the end we failed to get a licence. The licensing justices of Westminster in their 'wisdom' deemed that as a women-only club, we could not have a licence because we did not have a gent's toilet. It was inconceivable to them that we would not, sooner or later, let men in! The licence failure spelt the death knell for the café. Economic reality had to overcome sentiment. The café covered its direct costs, but never its overheads. Furthermore, the anxieties about it were pulling all our thoughts and efforts away from the bookshop, which was the viable and functioning part of the business. When Suzanne, our fourth worker, decided to take time off to travel, we felt we could not offer a job that was so much under review. In August 1985 we closed the café.

Running the Silver Moon café for fifteen months had thrown up some interesting attitudes. At its best it was exhilarating, but it had its downside too. The attitudes of women customers to the women serving in the bookshop and café differed remarkably. In the café one often became wallpaper, a functionary putting the cake on the plate or the coffee in the cup. In the bookshop, one's service was seen as more advisory and knowledgeable. In the café nearly all our food was home-made, woman-made, and with very good ingredients. It was also competitive in price; cheaper than the food sold in most of the sandwich bars down the road. Nevertheless, time and time again we would hear 'It's lovely to have a place that's central, but your food/coffee is so expensive'. We were acutely aware that women's average earnings are considerably less than those of men and that many of our customers were unemployed, but conversely we often got profoundly depressed by the customers' failure to understand the economic facts of paying rent, rates, overheads, and the persistent undervaluing of our own efforts and those of our women suppliers. Finally, the café as women-only space was a red rag to a bull. We were reported to the EOC for sex discrimination – an inaccurate and easily thrown out charge. We suffered frequent aggressive outbursts from men and even from women in the shop. We were sad when we closed the café, but not so sad.

A second major area of change and learning, to which I have already referred above, was that of job rotation and the theory and practice of working together. We were all working so hard that we had devoted little thought to this important issue. What was our experience? Our company had been formed in March 1984, but although this gave us a legal entity it offered no indication or guide as to how we would choose to work together. We had made various assumptions, namely, that there would not be a managing director and minions, we assumed equal pay and holidays, job rotation, skill sharing, equal hours and benefits, commitment, and responsibility. Having worked in unsatisfactory hierarchies before, we were all looking for equality of risk and effort, responsibility and reward.

Taking, first, the issue of our choice of work pattern. We had decided on job rotation. This was a concept much advocated in certain parts of the women's liberation movement. Job rotation had developed from the view that job specialization involved holding on to skills, information, and knowledge, thus creating power bases that could be used by employee against employee or more obviously, within a hierarchy, to set one person above another. In response to this, the concept of job rotation was designed to share knowledge, and prevent the accumulation of power. Furthermore, by learning and sharing many skills it was intended to de-mystify certain tasks. For example, in our context, if everyone at some time paid the wages, did the VAT return, made up the cash book, checking 'actuals' against 'budgets', then financial administration would become an easy companion rather than an alien focus of power. Similarly if everyone served on the till, or in the café, dealing for eight and a half hours a day with constant queries, demands for tourist information and washing-up, each of us would intimately understand the rewards and stresses of that particular job.

We chose job rotation for a mixture of reasons. We had all been dissatisfied with traditional work practices and were resistant to replicating them at Silver Moon. Previously we had been employees; now we had virtual *carte blanche* to try something new; a huge opportunity set against a background of reaction coupled with inexperience. We were founding a new venture and were very idealistic. Moreover, job rotation was the political currency of the day, and this external expectation influenced our thinking. It was something of a pendulum swing from job specialization to job rotation. How did we fare?

We started at the end of May 1984 with full job rotation on a two weekly cycle. There were four jobs: (i) till; (ii) administration; (iii) café; (iv) floater – who did lunch and tea reliefs, ran errands, and provided general back-up wherever it was needed. By September 1984 we had an easily identifiable crisis of communication and accountability. We were losing approximately one working day out of ten per person, because the first morning and the last afternoon of each fortnight was taken up with 'nesting in' and 'handing over' respectively. Given our intensely crowded working conditions, perpetually succeeding to someone else's workspace was deeply irritating. It felt as though just as you had settled to a job you enjoyed and did well, you had to transfer to a job that you did not enjoy as much or did less well.

There were also profound problems of accountability; e.g. if A queried an invoice in June, did B in July, without the benefit of memory, have the right information to act on? We were accumulating little messages, most of which were inadequate. Similarly, and just as critical from the customers' point of view, they never knew who they were dealing with. Communication on customer orders got blurred as the woman who had started the process went off to the café for two weeks. A third example was stock ordering. Our stock levels behaved like yo-yos as the ordering process passed from person to person and inevitable likes and dislikes crept in. The running of the shop was becoming dangerously sloppy. In September 1984 we ended job rotation, except for the café. We divided out specific tasks and responsibilities according to skills and preferences. Everyone still did two weeks in the café in rotation. Because it was each person's least favourite job, we felt we should still take turns. The shop began to function more smoothly. It was better for the customers and for us.

Equality and power

We also faced more comprehensive challenges in terms of the theory and practice of working together. What levels of equality did we have? What were the job/power relations of Silver Moon? On the one hand we had a team of totally dedicated women, each magnificently committed to the project; each working incredibly hard, bringing in skills, ideas, and effort. On the other hand, by our opening in May 1984, we already had significant imbalances; (i) length of involvement in the project – two years, one year, and two months; (ii) three full-time workers and one part-time worker; (iii) financial imbalances – is dedication of labour equal or not equal to dedication of labour *plus* financial contribution?; (iv) risk imbalances – three out of four of the workers were personally responsible for heavy financial guarantees and, of the three guarantors, one had no tangible assets, so that in fact the risk genuinely fell on only two of us.

The issues gradually surfaced after April 1983, when the team grew from the original two to three. It was suggested that we examine and deal with these tensions via workshop sessions. The suggestion was not taken up, partly due to a fear of confronting our feelings and partly due to the intense pressure of 'concrete' problems such as builders, fund raising and buying equipment and stock. The issue of an appropriate feminist way of working was swept under the carpet.

It surfaced again in March 1984, prompted by the interviewing for our fourth worker. Three of us had worked for a year with no formal structure and we were not entirely content with this. It called to mind the discussion put forward by Jo Freeman (1970) in her 'Tyranny of structurelessness' in which she criticized the women's liberation movement (and other radical movements) for advocating structurelessness as a solution to the problem of oppressive structures. Freeman argued that structurelessness is an illusion and organizationally impossible. The lack of a formal structure, she says, means not structurelessness, but the uninhibited interplay of informal and unacknowledged structures.

Having swept this issue under the carpet a year before, we still did not deal with it fully. We developed a dual structure. On a day-to-day basis all workers at Silver Moon would work equally and, if possible, by consensus. Underlying this was the 'bottom line', in that the three 'founder members' as we were already calling ourselves by March 1984, i.e. those who were responsible for the financial guarantees, had the final say. This *modus vivendi* has worked more or less well. There were worries that 'bottom line' power would intrude into day-to-day working and it does somewhat. We have had our share of problems: problems over quantity and quality of work input; problems over full- and part-time working; communications problems caused by time pressure, which is constant and frequently intense, and by abrupt personalities (usually mine). Use of the term *modus vivendi* is deliberate, because to say solution would have overstated the case. We exist with contradictory structures which reflect the real imbalances between the 'founders' and the subsequent workers.

With regard to such working relations Silver Moon is a living case study of a major theoretical problem of the women's liberation movement. What is equality among women? We come to the women's liberation movement steeped in our differences of class, race, sexuality, education, skills, financial resources, dependants, etc. Can we be fair and equal to each other? It seems a theoretical nut that the women's liberation movement has yet to crack – if it wants to, if it can.

At Silver Moon our experience has been fluid and changing. When Jane Anger, our third founder member, left in October 1986, we expanded from three full-timers plus one part-timer to two full-timers and five part-timers. This led to a significant realignment of the power balances. In February 1988 there was another change to three full-timers and three part-timers. Problems over time commitment resulted from having more part-time staff; e.g. if someone is working two days a week to support her writing or her college studies, is it justifiable to spend one evening per week on a staff meeting? We changed our meetings from weekly, in the mornings before work, to monthly in the evenings. With more part-timers there were problems of organization. We tried to resolve these by restructuring the staff meetings and by including a meal. Adding a meal and socializing to the staff meeting helped everyone to get to know each other; unfortunately it also increased the pressure as the evening wore on and everyone got more and more tired. Consequently we are now trying a new format: monthly staff meetings for business and quarterly dinners for fun. More part-time workers also increased our communications problems. Our deliberate informality occasionally resulted in people not receiving the information they needed. Rather to my surprise the solution to this has been traditional office paperwork, i.e. inter-staff memos and the pre-meeting circulation of agenda.

All this growth and change has taken place against the constant pressure of running a business in which we need to be able to make quick responses. Understanding and caring for the needs of those who work together is vital; *so too* is providing the best possible service to our customers. Silver Moon exists to bring women's writing to its readership and if we do not do that well we will fail. We always have to bear in mind that we serve the customer first. That is what the women (and men) we serve want – not to come second to a display of collective angst.

The past four years have been full of challenges; a time of testing traditional and alternative ways of working as we learned more and as circumstances changed. In retrospect, we were foolish not to have addressed these questions sooner and more profoundly. We had to learn the hard way through our mistakes, to make many changes and to evolve our present style of management – yes, we even use the term. Decisions about fundamentals, such as hiring, financial planning, and overall policy, are made, after consultation, by the two women who guarantee the lease. Everything else – publicity, author readings, window displays, organization in the shop, buying books from publishers, budget information – is open to everyone. This is a revised *modus vivendi* which currently seems satisfactory. Decisions are shared and made quickly; staff are involved without overload; there is more clarity of communication and better control. It has been hard going; a pragmatic evolution. The result appears to challenge the traditional hierarchies of capitalism as well as the dogma associated with collectives and consensus; we have ended up somewhere in the middle.

Reaching out

Having discussed the problems at length, I want to conclude on an up-swing. As we have grown and become more confident we have been able to initiate some very exciting additions. In 1987 we ran our first creative writing course. We have now organized three, all of which have been hugely popular and over-subscribed. Clearly, there is an eager demand to which we are ideally suited to respond. Writing courses will continue to be in our calendar. We also organize readings and discussions which have varied in content from poetry to detective fiction. In each year's programme we aim for a balance of fiction and non-fiction, and we always ensure good access to and by lesbian and black women writers. Our invited authors have ranged from relative unknowns to 'household names' such as P.D. James and Fay Weldon. Similarly, we have received authorial support by way of signing sessions from internationally acclaimed authors such as Margaret Atwood (shortlisted for the Booker Prize) and Toni Morrison (winner of the Pulitzer Prize). When Maya Angelou did a signing for us we had a line of people stretching for 75 yards down the Charing Cross Road pavement – a magnificent sight!

One of the most important developments of which we are justifiably proud is Sue Butterworth's creation *The Silver Moon Quarterly*. This is an eight page publication with reviews, book notices, and news from the shop. We mail it world-wide. Not only does it create sales of feminist books for us (and no doubt other shops), but it reaches out world-wide with information and news, giving a very important sense of connectedness and feedback.

Running a feminist bookshop is so much more than putting the books in the bag and the money in the till. We are also an information point and resource centre. Ten telephone calls a day (at least) attest to people using us for reference; everything from the addresses of women's centres to what music is playing where this week (though we do try and draw the line at having to check women's thesis footnotes for them!). We also give publicity to numerous women's causes and services by making available leaflets in the shop and on our noticeboard. Silver Moon networks just by existing. How often I have heard a customer say 'I've never seen so many women's books in one place!'. Within our display, we particularly highlight lesbian books and black women's writing on the main floor of the shop – not hidden in a discreet or uneconomic corner, but confident and featured. Publishing and commerce are as white, male, and heterosexist as the rest of society, so we enjoy saying 'We're here too!'. The networking and drawing together of resources for our customers is highlighted by our usefulness to teachers and librarians. The bringing together of thousands of feminist, lesbian, black women's, anti-sexist, and anti-racist books makes it easier for teachers and librarians to view and select. By the hard work and dedication of teachers and librarians more of these books are in schools and are available for general public access through libraries.

Measuring where we are against the aims we set ourselves, the assessment is good: (i) a living wage – we started with three and three-fifths jobs and now have four and two-fifths – all are paid and the conditions and flexibility compare favourably with elsewhere in the trade; (ii) to aid the spread of feminist ideas and to generate income for women writers – I believe that our sales have expanded the market for women writers, we have helped put royalties in women's pockets and have aided the viability and advance of women's publishing, furthermore we have given a market place for books, e.g. lesbian books and books by black women writers that other outlets decline to stock; (iii) as central a site as possible – the Charing Cross Road is the premier book selling street in the UK, we are accessible to our London customers, we are easily visited by tourists from out of London and abroad, we have customers from Alaska to Zimbabwe; (iv) above all else we wanted – and we have – autonomous control of our own endeavours. The creation of Silver Moon is one way, among many, of applying our feminist principles within a capitalist context.

Finally, is it worth recounting?

Yes, in a brief three point answer. First, when we were starting work on Silver Moon it felt as though we were re-inventing the wheel at every turn. I would have welcomed the opportunity to read of similar experiences. Second, in the last four years we have answered numerous enquiries from women and women's groups as to how we started, what problems we had to meet and solve, and what our experiences were. Clearly, there is a demand for information; there is a need to know how alternatives can be created. Finally, as a basic principle, women's work should be recorded. What we do when we set out to challenge the status quo is important. The changes we make, whether agreed with or not, should be a matter of record, not consigned to oblivion. As Amelia Earhart (1937:2) said 'thereby establishing themselves as persons, and perhaps encouraging other women towards greater independence of thought and action.'

Acknowledgements

My thanks to Sue Butterworth, without whom none of this would have been possible, and to Thea Sinclair, who would not let this fish get away.

References

Arts Council (1983) Letter from Marghanita Laski, Chairman (*sic*) of the Literature Panel.

Arts and Recreation Committee (1983) *Report by the Director of Recreation and the Arts*, London: GLC.

Bookseller, The (1983), London: J. Whitaker & Sons Ltd.

Earhart, A. (1937) *The Last Flight*, New York: Putnam.

Federation of Radical Booksellers (1984) *Starting a Bookshop*, Lancaster: FRB.

Freeman, J. (1970) 'The tyranny of structurelessness', in *Untying the Knot, Feminism, Anarchism and Organisation*, London: Dark Star Press & Rebel Press.

Garnham, N. (1983) *Concepts of Culture, Public Policy and the Cultural Industries*, London: GLC.

Greater London Council (1982) *Report by Head of Legal Branch to the Arts and Recreation Committee re. Draft Policy Statement for the Financial Support of Community Based Bookshop Projects in Greater London*, London: GLC.

—— (1983) *Bookshops Review of Policy* Report by Director of Industry and Employment and Chief Economic Adviser, London: GLC.

—— (1984) *A Guide to GLC Grant Aid for Voluntary and Community Organisations*, London: GLC.

Women in Libraries (1983) *Newsletter* 11.

Name index

Abdel-Fadil, M. 108
African Training and Research
   Centre for Women 172
Afshar, H. 105
Alday, L. 80
Alexander, S. 43
Amsden, A.H. 5
Angelou, M. 230
Anger, J. 214, 228
Antoniou, C.L. 203
Aquino, C. 96
Armstrong, P. 12, 14, 62, 66
Arrufat, J.L. 12
Arts and Recreation Committee 221,
   222
Arts Council 220
Ash, J. 94, 97
Atwood, M. 230
Awanohara, S. 90

Barnett, H. 82
Barron, R.D. 150
Barry, K. 87, 89, 98–9
Beale, J. 151
Beck, L. 105
Becker, G.S. 29
Beechey, V. 10, 11, 39
Beneria, L. 7, 10, 175, 177
Bhachu, P. 12
Bondfield, M. 45
Bookseller, The 218
Boserup, E. 176
Boulding, E. 10
Bowler, L. 132
Bowman, G. 199

Brandt, V. 84
Braverman, H. 35
Broadbridge, A. 12, 15, 16, 42, 62
Brownmiller, S. 89
Bruce, J. 188
Bruegel, I. 7, 10, 11
Bryan, B. 11
Bryceson, D.F. 88
Bukh, J. 177
Butterworth, S. 214, 230
Buvinic, M. 188

Cain, G. 7, 8, 9
Campbell, B. 139, 142–3
Campbell, J.K. 200
Carlin, N. 130, 139
Castelberg-Koulma, M. 11, 17, 20,
   84, 92, 100, 119, 190
Cavendish, R. 126
Chang-Michell, P. 84
Chib, S.N. 94
Chiplin, B. 61
Cholmeley, J. 20, 208
Claire, R. 92, 98, 100
Clark, A. 43
Cliff, T. 126, 131
Cockburn, C. 2, 9, 14, 30–2
Cohen, E. 81, 83, 87
Collier, P. 6
Cottingham, J. 92, 98, 100
Craig, C. 12, 13, 66

Dale, T. 44
Davis, K. 90
Davis, R. 216

233

Delphy, C. 144
Dennis, N. 134
Department of Employment 42, 50, 150
Dixon, R. 183–4
Doeringer, P.B. 28
Dworkin, A. 214

Earhart, A. 231
Ecevit, Y. 11–12, 14, 16, 18, 36, 48, 50, 153
Economist, The 92–3
Ehrenreich, B. 90
Elliott, C.M. 172
Elson, D. 13, 62, 64, 66, 86, 88
Erder, L. 58
ESCAP\FAO 187
Espin, O.M. 200–1
Evans, J. 131
Evans, M. 215

Fanon, F. 79
Far Eastern Economic Review 80, 95
Federation of Radical Booksellers 217
Fine, B. 130
Firestone, S. 144
Freeman, J. 228
Friedl, E. 199
Fryer, R.H. 151

Gagnon, J.H. 81, 83
Game, A. 2, 46, 49
Gardiner, J. 131
Garnham, N. 215
Goldman, E. 224
Golley, L. 80, 87
Gott, R. 99
Greater London Council (GLC) 215, 219, 220–1
Gregor, S. 202
Gronau, R. 10
Grossman, R. 86
el-Guindi, F. 107

Hakim, C. 7
Hamermesh, D.S. 4, 8
Hantrakul, S. 80, 82, 85–7, 95, 97

Harris, O. 11
Harrison, M. 151
Hartmann, H. 32–3, 72
Harwood, C. 131
Heath, E. 129
Heckman, J.J. 4, 10
Hein, C. 61
Herzfeld, M. 198
Herzog, M. 62
Heyzer, N. 13, 62
Higgins, J. 151
Himmelweit, S. 10
Hirschon, R. 199
Holcombe, L. 43–5, 49
Holden, P. 98
Hoodfar, H. 16, 105, 108, 110, 120
Huang, N.C. 60
Hunt, J. 149
Hunt, P. 126, 140
Huntington, S. 176

Ingham, J. 139
ISIS 90, 92

Jain, D. 184–5, 190
James, P.D. 230
Jefferys, J.B. 43–4, 48
Joekes, S. 62
John, A. 130
Josephides, S. 11
Joshi, H. 4, 6, 10

Karl, M. 192
Keddie, N. 105
Kikue, T. 91
Killingsworth, M.R. 4, 10
Kirsch, A.T. 85
Knight, J.B. 6
Koray, T. 57
Koussis, M. 199, 201

Lancaster, K. 45
Lee, W. 16, 17, 19, 202
Lele, U. 175
Lenze, I. 80, 90, 95
Leonard, A. 11, 19, 127–8, 169
Leuthold, J. 4
Lever, A. 13

Lilley, M. 133
Lindbeck, A. 8
Lindsey, K. 83
Livas, H. 206
Livingstone, K. 215
Loach, L. 132, 143, 146
Luck, M. 11, 14, 16, 17–18, 50, 53, 65, 150, 169
Lyon, J. 19, 100, 209

McCrindle, J. 139
McGregor, I. 129
Mackintosh, M. 11, 32–3
MacLeod, A. 106, 110, 112, 116, 119–20
Macurdy, T.E. 4
Magas, B. 142
Mallier, A.T. 6
Marcos, F. 96, 98
Martin, J. 54
Martineau, H. 214
Marx, K. 125
Matsui, Y. 91
el-Messiri, S. 108, 117
Millar, R. 130
Miller, J. 146
Millett, K. 83, 88, 90, 144
Mincer, J. 5
Mingmongkol, S. 95
Mitter, S. 10, 13
Mohun, S. 10
Molyneux, M. 10, 99
Montgomery, M. 10
Morrison, T. 230
Moser, C. 10
Musa, N. 106

Nabarawi, S. 106
Nashat, G. 105
Nasser, G. 107–8
Neumann, A.L. 81, 86–7
Norris, G.M. 150

Oakley, A. 43, 127, 137
Ocampo, S. 87, 92, 95
Ocampo-Kalfors, S. 95
O'Donovan, K. 15
Office of Population Censuses and
Surveys 42, 149–50
Okonjo, K. 188
Olesen, T. 214
Ong, A. 85

Palmer, I. 193
Papandreou, G. 203
Papanek, H. 174
Park Chung Hee 96
Pastner, C.M. 104, 106
Pearson, R. 13, 62, 64, 66, 86, 88
Perkins, T. 11, 39
Perpinan, M.S. 96
Phelps, E.S. 29
Pheterson, G. 91
Philipp, T. 107
Phillips, A. 13, 31, 88
Phoenix, A. 11
Phongpaichit, P. 80, 82–3, 85–8, 92, 95, 98, 99
Piker, S. 85
Piore, M.J. 28
Polachek, S. 5
Pollert, A. 62, 126
Porter, M. 125, 126
Pringle, R. 2, 46, 49

Read, M. 152–3
Reagan, R. 98
Recchini de Lattes, Z. 175
Reditt, J. 80
Rees, A. 8
Rees, T. 152–3
Reich, M. 9
Richter, L. 96
Roberts, B. 57
Roberts, C. 54
Rogers, B. 175
Rosser, M.J. 6
Rowbotham, S. 131, 139
Rubery, J. 9, 32, 35, 72
Rugh, A. 110, 112, 120

Sadat, A. 108
Sanday, P. 193
Sanders, I. 205, 207
Sayigh 104
Scott, A.M. 108

Shaarawi, H. 106
Shorter, F.C. 120
Sloane, P.J. 61
Snower, D.J. 8
Somerville, P. 10
Spender, D. 144, 213, 214
Stageman, J. 151–2, 167
State Institute of Statistics 68
Stead, J. 127, 141, 146
Sudworth, E. 96
Sullivan, E.L. 108
Suzuki, Z. 98
Szyszczak, E. 15

Tabari, A. 104
Takazato, S. 91
Taubman, P. 8
Taylor, B. 13, 31, 97, 131
Thanaret, S. 85
Thanh-Dam, T. 80, 82–3, 87–8, 93
Thepanom 80
Thitsa, K. 79–80, 82, 84
Thomas, B. 6
Tinker, I. 175
Tongudai, P. 86
Topcuoglu, H. 60
Trades Union Congress 150
Trussell, J. 10
Tucker, J.E. 108, 117

Turner, L. 94, 97

UNICEF/Ministry of Community
  Development and Women's
  Affairs 178–9

Villariba, M. 80

Wachter, M.L. 8
Wacjman, J. 126
Wainerman, C.H. 175
Walton, J. 16, 18, 75
Weldon, F. 230
Westwood, S. 12, 62, 126
Whitaker, W.B. 45
White, C. 99–100
Wikan, U. 200
Williams, J.A. 112, 116–17
Winstanley, M.J. 44
Women in Libraries Newsletter 216
Wood, R. 93–4, 96
Woolf, V. 214

Yeganeh, N. 104
Young, K. 10, 11

Zabalza, A. 12
Zaim, S. 60
Zimbabwe Women's Bureau 178–9

Subject index

absenteeism 67
accuracy 12, 62
Africa 177–83, 192
Afro-Caribbean women 11
agricultural work 19, 172, 174–7, 186–7, 192
agro-tourist co-operatives 202–11
alienation from trade unions 161–4
alternative working practices 3, 19
Ambelakia, 203, 204–5, 207, 208–9, 211
American Society of Travel Agents 98
Americans *see* United States
AMUL co-operative 186
Anti-Streetwalking Ordinance 95
Anti-Sweating League 149
apprentices 43
Arts Council 220
Asian Development Bank 93
Asian Women's Association 98
Association of University Teachers (AUT) 18, 36
Aylesham, Kent 132–4
Aylesham Women's Support Group 126, 146

Bangkok 79–80, 87, 89–92, 100
Bangladesh 183
banks *see* savings
Barnsley Women's Action Group 132
Betteshanger 132–4
birth rates 183
black women 11, 15
bookshop 20–1, 213–31

Brazil 176
Britain: equal pay legislation 14; occupational segregation 7
British Coal 134
British Printing Corporation 213
British Steel Corporation 129
Buddhism 84
Bursa province, Turkey 57
Business Guarantee Scheme 221

Cairo 16, 105
capital intensive production 69
capitalism 43
car industry 76
career ladder 1, 8, *see also* promotion
carpet weaving project 183
Catholicism 84
Centres for the Restoration of the Dignity of Women 99
Charing Cross Road 218–20, 231
Charity Commissioners 223
child care 5, 109, 110, 137–8, 147, 152–3, 183, 191
child prostitution 92
children, number and age 4, 10
choices 6
Christian Council of Japan 98
City of Westminster 216, 220
Clark Air Force Base 89
class 15, 30, 106–8, 112, 131–2, 142–7
class struggle 125–6
Clause 28 (Local Government Bill) 216
clothing industry 12

coal industry 129, 133
Collective Labour Agreements, Strikes and Lockouts Law 73
colonialism 176, 178
commission earnings 50–1
conditions of work 45, 47–8
Confucianism 84
consciousness 3
Conservative Government 129
consumer theory 45
continuity of employment 152–3
control 3, 68–72, 185–90, 195
co-operatives 20, 185–8, 202–11, 223
Cortonwood Colliery 129
craft workers 43, 72, 184–5
credit: groups 183, 188; provision 182
culture: clothing styles 116–17; Greek 197–202; role of 1, 11, 15; Thai 81–2; Turkish 58–62, 67–8, 73
Cypriot women 11

dairying scheme 186
demographic changes 4
department stores 3, 18, 44–6
dependency 68, 149–50
deskilling 53
development planning 172–4, 194–5
dexterity 12, 62, 64
discrimination 4
division of labour, gender/sexual: Hartmann's analysis 32–3; in Britain 7; in Greek co-operatives 208–9; in the home 17–18, 32–3, 39–40, 108–10, 137–8, 141, 147, 158–61, 189–90, 194; in library work 27–8, 38; in mining community 130–1, 134–5; in shop work 44, 49; in Turkish factories 58, 62, 70–2; Mackintosh's analysis 33; segmented labour theory 7
domestic labour: effect on employment 17–18, 32–3, 39–40, 189–90, 194; effect on union activities 158–61; in Egypt 108–10; in mining community

137–8, 141, 147; Marxist-feminist analysis 10
dowry 198, 199
dual labour market theory 25–30, 32, 35–6
Dusan, Korea 187, 189, 190

Eastry Rural District Council 133
Ecumenical Coalition on Third World Tourism 98
education 5, 12, 64–5, 107, 167
educational qualifications 30–1, 51, 65, 153, 167
EGE 206
Egyptian women 104–22
Employment Act (1980) 129
EMPOWER 97
Equal Opportunities Commission 225
equal pay legislation 14, 107–8
equality and power 227–9
Equality? survey 152–3
ESCAP studies 187, 190
European Community (EC, EEC) 53, 129

family honour 118–19, 200–2
Family Law Act 199
'family wage' 68, 149
Farmers Club 187
farming *see* agricultural work
Federation of Radical Booksellers 217–18
feminists 98, 100, 106, 125–6, 142–5, 214–19
food processing industry 65–6, 73
Friends of Women group 98

gender: characteristics 15, 62–4; class and 147; division of domestic work 17–18, 32–3, 39–40, 137–8, 141, 147; divisions 15–16; Greek expectations 198–202; ideology 3, 11; labour market 2; stereotypes 3, 19, 182; roles 108–10; subordination 71; Turkish factory job segregation 62, 70–2
German tourists 80

Ghana 177
Greater London Arts Association 220
Greater London Council (GLC) 215,
    218–22
Greater London Enterprise Board 220
Greece, tourism in 17, 20, 197–211
Greek women 11, 17, 20, 84,
    197–211
Greenham Common 141
Groningen Women's Studies
    Conference 95
Gujarati women 12, 183, 186

handicrafts, traditional 184–5
harijans 189
Harrods 44
holidays 47–8
homosexuality 216
household income 182, 193–4
human capital theory 5, 7, 12

income generating projects 180–1
India 176, 183–6
Indonesia 176
industrial action, 3, 150–1, 166–7,
    170
instability of employment *see*
    turnover of workers
internal/external labour market 7–9,
    28
International Feminist Network
    Against Female Sexual Slavery 99
International Labour Office World
    Employment Conference 173
International Tourist Year 93
International Women's Year 172
International Workshop on Tourism
    98
Iran: deveiling 106; veiling 104–5
Islam 105–6, 110–11, 119, 121

Jamaica 177
Japanese tourists 80, 98
job: competition theory 7–8;
    satisfaction 51; rotation 226–7
jute works 183

Kamaki phenomenon 197, 199

Kent: County Branch of NALGO
    154–68; miners' strike 19, 125–47
Koran 105, 119
Korea 187, 189, *see also* South Korea

Labour Government 129
labour intensity 13, 15, 67–9
Labour Law 91 of 1954 107
labour market: dual *see* dual;
    gendered *see* gender; segmented
    see segmented; structuring 15–16;
    supply and demand *see* supply
Labour Party 139, 147, 155, 166
Law on the Traffic in Women and
    Girls 85
Law Prohibiting Decadent Acts 86
lesbians 216–17
library workers 14, 17, 25–40
Lijjat pappad industry 185–6
livestock project 187
Local Government Bill 216

machinery, factory 13, 14, 63–4,
    65–6
machismo, 198
Mahila Mandal project 189
mail-order brides 82, 92
Malaysia 187, 190
managerial positions 43, 68–9,
    156–8, 185–6
Manila 81, 86, 89, 100
market forces 1
marriage: in Egypt 109–10, 120,
    121–2; in Thailand 81–2; in
    Turkey 59–61, 76–7; Kent miners'
    strike 138–9; mail-order brides 82,
    92
Marxist-feminist analysis 10
materialist perspective 33
Mhadubani painters 184–5
milk co-operative scheme 183
miners' strike (1984–5) 19, 125–47;
    women's role 134–5
Mines and Collieries Act (1842) 130
Ministry of Community
    Development and Women's
    Affairs 180
Mozambique 182

muhaggabat 114, 123 n.14
Mung Ho group 189
Muslim women 104–5

National Association of Local
    Government Officers (NALGO)
    18, 36, 151–7, 165, 167, 170
National Coal Board (NCB) 129
National Health Service (NHS) 11
National Union of Journalists 213
National Union of Mineworkers
    (NUM) 128, 129–31, 133, 136
National Women Against Pit
    Closures Conferences 141
National Women's Organization 126
Nepal 183, 189
New Earnings Survey 50
Nicaragua 188
Nigeria 188

Olongapo 80, 87, 89, 92, 95

Pacific Area Travel Association 93
Pan-Hellenic Socialist Movement
    (PASOK) 203
part-time work: bookshop 228–9;
    effects 10–11; library workers 17,
    27–8, 31, 33, 37–9; shop workers
    42, 53; TUC figures 150; Turkish
    system 61
passivity, female 68, 70–1, 90
patience 62
patriarchal control 71, 76, 88
patriarchy 33
Paving Act 219
pay levels: gender differences (sales
    assistants) 50–1; minimum 68;
    'perfect market' explanation 4–5,
    6; women's 3, 5
Philippines 79–81, 84, 86–7, 89,
    94–6, 187, 189
picketing 131, 132, 136
Plan for Coal (1974) 129, 130
Playboy 90
political representation 179–80
politicization of women 139–42,
    145–7

polygyny (polygamy) 81–3, 181
Pomum Tourist Resort Project 94
primary/secondary labour market
    sectors 8–9, 13, 25–6, 28–9, 36,
    150
printing industry 35
productivity 4–5, 67
professional qualifications 26, 30–1
promotion opportunities 37–8, 39
property, women as 82–3
prostitution: child 92; customers
    89–92; nature of 81–3; racist
    attitudes 19; reasons for entering
    83–8; responses to 97–100
Prostitution Prohibition Act 85

qualifications *see* educational,
    professional

race divisions 15–16
racist: attitudes 19; stereotypes
    15–16, 17, 19, 201–2, 211
reformatories 97, 99–100
reserve army of labour 10
retailing 42–54, *see also* sales
    assistants
rice saving scheme 187
Rosie Reizen travel advertisements
    90

Saigon 99
sales assistants 12, 15, 42–54
savings: bank accounts 182, 187;
    clubs 180; credit groups 188;
    Sisters Savings Scheme 186
Schools for New Women 100
secondary labour force 150
segmented labour market theory 1, 7,
    8–9, 13
segregation, occupational *see*
    division of labour
Self-Employed Women's
    Association (SEWA) 190–2
Seoul 86, 89
sexual harassment 70, 88
sexuality: as commodity 17; Greek
    198–202

shame 199–200
shift work 61
shop stewards 18, 73, 75–6, 149–70
shop workers *see* sales assistants
Sikh women 12
Silver Moon Quarterly, The 230
Silver Moon Women's Bookshop
  213–31
Sisters Saving Scheme 186
Sisterwrite 224
skill and pay: factory workers 12;
  perceptions of 12–15; sales
  assistants 12, 48–51; women's
  jobs 3, 5
skill: definitions of 3, 12, 30–1,
  65–7; educational attainment
  64–5; sales assistants 43–4, 48–9;
  Turkish factory work 62; types of
  30–1
Snowdown 132–3, 136
socialism 100, 107, 125, 142, 180
South Africa 177
South-East Asia, sex tourism in 3,
  16, 79–100
South Korea 79–80, 84, 86, 88, 92–5
South Korean Church Women
  United 98
South Vietnam 79–80
State Woollen Mill, Bursa 59
strength 62–3
strikes *see* industrial action, miners'
  strike
supermarket employees 45
supervisory jobs 62, 66, 68–72, 156
supply and demand (labour) 4, 6, 15

Tamil Nadu 189
technology 13, 35, 53, 176
textile industry 58, 63, 65, 73
Textile Labour Association (TLA)
  191
Thailand 79, 81–2, 85–8, 94–5, 189
Third World Movement Against the
  Exploitation of Women 98
Tilmanstone 132–3
tourist industry 17, 20, 93–7, 197–8
trade unions 1, 6, 9, 13–14, 16, 18,
  35–7, 39, 72–6, 149–70, 190–2

Trades Union Congress (TUC) 149,
  151
training 5, 12, 15, 37, 167–8,
  169–70, 210
Turkey: deveiling 106; factory
  workers 3, 12, 14, 16, 18, 56–77;
  union activity 72–6, 153;
  woman's place 58–62, 67–8, 73;
  women 11, 36
turnover of workers 32, 67

Union of Shop, Distributive, and
  Allied Trades (USDAW) 48, 50
United National Research Institute
  for Social Development
  (UNRISD) 1172
United Nations: Conference on
  Women 172; Convention for the
  Elimination of Discrimination
  against Women 99; Convention
  for the Suppression of the Traffic
  in Persons 99; Economic
  Commission for Africa 174;
  General Assembly 93; Plan of
  Action for the Integration of
  Women in Development 179
United States: attitude to prostitution
  90; Department of Commerce 93;
  Department of Labour 174;
  servicemen 79–80, 89; tourists 80

veiling 15–16, 104–22
Vietnam 99–100
Vietnam War 19, 79–80, 93

wages *see* pay
We Forum 95
West Africa 177
Whiteley's store 50
widows 74
wives: in Egypt 110–12, 121; in
  Thailand 81–2; in Turkey 58–62,
  67–8, 73; in Zimbabwe 178, 181–2
Women Against Pit Closures 141,
  143
women as property 82–3
Women's Co-operative Guild 149
Women's Farmers Club 187

women's liberation movement
142–5, 157, 223
Women's Press, The 215, 219
World Bank 19, 93–4

young women 74–5, 183

Zambia 182
Zimbabwe 178–83
Zimbabwe Women's Bureau 178,
179, 180